THE EVOLUTION OF
MODERN INDUSTRIAL ORGANISATION

THE EVOLUTION OF MODERN INDUSTRIAL ORGANISATION

by

F. J. WRIGHT, M.Sc. (Econ.)

Senior Lecturer in Economics and Government, Department of Commerce and Management, Norwich City College

THIRD EDITION

MACDONALD & EVANS, LTD.
8 John Street, London, W.C.1
1967

First published 1954
Reprinted 1955
Second edition 1957
Reprinted 1958
Reprinted 1960
Reprinted 1962
Reprinted 1964
Third edition 1967

©

F. J. WRIGHT
1967

Printed in Great Britain by Richard Clay (The Chaucer Press), Ltd.,
Bungay, Suffolk

PREFACE TO THIRD EDITION

THIS book, which has had considerable success in its previous form as a textbook designed for the use of students preparing for various professional examinations, has now been revised and enlarged to give it a wider appeal. It is hoped that it will prove useful not only to those studying for professional examinations requiring a knowledge of modern economic history but also to G.C.E. students, Engineering Sandwich Course students—all those, in fact, interested in the study of economic and social history, especially those events leading immediately to the economic and social organisation of the present day.

F. J. WRIGHT.

CONTENTS

LIST OF CHARTS

CHAPTER I

INTRODUCTION

IT is not necessary to stress the importance of the study of history to the student of industrial affairs. He recognises that although history does not repeat itself, since the circumstances of life change with the years, the roots of the present are in the past; that if men and women had not thought and acted in certain ways in the past, our material and spiritual environment would be different from what it is today. He recognises that geographical and social factors have influenced the kind of life he leads, that climate has had an important effect upon the way his ancestors behaved, and upon the way he behaves. The temperate climate of Britain has had its response in economic behaviour—*e.g.* the way in which the British people developed their textile manufactures; climate has influenced the way in which the Americans have used their land to grow various types of wheat.

Nevertheless, it is too easy to see events in a wrong perspective. For many years academic historians assigned too great an importance to deeds and sayings of minor kings and political figures while neglecting the broad stream of events in which these personages played a very small part. Not until H. G. Wells's *Outline of History* caught the attention and imagination of the general public did thousands of ordinary men and women succeed in seeing many historical events in something like a true perspective.

The student of industrial affairs who is engaged in the workaday world of manufacturing things or distributing commodities is similarly inclined to get his perspective wrong when studying modern industrial organisation. Too often he is inclined to imagine that the history of the world can be divided into two periods—Before the Industrial Revolution and After the Industrial Revolution—separated by a series of events that made history before the Mechanical Age quite irrelevant to his life and work. For him, the history of modern industrial organisation began in the late eighteenth or early nineteenth century.

He is right to the extent that the modern western world became a different kind of civilisation after the events usually spoken of as the Industrial Revolution began; but it is a mistake to imagine that what is happening in the industrial world today has no reference to what happened in, say, the Middle Ages. Long before the Middle Ages drew to their close, there were at work forces helping to shape

1

the Britain of today. The rigid patterns of life were being broken up; the hold of the feudal lord over the lives of those who worked for him was declining. The Black Death, 1348–49, hastened a process of change which came to a crisis in the Peasants' Revolt, 1381, and which liberated the peasants from the fetters of feudalism and which laid the foundation of the woollen trade. The establishment and expansion of towns, and the rise of a merchant class and of capitalist employers, were steps in a process of development the implications of which are still being worked out in the political as in the economic sphere.

The study of economic history, of the ways in which the community as a whole has sought to make a living, is but one aspect of the study of society as a whole. Political developments are inextricably bound up with economic and social developments generally. It is neither expedient nor desirable to separate the political history of trade unionism from its economic aspects. The philosophy which found its economic expression in mercantilism must be studied in relation to its political background and the general social life of the times. This 'mercantile doctrine' is a philosophy—the desirability of building up a 'favourable balance of trade' by increasing exports and restricting imports and making the foreigner pay for the difference—which is not dead today; in one form or another it is expounded from time to time by people who believe that it is possible to make the other man pay for what we want.

The study of economic history may not prevent us from falling into errors which have plagued our forefathers, any more than a study of psychology will prevent us from making fools of ourselves occasionally; but at least it gives us far less excuse for glorying in our ignorance. It is said that the realisation of ignorance is the beginning of wisdom; and it adds to our ability to deal with modern industrial problems if we realise, for example, that 'scientific management' is not a recently invented tool which will serve as a magic talisman to solve our modern industrial troubles but a handling of problems or organisation which was experimented with at least as long ago as the time of Robert Owen (1771–1858). There were 'labour troubles' in the days of the Gilds. The local 'squire' still exists in parts of England. The worker in a modern industrial town which did not exist until the Industrial Revolution threw it up may be handicapped by his very modernity in looking at modern industrial problems in the right way. He needs to get outside his own factory, his own town, his own industry, his own times, to see his own particular trade union problem in its proper perspective.

On the other hand, a too academic approach is to be avoided. It may be that the philosopher, in comfortable circumstances of affluence, or sitting in safe seclusion in his University chair, away from the heat and toil of life, may succeed in 'seeing things together,' looking at things in their right proportion, achieving that attitude of scientific detachment which Plato regarded as the hall-mark of the truly educated man. It is equally possible that an academic thinker, obsessed with the idea of his own cleverness and hampered by a feeling of intellectual superiority to the rest of the human race, may lose the thread of truth while pursuing the labyrinthine mazes of the higher thought; the writer once heard a distinguished historian declare that there was no such thing as the Industrial Revolution—a view containing a germ of truth in that the Industrial Revolution was but the culmination of events which had their inevitable end in a plethora of inventions and the rapid reorganisation of the life of mankind, but surely sacrificing a sense of proportion to the effect gained by a picturesque exaggeration.

If it were possible for a writer to state the truth adequately in a book on industrial history or on any other subject, there would be no need for any more books to be written, once the truth had been stated in a standard work. But every age brings its own way of looking at life; readers look for new methods of presentation, of stimulation to thought, as well as for information on recent discoveries or more accurate assessment of facts. That is why to the writing of books there is no end, why even mathematics and philosophy have every year new books seeking to expound facts and principles afresh.

The student of modern economic and industrial organisation seeks a way of understanding his own place in the industrial scheme, of finding out how he and his colleagues and their body of ideas and practices fit in the story of the history of his country and his age. This is quite a legitimate aspiration, since the most important thing in this world is the individual person; the worker in industry is the most important fact in industry, just as the ordinary citizen is the most important fact in politics. All the learning and philosophising and studies of government and constitutions and economic theories fail if they obscure this vital fact. It is the fact behind all the search for a theory of democracy, the motif of the hundreds of years of struggle and bloodshed in our country's history.

It is to this task of trying to see the significance of our modern age in relation to the unfinished, continuing story of industrial life that we are to apply ourselves.

Industry may be defined as the group of processes by which economic goods are obtained from raw materials, comprising extractive, manufacturing and constructive activities. Sometimes agriculture is spoken of as an industry, sometimes the expression 'agriculture and industry' is used. It is convenient to regard agriculture as an industry. It is important to have in mind when one uses the term 'industry' a careful idea of the scope of the term; the 'motor industry' comprises processes in which a number of different commodities are produced. The same comment may be made on the use of the terms 'textile industry' and 'shipping industry.' Here, as in everything else, common-sense usage will do no harm.

Since trade, transport and distribution, banking and financial activities, insurance services, and all those services generally spoken of as 'commercial,' are intimately connected with industry, no survey of economic development could be adequate without a consideration of the part played by those services in the scene as a whole. Without them, industry on any large scale could not begin to be organised.

Man needs bread, but he does not live by bread alone. Industry and commerce are not ends in themselves; they are the means by which Man may live, and live more abundantly. Modern societies use the fruits of industry and commerce to conquer want in the community generally, to fight disease, ignorance, squalor, idleness—the Giants which Lord Beveridge spoke of in his famous Report, *Social Insurance and Allied Services.**

But social services and social security generally are not ends in themselves, as some devoted professors of social studies would have us believe; the Swedes have found this out and the British are coming to see it. They have all these things and the Kingdom of Heaven has not been added unto them.

There is no point in the study of history unless it leads men and women to better, more satisfying lives. This object is the more likely of achievement if more recent history, of relevance to the conditions of the current social, industrial and economic scene, is studied with understanding of the implications of events and with a sense of the proportion in which those events loom in importance. This sense of proportion is the characteristic of Plato's 'educated man', and its attainment is one of the most difficult operations in education.

Paradoxically, it is of the most immediate importance to the study of modern events when one surveys human history as a whole, for then we see that Man, and particularly modern man, is a newcomer to this world, still struggling, in spite of his achievements in nuclear physics and modern production methods, with the limitations, the prejudices, the passions, the blindness, the self-centredness, that afflict the very young. He still has to learn humility.

That is why we begin our study with a look at the time proportion, the essential similarities of modern man with his predecessors. The lathes, the milling machines, the electrical devices, the computers, are still merely extensions of the physical man's hands and eyes and brains. Man does not create; he is the created.

Two thousand years ago, in A.D. 79, the town of Pompeii, near Naples, was suddenly cut off in the midst of its industry and com-

* Cmd. 6404, 1942.

merce, its pleasures and vices, and buried under twenty feet of ash erupted by the volcano Vesuvius. Modern methods of excavation have revealed much of the life of the ancient Pompeians. The tourist can walk along the streets of the excavated town, see the houses of the merchants and rich citizens and ordinary folk. He notes with astonishment the existence of those comforts and luxuries which he imagined were peculiarly modern—the reception and dining-rooms, the central heating arrangements. The traffic problem necessitated a one-way system for some streets. Election notices and propaganda—painted on walls in letters a foot high—remind him of similar displays in his own time and language. The mosaics and paintings—and it is from the Pompeian paintings that the historian has gained much of his knowledge of the art of ancient Rome—tell of a civilisation and culture in many ways and at least for some people superior to his own. And if he looks for another kind of correspondence in ways of life— apart from the numerous scribblings of an amatory and more lowly nature not unknown in the streets of a modern town—he will learn that in the reign of the Emperor Nero a riot broke out at the amphitheatre between the Pompeians and the neighbouring Nucerians concerning their partisanship of this or that gladiator in the arena, that many people were killed and injured, that much damage was done; and he will remember similar occurrences in his own time—such as that, for example, in May, A.D. 1964, when a riot broke out over a disputed goal in a Peru–Argentina football match at Lima, and hundreds of people died or were injured in the panic accompanying the stampede towards the exits.

Exhortation and incitement to be good and clever are not of much avail in an area in which there is much mental poverty in spite of and perhaps even because of broadcasting and television and other forms of mass communication. It is only facts which will prevail; and experience has provided us with past facts. This book is an essay attempting to set out the facts relating to industrial and social organisation as they have occurred, mainly in Britain; and it presumes in places to interpret the facts, to give an appreciation of the significance of the facts. The interpretations of various people are apt to vary; but if they are honest interpretations, this fact itself makes for a reasonableness which will guide people towards a true interpretation of the significance of the industrial and social events in our history.

CHAPTER II

THE EARLY HISTORY OF MAN

1. EARLY MAN AND STONE INDUSTRIES

Until 1959 the earliest human or sub-human remains discovered had been those of the Java sub-man, *Pithecanthropus erectus*; in 1891 Professor Dubois found on the banks of a river in Java the roof of a skull, two molar teeth, more simian than human, and a thigh-bone. No implements were found with the remains.

In July 1959 an expedition under Dr Louis Leakey, working in the Olduvai Gorge in Tanganyika (now Tanzania) found a human skull which was estimated to be at least 600,000 years old. Previously held ideas on the antiquity of the human race were revised; it now appeared that our earliest forefathers existed as men perhaps a million years ago or even earlier.

A million years is a very brief period in the history of the world. A glance at Chart 1 will show that Man is a relative newcomer to the world stage. However far archaeological discovery pushes the date of his emergence back, very soon on the scale of world history he disappears into an unknown remote creature of whose nature and physical make-up we have no conception. We know only that for countless aeons, during which other forms of life came into being and disappeared in their turn, there was no trace of humanity at all.

Man probably appeared at the end of the Pliocene Age or the beginning of the Pleistocene, when the climate was temperate. But he was hardly a 'true' Man. By that time, say about 700,000 or 800,000 years ago, the great reptiles had long gone: they could not adapt themselves to the changed conditions. It was the characteristic of Man's ancestor that he could adapt himself. The struggle for survival must have been hard at times, especially for a small, monkey-like creature facing the snows and ice of the Ice Ages. It was his brain, and even more his mind, which enabled him to adapt himself. His numbers were probably small—sub-human and human remains are astonishingly rare—but he lived, and multiplied, and obtained dominion over his environment.

The ancestor of Man learned to fashion tools and weapons as the first stage of that dominion. Eoliths ('dawn-stones') have been found which seem to bear some evidence of having been rudely fashioned, though it is difficult to distinguish between natural effects

6

Geological Age	Characteristics	Duration (approx. millions of years)	Era
ARCHAEN	No life		
PRE-CAMBRIAN	First signs of life	?	
CAMBRIAN	The oldest rocks containing well-characterised fossil fauna —crabs, sponges	100	
ORDOVICIAN	Grit, shales, limestones, mud; shellfish	60	
SILURIAN	Sandstones, shales; crustaceans	50	PRIMARY
DEVONIAN	'Old red sandstone.' Fishes	50	(PALAEOZOIC)
CARBONIFEROUS	Coal measures. Gigantic plants, insects	80	
PERMIAN	'New red sandstone.' Fishes, marine reptiles. Ferns	45	
TRIASSIC	Limestones. Fishes, amphibia, reptiles. Trilobites	45	
JURASSIC	Marine clays. The age of reptiles	45	SECONDARY (MESOZOIC)
CRETACEOUS	Chalk formation. Fishes. Huge land reptiles	65	
EOCENE	Disturbances of earth's crust; Mammals, hoofed beasts		
OLIGOCENE	Marls and clays. Lakes		TERTIARY (CAINOZOIC)
MIOCENE	Final uplifting of present mountain chains	20	
PLIOCENE	'Crag'; marine shell-banks		
PLEISTOCENE	Ice Age. First appearance of Man	1	QUATERNARY

CHART 1—*The Geological Age. Estimates of the duration of the eras vary. The above figures are very approximate.*

as from grinding in the beds of rivers and human artifacts. Eoliths have been found at Ipswich beneath the boulder clay and at Cromer on the foreshore. This is the period to which *Pithecanthropus* belongs.

The Pleistocene Age was one of the Glacial Ages interspersed with milder interglacial periods. The first Glacial Age reached its maximum about 500,000 years ago; the second about 400,000 years ago, the third 150,000 and the fourth about 35,000 years ago. At the beginning of the Pleistocene Age, Man's ancestors learned to fashion 'rostro-carinate' tools or 'eagle's-beak' flint tools: roughly triangular stones, with one face flat, the other roughly shaped into a beak-like form, with a rounded end, suitable for holding.

Flint implements which are of undoubted human or sub-human design and workmanship occur in the second Glacial Age. Archaeologists refer to the Palaeolothic or Old Stone Age, characterised by unpolished chipped stones; and designate the types of tools by the names of the places where they were first discovered. Thus, Strépy tools refer to the worked flints first found on the gravels and terraces on the banks of the Somme near Strépy, in Belgium; they are roughly flaked and are the work of the Palaeolithic hunters who made hand-axes, scraping tools and other crude implements, poor weapons compared with those of the teeth and tusks of their contemporary animals the hippopotamus, rhinoceros, elephants and sabre-toothed tiger—the last of the fearsome co-hunters in which the excessive development of one feature, its great curved tusks, was its own undoing. Man used his brain to make tools and weapons as adjuncts to his body, but extraneous to it.

The various stages in the development of tools were not contemporary everywhere, nor do the various types of tools so much represent periods of development as stages in which the forms represented changes in ways of life. The early periods are too remote and the evidence too sparse to give us any indication of social life. Probably social organisation was extremely elementary—a kind of family or tribal life.

The Acheulian and Chellean types of flint working, called 'industries' by the archaeologists, and not unfancifully comparable with the industries of modern times in their influence upon the lives of the people living in those cultures, were named after the types of tools found respectively at S. Acheul, on the Somme, and Chelles on the Seine, near Paris. They were 'core' industries: the flint worker knocked off chips from a lump of flint until he reduced the lump to a convenient size and shape, sharpening the edge. A Chellean tool is almond-shaped with a butt for handling; the Acheulian tools are thinner and flatter. These Early Palaeolithic men lived in an interglacial period, but the climate was moving towards the third Glacial Age.

In 1907 a jawbone was found in a sandpit of Chellean age near Heidelberg; the teeth were human. But 'Heidelberg Man'—or brute—remains a mystery.

Thousands of years later, in the last interglacial period and just before the onset of the fourth Glacial Age, there lived Neanderthal Man, so called because remains of him were first discovered in the Neanderthal Cave, near Düsseldorf, in 1857. Because similar remains were found at Le Moustier in 1909, the type of flint-working practised by Neanderthal Man is also called Mousterian. It was a 'flake' industry; a piece of flint of the whole length of the core was struck off, showing the 'bulb of percussion' on one side, where the stone was fractured, the other side being worked. It appeared that Neanderthal Man buried his dead with flint tools and food. He may have disappeared as the approaching cold drove him towards the caves and he found himself unable to withstand the climate or to provide for himself; or he may have been exterminated by the Cro-Magnon men of the Late Palaeolithic Age, the first 'true' men: a tall, well-built race, leaving evidence of very considerable skill in the making of flint and bone implements, of artistic ability in the making of statuettes and in the painting of pictures on the walls of caves; they buried their dead with reverence. The Cro-Magnon is the name of a grotto in the Dordogne. The Cro-Magnons were the ancestors of the Nordic and Mediterranean races; the tourist who visits Mentone can see skeletons of his remote and direct ancestors in the little museum near the Cave of the Red Rocks on the Italian border, the Grimaldi Cave. Here were found also skeletons of a negroid race, the Grimaldi race. It is suggested that these, together with perhaps a third race, represent the prehistoric ancestors of the major races of Mankind.

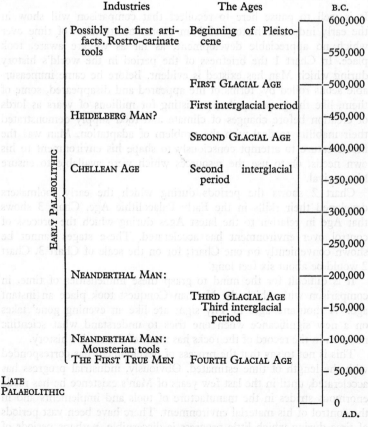

Industries	The Ages	B.C.
Possibly the first artifacts. Rostro-carinate tools	Beginning of Pleistocene	600,000
		550,000
	FIRST GLACIAL AGE	500,000
	First interglacial period	450,000
HEIDELBERG MAN?		
	SECOND GLACIAL AGE	400,000
CHELLEAN AGE	Second interglacial period	350,000
		300,000
		250,000
NEANDERTHAL MAN:		200,000
	THIRD GLACIAL AGE Third interglacial period	150,000
NEANDERTHAL MAN: Mousterian tools		100,000
THE FIRST TRUE MEN	FOURTH GLACIAL AGE	50,000
		0 A.D.

EARLY PALAEOLITHIC

LATE PALAEOLITHIC

CHART 2—*The Early Industries of Man*

The Later Palaeolithic Period is divided into three Ages, the Aurignacian, Solutrean and Magdalenian. The Aurignacian men were the 'reindeer men'; they fashioned arrow- and spear-heads and bone implements out of reindeer horns, made drawings on them, and painted on the walls of caves. The Solutré people produced beautiful lance-shaped flints; the Madeleine people continued to use flint for borers and scrapers, but turned more to bone and ivory for other implements such as needles, while still turning out large numbers of finely made small flint implements, like arrow-heads.

With the Azilian Age, during which flint workmanship deteriorated and the people painted pebbles with probably magical significance, the Later Palaeolithic Age moved into a transitional and somewhat degenerate stage.

2. TIME SCALES

It is well to pause here to recollect that comparison will show in the early industrial history of Man enormous stretches of time over which no appreciable development, as far as we are aware, took place. In Chart 1 the briefness of the period in the world's history during which Man has existed is evident. Before he came immeasurable aeons rolled by; forms of life appeared and disappeared, some of them, like the giant reptiles, persisting for millions of years as lords of creation before changes of climate and food supply demonstrated their inability to deal with the problem of adaptation. Man was the first creature to attempt consciously to shape his environment to his own needs, or to use the resources which were available to ensure his survival.

Chart 2 shows the periods during which the early toolmakers developed their skills in the Early Palaeolithic Age. Chart 3 shows that Age in relation to the latest Ages during which the process of control over environment has accelerated. These stages cannot be shown conveniently on one Chart; for on the scale of Chart 3, Chart 2 would be about six feet long.

It is difficult for the mind to grasp these immensities of time, in comparison with which the Norman Conquest took place an instant ago. 'A thousand ages in Thy sight are like an evening gone' takes on a new significance when one tries to understand what scientific research in the record of the rocks has made of the earth's history.

This is not to say that the process of development has corresponded with the length of time estimated. Obviously, industrial progress has accelerated, until in the last few years of Man's existence he has made enormous strides in the manufacture of tools and implements and in the control of his material environment. There have been vast periods of time during which little progress is discernible, perhaps periods of

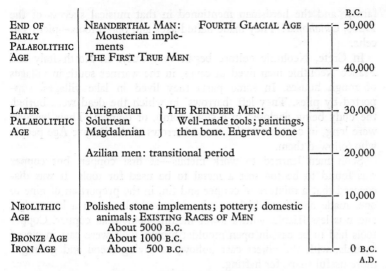

			B.C.
END OF EARLY PALAEOLITHIC AGE	NEANDERTHAL MAN: Mousterian implements THE FIRST TRUE MEN	FOURTH GLACIAL AGE	50,000
			40,000
LATER PALAEOLITHIC AGE	Aurignacian Solutrean Magdalenian	THE REINDEER MEN: Well-made tools; paintings, then bone. Engraved bone	30,000
	Azilian men: transitional period		20,000
			10,000
NEOLITHIC AGE	Polished stone implements; pottery; domestic animals; EXISTING RACES OF MEN About 5000 B.C.		
BRONZE AGE	About 1000 B.C.		
IRON AGE	About 500 B.C.		0 B.C. A.D.

CHART 3—*The Later Prehistoric Ages*

stagnation, even of retrogression; for the story of human life is not one of steady progression: in the first half of this century a European country reverted to the depths of barbarism.

It is well to reflect that although industrial and technological progress has been so marked in men's very recent history, in many ways in social organisation, in psychic and spiritual development, in the control of Man's own prejudices and passions, in the subjugation of animal ruthlessness, in the manifestation of self-preservation and the satisfaction of sexual needs, progress has been very slow. That sense of proportion which Plato spoke of as the hall-mark of the educated man is still something about which education in practice, in the fury and struggles of an industrial society, knows little.

3. THE DAWN OF INDUSTRIAL HISTORY

Neolithic man, the New Stone Age men, polished their stones, made pottery and domesticated animals. Probably they came from Asia— times and places are still not precisely established in our history. They were hunters, like the Palaeolithic men, but as the climate became milder they settled down and took up pastoral farming and agriculture, perhaps intermarrying with the earlier races. Some peoples became nomad, others pastoral: there is no wholeness in Neolithic men, no simple pattern. Their ways of life were as various as our own; probably in those early days there was the rivalry between the farmer and the herdsman mentioned in that musical success of the 1950s, *Oklahoma*! They made hafted axes and bored tools—picks and celts.

In Crete, Neolithic culture began very early. In North Italy and France Neolithic men lived in caves, in the warmer south in villages of rough houses. In some parts they lived in lake villages, supported by piles. They left 'barrows' in which the dead were buried, the body being enclosed in a stone tomb, or dolmen. Their barrows were long, in contrast to the round barrows of the Bronze Age people who followed them.

Soon men learned to work metals—at first copper, but copper was found to be too soft a metal to be used for tools. It was discovered that a mixture of copper and tin, in the proportion of nine to one, made an alloy which was harder, could be given a keen edge, and was less friable, with a lower melting-point than copper. Copper tools had to be cast in open moulds; bronze tools were cast in closed moulds, with the object cast hollow, so saving metal and getting a more useful shape for hafting.

Stone continued to be used for rough work such as farming, and for arrow-heads; it was, of course, much more readily obtainable. But bronze gave into men's hands a formidable weapon, and organised war became a means of obtaining power and wealth and living-space and sexual dominion and slaves. The 'bell-beaker' people—their type of culture characterised by this kind of pottery—flooded across Europe, fighting, conquering, exterminating.

The Bronze Age was the age not only of the bronze tools of which the celts were characteristic, of the swords and daggers and spears, of utensils like buckets and ploughs, of decorated chariots and beautiful gold ornaments, but also of the great stone monuments, the megaliths, like Stonehenge, still presenting problems relating to their purpose, whether religious or otherwise, their methods of transport and erection.

The 1500 years of the Bronze Age men gave place to the Celtic period. The Celts were fair-haired, blue-eyed people who brought with them a new and terrible metal: iron. They spread Iron Age culture with the considerable aid of the swords they fashioned—the Hallstatt period is characterised by the leaf-shape swords the invaders used; a later culture is called La Tène, from a settlement near Lake Neuchatel.

The wars and disturbances of the Celtic invasion resulted in the settlement in Britain of the Gaelic-speaking peoples of Scotland and the Isle of Man, the Erse-speaking people of Ireland, the Brythons—who were to be driven into Wales by the Belgae, called Gauls in France. The Celts buried their leaders with chariots; they built hill forts and lake dwellings (as at Glastonbury); they worked in enamel;

they made bowls and pottery, using a lathe; they lived in circular wattle-and-daub huts. They spun with a distaff and spindle, and made clothes of fustian and linen.

So we come to the beginning of recognisable history, with remains of forts and huts and implements scattered about Europe in more definitely identifiable forms than those which the prehistoric peoples have left us to interpret. It was the beginning of the history of the school-books, the history of the Ancient Britons whom the Romans encountered, the Gauls, the Germanic tribes. The great first flush of invasions and the settlement of European peoples were over. From now on 'history' was to be the story of developing industry, of consolidation of people into ranks and status and occupations and ways of life and thought which have to a great measure persisted up to our own times.

4. THE GREEKS AND THE ROMANS

But first there were to be two great surges of the human spirit in Europe which affected in two different ways the course of historical development.

The first was a bright flame of culture and mental awakening of men which has never been put out, though it has burned low at times. At the time when the peoples of Europe and the near East were settling down into a routine of peasant agriculture and simple metal-working not so very different from that of their remote ancestors, a wave of people from a colder climate to the east reached Greece about 2000 B.C., using the bronze swords and shields and light horse-chariots that had brought them the mastery over the lands they had passed over.

The *Iliad* of Homer gives us a picture of the habits and social organisation of these people in the last years of the Mycenaean era, about 1600 B.C. Mycenae, whose royal graves have yielded a great quantity of gold and precious objects, was a Cretan colony. The palace of Gnossos, the home of the legendary labyrinth with its fearsome bull-headed monster, shows us a system of drainage and sanitation not to be surpassed—or regained when the Minoan empire was destroyed— for about 3000 years. Modern archaeology has discovered that the heroes of the Trojan War were not as mythical as had been imagined; there had been, in fact, several Troys. Even the beautiful Helen probably existed—as a personification of Greek women stolen by the Trojans.

Successive wars waged by conquering peoples armed with the superior iron weapon have left a fragmentary and confused record. But, at last, by about the end of the eighth century B.C., a collection of city-states emerged: cities governing themselves or being governed by a king. The form of government is not so remote from current experience: the city of Geneva is, after all, a republic, a city-state; and in the *Landsgemeinde* cantons of Switzerland the citizens meet together and elect the magistrates with a show of hands. The largest *Landesgemeinde* canton, Appenzell Outer Rhodes, has more than 10,000 voters, and every citizen is expected to come to the main square and give his vote.

Nor is there lacking in ancient Greece a parallel to the unique geographical features which have done so much in making Switzerland a country of small republics with democracy springing from the will of their citizens. The broken and indented coast-line, the mountainous country, tended towards an isolation of populations. The threatening sea power of the Phoenicians was broken. The use of an alphabet favoured literary communication. The genial climate encouraged outdoor life. The institution of slavery favoured the formation of an aristocratic leisured class who could give itself to culture, the development of the spirit, the discussion of political forms, the pursuit of science. A favoured few enjoyed a way of life which could be enjoyed by all in our own day, now that machines have replaced the slaves—a way of life, that is, to all who desire it, for not all wish to dwell in the heights.

It was a potential paradise marred by internecine strife between the city-states, by wars and the human defects of envy, jealousy, resentment and sheer mental limitation. The Greeks, like the Romans, could not survive because the world of the powerful and intellectual was too narrow, and the institution of slavery was a cancer devouring Greek integrity. But in its flowering, Greek civilisation was a force which changed the life of the European world.

Of the development of Greek thought in philosophy and politics it is not the place to speak in this book. For centuries the academic world has been discussing the ideas of Plato and Aristotle on the government of the State and the meaning of 'democracy.' Nor can we pause to consider the classic sculpture, the temples, the art which still astonishes the tourist who gazes upon the ruins of the Acropolis, the temples of Paestum.

What is of relevance to our present study is Greek science, which reached its greatest achievements in the fifth century B.C., the beginning of the age of 'classical' Greece. While the people of our own country were walking in the mists of a struggling barbarism, the Greeks —or the philosopher–aristocratic section of them—came near to modern conceptions in their ideas of the structure of the universe. Thales, who had learnt his mathematics in Egypt and his astronomy in Chaldea, predicted to within a year the solar eclipse of 585 B.C. Pythagoras discovered the correspondence between the principal intervals of the musical scale and the ratios between lengths of string at a given tension. Anaxagoras propounded a theory of a spherical universe; Leucippas anticipated the atomic theory. Hippocrates of Cos became the most well-known of physicians. The existing body of knowledge about the world and its life was set down by Aristotle (384–322 B.C.), whose works were raided subsequently by the seekers of knowledge emerging from the thraldom of the Middle Ages. Aristotle was the first European, as far as we know, to insist on the value of organised research in the gathering of knowledge. He represented the freeing of the human mind from the bonds of myth and superstition which had troubled the great civilisations of Egypt and Chaldea.

Aristotle was the tutor of Alexander the Great; and it was Alexander who, by his attempt to conquer the world, carried Greek culture to the East and received Babylonian and Egyptian contributions in return. Until the establishing of the Roman might in the first century B.C., Greek culture dominated the Western World—and indeed played a significant role in what the Romans could boast as their culture.

The death of Alexander the Great in 323 B.C. was followed by conflict between his generals. Ptolemy, who had Egypt as his share of world conquest, raised Alexandria to the place of cultural centre, rivalling Athens; and Greek science advanced steadily. Archimedes studied hydrostatics—if indeed he did not invent it—and Euclid became pre-eminent in geometry. Herophilus in effect discovered the circulation of the blood. Pytheas discovered that the moon caused the tides. Hero invented a steam-engine, the prototype of the models which an enterprising modern manufacturer makes for schoolboys treading the path of the history of science.

But the Greeks were philosophers and academic thinkers, not practical scientists. It is said that they despised the practical application of the scientific principles they discovered, treating their researches as a rich erudite scholar would treat his hobby, the satisfying of a gentlemanly curiosity.

Why, after all, should Hero's steam-engine have been used as the precursor of a Greek Industrial Revolution? The Greek philosophers, the scientists, belonging to a privileged class, were comfortable as they were, with slaves performing the dull routine tasks and supplying mundane needs.

Greek science faded and died. Constant warfare between the city-states, the increase of a poor proletariat, growing unrest among the slaves, helped to cause confusion and decay, taken advantage of by the determined practical Romans. Greek science could not master the problem of malaria which led to the abandonment of such sites as the Sybaritic Colony at Paestum—neither, in fact, could the practical arts of the Romans: they had to leave Ostia, the port of Rome, to a similar fate.

Greek civilisation as a physical thing vanished. As a spirit, an inspiration, it lived on.

If it can be said that the Greeks' great gifts to subsequent civilisations were the initiation of the scientific spirit of enquiry and investigation of facts, the invention of Political Science, and their unsurpassed art in stone, it may be equally urged that the contribution of Rome to human development in the West was the conception and establishment of law and order. The Romans had extraordinary gifts as soldiers and administrators. They borrowed their scientific theory and art and even their mythology from the Greeks; they applied Greek science in their engineering and architecture—without adding very much to the body of scientific knowledge.

But they did evolve a practice of administration and a body of law which, like Greek philosophy, has left an enduring mark on the world.

The Roman arms conquered the known world, and with them went Roman law and discipline and villas and central heating. Barbarous tribes were chastened and brought within the Empire and civilised. The idea of a Roman peace and a Roman law and a Roman civilisation was spread throughout Europe, to linger on, after the adoption of Christianity, in the conception of a Holy Roman Empire uniting all men.

But, like the political organisation of the Greeks, the Roman State had a rotten and crumbling foundation in the institution of slavery. The rulers of the Empire degenerated; corruption and greed and a narrow bureaucracy weakened the administration, the Emperors were sometimes maniacs or generals elevated to the purple by a soldiery desperate for leadership. The proletariat was fed on the spoil from conquered peoples. The old ideals of the Republic, *pietas* and *gravitas*, were subjects for merriment.

The neglect of the pursuit of science had left the Romans with no technological means to overcome the hordes of barbarians which poured over the Empire; there were no guns or adequate means of self-defence. In any case, the spirit was gone. In A.D. 410 Rome itself was captured by a Gothic king. In the seventh century A.D. the library at Alexandria was destroyed by the Arabs, and the lamp in the East went out.

In the West the Roman Empire crumbled into barbarism; the city of Rome itself decayed—for the newcomers were no dwellers in cities —and its ruins intrigue the modern traveller. The Western World lapsed into the Dark Ages, illumined only by the flickering gleams of learning of the cloister, such as that of the Venerable Bede, who at Jarrow gathered together the knowledge which he found available and wrote it out in Latin.

In the East a Roman Byzantine Empire owed more to Greek culture than to Roman, though it maintained the tradition of Roman law.

CHAPTER III

THE MIDDLE AGES

1. THE BEGINNINGS OF THE FEUDAL SYSTEM

Now we narrow our field of view and enlarge the details of events to see them in the perspective of our own times. We have seen in pre-historic times the beginnings of the division of labour, of specialisation; there were flint-implement 'works' in the New Stone Age, as at Grime's Graves, in Norfolk. But though archaeologists speak of stone and horn and bone 'industries,' and though there must have been some sort of organisation of the work of prehistoric men, industrial organisation was in a rudimentary state. The Romans had manuscript-copying 'factories'; evidence of woollen-garment processing is abundant in the excavated town of Pompeii which perished nearly 2000 years ago, and fish sauces and relishes were a Pompeiian specialty.

But whatever tendencies there were towards the spread of industrial organisation were wiped out as the old Roman Western World was destroyed. When the scene clears again we find that industry and social organisation have moved along a somewhat different path from what has gone before.

The break-up of the Roman power was followed by the division of Europe into a number of self-contained communities, each under the sway of a king or prince or lord. The Feudal System existed in England even before the Norman Conquest; but the Normans introduced a more definite political feudalism, a political system by which the king was regarded as the owner of all the land in his kingdom, parcelling out land to his followers, the nobles and barons, in return for their acknow-ledgment of him as their liege lord, the promise of the provision of military service, and their services in helping to govern the kingdom. Great lords let out land to lesser lords on similar conditions.

This was the political structure of the feudal state. The economic aspect of it was the manorial system. The ultimate unit in the feudal structure was the manor. A great noble would hold many manors, and the lord of the manor would owe allegiance to him. The system was a useful and perhaps inevitable one in view of the troublous nature of the times; and after the Conquest Norman lords replaced Saxons in most manors. William wielded a heavier hand than did the Saxon kings; the Norman lords were perhaps of a fiercer kind than the Saxon;

17

but there was no great revolution in the nature of work generally: the Feudal System in itself discouraged change.

2. THE FEUDAL SYSTEM AND THE MANORIAL SYSTEM

It is because the Feudal System and its economic counterpart, the Manorial System, constitute a striking contrast to the expanding economy of the nineteenth century and to the spasmodic progress of the twentieth that it is profitable for the student of industry to consider them. They illustrated a policy of No Change. It was a policy which, politically, was designed to retain the power of the nobility and the king—and king and nobles often quarrelled with one another on the question of their respective rights. Economically, the system was designed to support the lord of the manor by the labour of the peasants, in return for which they obtained his sometimes doubtful protection.

The systems were complementary: the Feudal System had its economic effects, and the Manorial System had its political effects; when anything happened, such as the Black Death, which had far-reaching economic effects, there was an inevitable reaction in the political sphere.

The population of England at the time of the making of the Domesday Book, 1086, has been estimated to be about 1,800,000. Eighty per cent of the population consisted of villeins, cottars (or bordars) and slaves; of these, nearly half were villeins. These classes were serfs, bound to the manor and unable to leave it without the lord's permission, except by becoming outlaws. The slaves became absorbed in time into the cottar class. The villeins and cottars had to perform *week-work*, *i.e.* agricultural work for the lord of the manor on two or three days a week, and work on *boon-days*, *i.e.* work whenever the lord of the manor might require it, though the number of boon-days was limited by the law, based on custom. These services were performed in return for the tenants' holdings, and the tenants also paid the lord a rent in money or kind or both. The cottars held less than the villeins, and frequently had time to spare to work for the villeins—they became a kind of medieval agricultural labourer class.

The lord's land was called the demesne. Freemen and socmen, constituting about 12% of the population, were not bound to the cultivation of the demesne as the villeins and cottars were. They later commuted what services they had to render into money payments. They could, if they wished, leave the manor. The distinction between freemen and socmen is not easy to draw.

The aim of Domesday Book was to survey the king's estate, *i.e.* his kingdom, so that William should know what his resources were, and how much more he could get out of them—in one sense he was a scientific manager, and certainly he was an able if ruthless administrator. He held a good many manors himself, and these were farmed by his bailiffs. The majority of the others were held by the Norman nobles, his *tenants-in-chief*. These tenants-in-chief sub-let such manors as they could not work themselves or leave in the hands of bailiffs to sub-tenants, *tenants in mesne*, who thus became lords of the manor; they included some English who had submitted to the Normans.

The government of the country was carried on by the services rendered to the king by his vassals; a great baron was usually appointed the sheriff, or king's representative in the shire, enforcing the king's rights, protecting his interests, being responsible for the collection of local revenues, for the maintenance of order and the administration of justice, and seeing that the military service due to the king was provided. The king's domain lands were always greater than those of the nobles; the feudalism made it difficult for the baron to cut himself away from the royal power. The king's military power was superior to that of any likely combination against him. It was therefore a political system more definite and more rigid than that of the Saxons, and to that extent Norman feudalism was an innovation in England. As William bestowed confiscated estates on his followers, lay and clergy, he built up a strong system of royal power. His Great Council of barons and bishops attended as a duty they owed not to the 'State' but to the king as the lord of his vassals.

The feudal system which was thus established in Europe between the eighth and eleventh centuries found its earliest and most complete expression in France. Its period of greatest flowering was from the eleventh to the end of the fourteenth century. Even today there remain survivals of feudalism in the laws and customs of many European countries.

3. THE MANOR AS THE UNIT OF ECONOMIC ORGANISATION

England at the time of Domesday Book was a country of rural communities, the richest and most cultivated parts being in the south-east. The manors were self-sufficing communities; roads were bad, and the forests were infested with outlaws scarcely less savage than wild beasts. It is doubtful whether a serf would wish to stray; he had security, with no fear of unemployment, and it was not in the interests of his lord to be excessively tyrannous. Noble and non-noble recognised the claims of custom, that raw material of laws; William I had promised that the English should keep their customs, and he kept his word.

It is not surprising, therefore, that after the disorder and violence that followed the break-up of the Roman Empire, the feudal system and the manorial system, with their promise of security and a settled way of life, should have lasted through so many centuries.

Conditions varied throughout the country, and it is now known that they were by no means so uniform as had previously been thought; but, in general, the organisation of the manor as an economic unit, a way of making a living, could be described as the organisation of production in a practically 'closed' economy, one in which there was little dealing with outside markets. Production was for the little community of the manor, and all concerned had their relations with other members defined by custom. Custom dictated the times of sowing, of enclosing the land to grow cereals, opening the land for common grazing. The custom was declared by the steward, the lord's representative, who presided over the manorial court.

The day-to-day management of the manor was entrusted to the bailiff; he directed the labour of the villeins, who were represented by an elected reeve—there is a parallel, if not a very close one, with the general manager–shop steward relationship of a modern business undertaking.

The land was divided into pasture and arable, and there were common rights over grazing. In general—though once again it must be stated that conditions and details of organisation varied throughout the country—the arable land was divided into two or three large open fields. The holdings of the tenants were distributed among these fields, so that the good and bad land was evenly divided out—a medieval policy of fair shares for all. A system of rotation of crops was practised; *e.g.* in the three-field system, Field A would grow wheat during the first year, Field B barley and Field C would lie fallow. During the second year Field B would lie fallow, Field A would grow barley and Field C would grow wheat. During the third year, Field A would lie fallow, Field B would grow wheat and Field C barley. In the two-field system one half of the land would be cultivated and the other half allowed to lie fallow, each half being cultivated in alternate years.

It was a system wasteful of land, and production did not reach a high degree of efficiency. Winter feeding of livestock by root crops was not known, so that most of the cattle were killed off and salted down on the approach of winter. Bread was produced from the wheat; malt and ale were brewed from the barley; the wool from the sheep was spun into yarn in the cottages and the yarn woven into a kind of rough cloth; the hides of the cattle were made into leather.

From the modern viewpoint, farming on the manor was of somewhat rough-and-ready nature. The tenants' holdings were in strips separated from one another by strips of unworked grass and turf and weeds which it was apparently nobody's business to keep down. There was no attempt made to improve the breeds of cattle. Large numbers of swine and poultry were kept, and pork and poultry-meat no doubt kept the tenant sometimes better fed than were unskilled workers of the nineteenth century.

Before the middle of the fourteenth century there was a considerable export of wool to the Continent. The Black Death of 1348–49 intensified the process of enclosing land for sheep-farming, and woollen manufactures later replaced raw wool as the principal commodity in the export trade.

4. TOWNS, FAIRS AND MERCHANTS

The system was not entirely self-sufficing and closed. Human nature is dynamic; and processes were at work tending to destroy the manorial system even before it reached its full flower. The very limitations of the manorial system encouraged the growth of forces springing up to counter these limitations. Such commodities as muslins, laces, ribbons, needles and thread, nails and weapons were obtained from markets and fairs and from the towns which were beginning to spring up near river fords and the meeting-places of trade routes. The village surplus might be disposed of in the neighbouring town to pay for the articles which the village could not make itself.

Thus money, unnecessary in a completely self-sufficing agricultural economy, came into use. This was an influence contributing to the decay of the manorial system. By the fourteenth century, it would seem that it was becoming common for peasants to commute their services for money payments. Men purchased their freedom for money; towns purchased rights from the lords, who, as they practised what were almost their sole accomplishments in the wars and crusades, and as they indulged in the expensive tastes acquired through their coming into contact with the luxuries and refinements of foreign countries, wanted more and more of this useful commodity.

The towns had sprung up at trade junctions, near cathedrals and monasteries, at river fords or at specially fortified places. About 80 towns are mentioned in Domesday Book; in 1377 about 40 of them had a population of over 1000. In the Middle Ages a few towns had populations of 5000–10,000; London's has been estimated to have been about 25,000–30,000. York and Bristol were the only other places with populations greater than 10,000.

The towns were at first entirely under the jurisdiction of the king and the nobles; but the perennial desire of the nobility for money induced them to grant charters giving the townspeople freedom to manage their own affairs. The ecclesiastical barons showed more sagacity and determination than the lay nobility in holding on to their rights, whether in relation to agricultural matters or to towns.

Towns bought the right to pay a fixed sum to the Crown in place of a number of taxes of various kinds; they chose their own mayors. A town would set up a borough court to deal with the general conduct of its affairs and with its legal business. A town would set up its own markets, though this profitable type of business—for the merchants paid tolls and charges—was often retained by the Crown, the Church or a baron.

Fairs were also held, many important ones annually, for the buying and selling of particular commodities, such as wool and horses. On the Continent certain fairs, such as the book fair at Leipzig, were of considerable importance right up to the outbreak of the Second World War; but most English fairs have degenerated into the 'fun fair' type.

In the Middle Ages fair officers had authority over the maintenance of order and the conduct of business transactions. Usages and customs relating to the conduct of business transactions, derived partly from the Roman law and partly from the practices of foreign markets, were developed—the 'Law Merchant.' There sprang up for the immediate settlement of disputes 'Piepowder Courts,' so called from the dusty feet (*pieds poudrés*) of the merchants who attended them, often from far away. These courts were not regarded with any great favour by the professional lawyers. The usages relating to British and foreign traders were declared and administered in the Courts of the Staple set up in certain foreign towns. In the reign of James I some of the usages of merchants were recognised as common law, but it was Lord Chief Justice Mansfield (1705–93) who by his labours caused the law merchant to be incorporated into the general body of the Common Law of England. Later, some of these usages formed the basis of statutes: the Sale of Goods Act, 1893, and the Bills of Exchange Act, 1882, in effect codified as Statute Law these long-established practices and usages.

Even in the Middle Ages, then, the merchant was coming to be a member of a new class in the English social scene.

5. THE GILDS

By the twelfth century the merchants were establishing in most English towns associations for the promotion of their particular trades. These associations, the merchant gilds, imposed a 'just price' and insisted on fair trading practices, and extended their interests to religious and 'friendly society' activities. In general, it may be said that members of the gild enjoyed the right to trade within the town without paying the tolls exacted from strangers. They were expected to deal fairly and honourably, to exact no more than a reasonable profit, to settle their debts. Enforcement of such requirements was made possible by the organisation of the gild, headed by an alderman and assisted by wardens and a council, and by the gild court. Such privileges as the gild enjoyed were granted by the Crown or by the lord of the manor.

Though it is generally stated that the ancient gilds cannot be compared with the modern trade unions, it does seem that they had points in common with union practice, as well as with the practice of modern masonic associations. It is true that the gilds were associations of masters, not of 'operatives'; that the wealthy merchants would become not only officers of their association but would also be likely to take office as burgesses managing the affairs of the town as a whole. Differences between the modern trade union and the gild are easy to see; nevertheless, these associations are not entirely dissimilar.

Perhaps the greatest contrast between the trade union and the gild is seen in the associations of craftsmen called the craft gilds, whose organisations, with the system of council and wardens, was similar to that of the merchant gilds. A somewhat later development than the merchant gilds, craft gilds arose as the division of labour in the towns resulted in the coming into being of craftsmen skilled in particular handicrafts. Some gilds were chartered by the Crown; others were under the control of the town authorities. They maintained standards of quality and workmanship, even punishing offenders for bad workmanship or sharp practices, ensuring a fair deal and a 'just price' for their products.

Within the craft there were grades of workmen: master-craftsmen, journeymen and apprentices. Journeymen were qualified workmen working in a master's workshop for wages (journée = day). Apprentices were young men engaged in learning the craft; an apprentice usually spent a few years as a journeyman when he had completed his training, and hoped to set himself up as a master eventually, by hard work and attention to his craft—helped perhaps, in some cases, by the expedient of marrying the master's daughter. There is a tradition that, conforming to the fashion of violence in the Middle Ages, apprentices would engage in rough games or pitched battles in the streets, using clubs and staves as weapons.

Master craftsmen were independent producers, working with their own tools and using their own capital. By the fourteenth century the craft gilds were sufficiently powerful to supplant the merchant gilds. They grew to be as monopolistic and exclusive as the merchant gilds; and journeymen realised that many among their ranks would never rise to the status of masters. They therefore formed associations of their own to get as high wages and as good conditions of work as they could. To this extent the associations of journeymen were the forerunners of the modern trade unions—at least of the skilled unions.

As for the masters, they grew more and more despotic and narrow; the gilds became ever more monopolistic and self-seeking, and adopted 'liveries' which could be worn only by the wealthiest and most powerful members: the modern 'livery' companies are descended from them. It was thus that they came to hinder the development of industry and commerce rather than help it. Industry grew in the new towns, where there were no gild restrictions; craftsmen settled outside the confining walls of the town. They lost a considerable amount of property in the Tudor period, the blossoming 'State' seizing it on religious pretexts; and the developing nationalism of the period caused their regulation to pass into the hands of the State.

As was the case with the manorial system, the gild system strangled itself with its own restrictions. It may be argued that a modern parallel exists internationally in the trade restrictions and barriers which have confused and confounded the world in the inter-war and post-1945 period—restrictions which such organisations of international machinery as the General Agreement on Tariffs and Trade, the 'Kennedy Round,' the European Common Market, and the European Free Trade Association have been set up to unravel.

6. THE WIDENING OF HORIZONS

Rural activity during the Middle Ages comprised not merely agriculture but also the weaving of wool in the cottages. Wool weaving in the towns grew to such an extent that by the thirteenth century England was exporting woollen cloth. At the close of the century there was a decline which was arrested by the immigration of Flemish weavers, some of whom became so substantial that they were able to employ workmen; and by the sixteenth century the woollen industry, now England's staple industry, was in the hands of capitalist employers: they purchased or grew their own wool and paid workers to weave it into cloth in the weavers' own homes. So it was that 'capitalism' and the 'domestic system' arrived.

In the meantime important things had been happening to agriculture. In the fourteenth century, in 1348–49, the Black Death hastened the decay of the manorial system and shattered the economic basis of the feudal system by sweeping away from a third to a half of the population of England. Labour became scarce; and the peasants responded to economic forces by disregarding the injunctions of the Government and moving to places where they could obtain the highest reward for their services. By so doing, they lost many rights and privileges, such as rights of common pasture and waste; and the era of the landless labourer had fairly begun. The lords went over to sheep-farming, enclosing the peasants' holdings. By the end of the fifteenth century villeinage had practically ceased to exist. Open-field cultivation continued to be practised for some time yet—and, in fact, it was carried on in a remote village or two until quite recent times; but the old manorial system was dead. A money economy had replaced the old barter-in-kind economy; subsistence activity had given place to the profit-motivated economy.

So far as dates are of any significance, the Battle of Bosworth Field in 1485 marked the end of the true Middle Ages, with their quasi-romantic chivalry, their violent, mail-clad barons, their frowning castles—whose defences were soon to crumble against the blast of gunpowder. For well-written fiction, based upon years of historical research, giving a picture of life in the Middle Ages, the reader may go to Sir Arthur Conan Doyle's *Sir Nigel* and *The White Company*.

In England a strong dynasty of sovereigns, the Tudors, with states-manship and tact, aided by Welsh sagacity and guile, held the baronage in leash—in any case, the old families had fairly successfully striven to wipe one another out during the Wars of the Roses. The policy of the Tudors—aided by the desire of the ordinary man, who was sick of the nobles' paralysing wars, for a strong government—had a unifying influence on the country and developed the growing spirit of nationalism, so that a man would be proud to call himself an Englishman rather than a Kentish-man or a Leicestershire-man. The Crown regulated commerce, at first by currency regulations and then by the establishment of uniformity in weights and measures. Mer-cantilism was born: the doctrine that a nation's wealth was increased by restricting imports but expanding exports and building up a 'favourable balance of trade.' It was nationalism running wild in the economic sphere—but economic thinking was somewhat elementary then; and, besides, there was need to arm by whatever manner men could against the might of Spain.

It was in Elizabeth's reign particularly that the Privy council ex-ercised an important influence on the economic life of the country: its influence was, indeed, an economic aspect of the growing spirit of nationalism, itself a by-product of the Renaissance.

Under the guidance of Lord Burleigh industry was protected; cloth-making came completely under the control of the home manufacturers, who were freed from their dependence on foreigners for the finishing processes, and were able to compete with the Flanders merchants in the markets of Europe. Burleigh granted monopolies and patents to those who introduced new processes, and encouraged the Protestant refugees whose skill proved invaluable in the woollen industry, in glass manufacture and in the manufacture of needles and cutlery. During the sixteeth century industrial progress was rapid.

To protect the country against the threat of Spanish power, Burleigh encouraged the shipping industry, directly by encouraging ship-builders and indirectly by encouraging the fishing industry, and under-took the maintenance of the supply of timber and of hemp and naval stores.

By the end of the reign of Elizabeth the privileges of the foreign

Period	Social and political background	Economic features
Prehistoric Old Stone Age: approx. 400,000–8,000 B.C. Middle Stone Age: approx. 8,000–3,000 B.C. New Stone Age: approx. 3,000–1,700 B.C.	Rudimentary social organisation Cave life Life poor and hard Superstition and magic	Hunting; fishing; collecting herbs and fruit Old Stone Age 'industries' —rough flint weapons New Stone Age 'industries' —polished stone weapons; pottery Beginnings of agriculture
Bronze Age: began in Britain about 1,700 B.C.	Bronze weapons; stone monuments Stable communities Hill forts Hut dwellings in stone circles	Metal-working Flocks and herds Domestic animals Weaving, ornaments
Iron Age: began in Britain about 500 B.C.	Lake and land dwellings: wattle-and-daub huts; thatched roofs Iron weapons; Chariots; Druids	Agriculture Flocks and herds Domestic animals Weaving, ornaments
Roman Occupation: 55 B.C.–A.D. 400	Military camps Roman houses; baths Strong military rule Road-building	Some trade
Dark Ages: A.D. 450–1066	Political anarchy Invasions Saxon kings. Feudal system	Saxon feudal and manorial system—self-sufficing agriculture Some shipbuilding under Alfred
Eleventh–sixteenth centuries	Norman feudalism 'Middle Ages' Beginnings of Parliament (but not modern representative system)	Manorial system Fairs. Markets Merchant gilds (twelfth–fourteenth centuries) Craft gilds (fifteenth–sixteenth centuries) Growth of towns

CHART 4—*Social, Political and*

Period	Social and political background	Economic features
The Tudors: 1500–1603	Strong central government Renaissance—revival of literature and the arts Government 'paternalism'	Economy mainly agricultural. Enclosures Handicrafts Shipbuilding Merchants of the Staple Regulated and chartered companies
1603–1700	Civil War, 1642–49 Bill of Rights, 1689 Constitutional monarchy established	Enclosures Expanding overseas trade Bank of England founded, 1694
1700–1800	Rise of new middle classes War of Spanish Succession, 1701–13 War of Austrian Succession, 1740–48 The Seven Years War, 1756–63	Britain becoming a great commercial nation Domestic system of industry Coal- and iron-mining Pottery industry Industrial Revolution
1800–1900	Napoleonic Wars, 1792–1815 1832, First Reform Act 1867, Second Reform Act 1872, Secret Ballot 1884, Third Reform Act Great increase of population Rise of large industrial towns Popular education Municipal reform	Spread of Industrial Revolution Inventions Factory system Trade Unionism. Free Trade, 1840–1914 Scientific managment in agriculture Combines in industry
Twentieth century	First World War, 1914–18 Rise of Labour Party Second World War 1939–45 Social legislation	Trade restrictions Birth of international economic organisations Beginnings of Atomic Age
	Increasing interrelation of State and economic organisation	

Economic Development in Britain

traders in England were at an end; the German merchants of the Hanseatic League lost their privileges in 1578.

In the realm of currency Sir Thomas Gresham, Elizabeth's finance minister, was entrusted with the task of putting on a sound basis again the currency, debased by Henry VIII. It is to him that Gresham's Law ('Bad money drives out good money') is attributed.

Colonial development was hardly a strong feature of the Elizabethan era; but chartered companies (also considered in more detail in Chapter V) were encouraged. It may be said that the 'Elizabethan Age' was one in which the economic foundations of England's subsequent expansion into a great commercial and trading power were firmly established. Mercantilist policy was not actively pursued during the reign: it was not until the time of the Commonwealth, in 1651, that the first effective Navigation Act was brought into operation.

By the fifteenth century the Venetians and the Genoese had assumed mastery of the trade routes in the Mediterranean; the trade with North Europe and Russia was mainly in the hands of the merchants of the Hanseatic League, a powerful body of merchants of German and Scandinavian towns. In England the Merchants of the Staple, dealing in the staple commodities, wool, hides, leather, tin and lead, formed an export association as early as the latter part of the Middle Ages. The export of cloth was the special concern of another type of association, the Merchant Adventurers, the members of which carried on trade individually or in partnership.

The trading routes to the Orient were through the Levant and Mesopotamia and down the Persian Gulf to India. The contact with customs and commodities different from their own widened the mental horizons of the merchants as the Crusades had widened the ideas of the knights; there was spice for the mind and there was spice for the body in such wanderings.

In 1453 Constantinople, the last outpost of European power in the East, fell to the invading Turks; and trade with the East was severely interrupted. Already the Portuguese had been speculating about distances and exploring ways and means of getting to India by going round the coast of Africa; in the fourteenth and fifteenth centuries they visited the Canary Isles, Madeira and the Azores. In 1487 Diaz rounded the Cape of Good Hope; and in 1497–98 Vasco da Gama sailed round the Cape to India.

It was the end of an age; these developments were rapidly shaping a new economic and political and social structure. Not that one can put one's finger on any year and say, 'This was the end of the Middle Ages.' The stream of life flows on, and the terms used by historians are merely conveniences to enable them to try to grasp the significance of a term of years; the expression 'Middle Ages' is a somewhat misleading and indeed peculiar one—what were they the middle of?

For convenience's sake, enabling us to try to see things in proportion, one can say, then, 'The "Middle Ages" were over; this is the beginning of a new era in human affairs.' But, indeed, it is like ending a chapter of an exciting book in the middle of pressing events in order to draw away for a space to see those events in relation to the broad stream of what has gone before.

CHAPTER IV

THE ACHIEVEMENTS AND SIGNIFICANCE OF THE RENAISSANCE

1. SCIENCE IN THE EAST

The burning of the library at Alexandria in A.D. 640 by the Arabs was a manifestation of the fanaticism which inspired the early Mohammedans in the conquering sweep of Islam, a sweep which carried them to Gibraltar and Spain. But religious fervour in the form of destruction of anything non-Mohammedan was diluted as the Arabs absorbed into their huge Empire peoples whose culture could not fail to influence their own—the Persians, the Syrians, the Moors, the Egyptians; the Jews in their traditional role as buffers between the Western and Eastern Worlds also fertilised with their ideas the field of energy of this conquering race.

In Europe, while the monks were poring over little-understood classical texts and records in their monasteries and the Christian Church fathers were persisting in their unshaken belief that the world was coming to an end very shortly and that interest in wordly things was a waste of time as well as being heretical, the Mohammedans developed an interest in classical works, and encouraged Greek learning. Greek texts, especially those concerned with the sciences such as medicine, astronomy, chemistry, were translated into Arabic; centres of learning were established throughout the Empire.

In the tenth century, when Britain was undergoing the battering of Saxon, Danish and Norman struggles and invasions, the Arabs built cities of culture and learning such as Cordoba and Toledo, and pursued studies of the greatest significance to our own age. They are credited with the discovery of the binomial theory and the solution of cubic equations. Just as the Greeks gave their own word to the study of Politics (*polis*=city-state), so the Arabs gave us the word Algebra and our system of numbers—so much more manageable than the cumbrous Roman figures.

Though their astronomy was befuddled with astrology, the Arabian scientists made useful observations and records (astronomy today owes much to the patient record-making of amateurs); eclipses were predicted precisely. Arabian chemistry was similarly confused with the search for a means of transmuting baser metals to gold which had

preoccupied thinkers in Alexandria; but nevertheless their experiments led to the discovery of many chemical substances and to the invention of new chemical methods and apparatus. One Ibn Sina
(A.D. 980–1036) (Avicenna) denounced alchemy in modern fashion.

The University idea was already in operation in the world.

It was, indeed, through Arab sources that many Greek works
reached Western Europe. Pope Sylvester II had spent some years as a
monk in Barcelona and on his return to Italy spread the new Arab
learning.

2. THE REVIVAL OF LEARNING IN EUROPE

The Arab advance into Europe was halted by Charles Martel, a
Frankish king. He defeated an army of Arabs and Moors at Tours in
732. His grandson, Charlemagne, Charles the Great, extended his
conquests to build an empire which stretched from France to North
Italy in the south and to the Elbe in the east. He was crowned
Emperor by the Pope in 800. At his death, his empire was divided between his three successors, one of whom, ruling the eastern part, comprising Germany and Austria, became Holy Roman Emperor. It was
a title which was borne by German princes from the time of Otto
the Great in 962 to 1806, by which time it was shorn of all meaning.

In spite of the attention demanded by his military activities,
Charlemagne found time to interest himself in art, architecture and
learning generally. His inspiration and encouragement, and the interchange of ideas and knowledge from the Crusades (Constantinople
finally fell to the Turks in 1453), resulted in a revival of learning in
Europe. The University of Paris was founded in 1101, Oxford in
1167.

But the learning in the Universities was that of the 'Schoolmen,'
engaged in studying such subjects as logic, rhetoric, theology and
metaphysics, and becoming involved in pedantic hair-splitting and the
juggling with words and ideas which still distinguishes the Arts side
of our universities today.

Nevertheless, in order to pursue their Aristotelian studies, the
scholars had to study Greek, and especially, since the existing trans-
lations, from Arabic into Latin, were unsatisfactory, the Greek original
texts, so that a better knowledge of the original Greek writings was
obtained.

The old Roman Empire, by the time the 'Middle Ages' had been
reached, had split into three parts. The south and east, from a part
of Spain and North Africa to Mesopotamia, was in Mohammedan
hands. The Eastern Greek Empire was ruled over by an Emperor at
Constantinople. The Western countries, with the Pope as spiritual
leader, was Western Christendom, with a spiritual tradition of a united

Europe interchanging its scholars and ideas but politically divided among the dukes and counts and princes of the Feudal system, owing allegiance to an Emperor striving for dominion, more or less successfully according to the characters of individual Popes and Emperors. The 'ordinary' man, the non-noble man, was squeezed between the tyranny of the Church, substantial enough in an age in which there was a real fear of hell and damnation, and that of his secular lord, demanding his material services and threatening his economic and physical existence. Until the rise of towns and gilds and associations or burgesses, the freeman and the serfs were helpless in the grip of a Feudal tyranny which, in the case of France, lasted right up to the Revolution.

The Normans introduced their brand of feudalism into England; but because of the tradition of local government and the common law derived from the Saxons' ancestors which William I had suffered to remain, Feudalism never reached the rigidity it attained on the Continent; and the system of centralised law introduced by Henry I and Henry II conflicted with the political aspirations of the barons, to culminate in a series of civil wars that eventually resulted in their own near-extermination by the barons themselves.

3. ROGER BACON

The psychological characteristic of the Middle Ages was respect for Authority, Authority not only in the political and ecclesiastical spheres but also in the inner world of ideas. The Schoolmen, accepting unreservedly the unverified statements attributed to Aristotle, dominated the thought of the Middle Ages.

But there was a flicker of the mental dawning that was to come with the Renaissance. Roger Bacon was born in 1214. He studied Greek at Oxford, went to the University of Paris, and returned to Oxford in 1250 to study particularly optics and chemistry, unorthodox pursuits which, since he was a Franciscan friar, brought him under the very deep suspicions of Mother Church. For ten years he was confined to a house in Paris. The election of a new Pope who was a family friend gave him the opportunity to regain his freedom. He wrote three books, the contents of which were sufficiently disturbing to the authorities to ensure for him a further period of confinement. He returned to the safer study of philosophy, and died in 1294.

The imaginative writings of Bacon, including descriptions of things to come in the shape of powered ships and flying machines, anticipate the similar and more expertly founded efforts of Leonardo da Vinci 200 years later. But his real significance lies in his insistence on the value of observation, experiment and deduction, that scientific method which was detested by the authoritarian Church which, if not really convinced of its own infallibility, realised the dangers to its organisation if free thinking was allowed to flourish.

Roger Bacon was not a modern in the sense that he was free from the cramping influence of veneration for established Authority—not that all 'moderns' are so free. He thought in medieval ways. But his medievalism was illumined by a spark that was to grow into flame which burned for a time with a great fire, so brightly that men caught glimpses of the eternal Truth, Beauty, Goodness, and translated them into human terms.

4. THE RENAISSANCE

The Renaissance was the Rebirth of Learning—Greek and Latin learning, in narrow terms; but it was much more than that. It was a freeing of the human spirit from the mental bonds of the Middle Ages: the reverence for authority and particularly that of the Church; the timidity and pettiness of the Schoolmen; the clinging to a security that fears the new and the unknown. It was no mere concentration on learning; it spread into art, literature, science, physical adventure, religion. It did not touch everybody—or we should be living in a different world today. But those whom the spirit did touch it transformed, and it transformed the age in which they lived.

It was no sudden process—we have discerned a spark of the new spirit in Roger Bacon in the thirteenth century; and Dante (1265–1321) produced his works before the Italian Renaissance came into full flower. But Europe was receiving the impact of the ideas revived and brought to her from the Arab world. It needed the breaking of the rigidity of the Feudal System to give the opportunity for men to expand their mental horizons and transform their social and physical environment.

The Renaissance was a rebirth of the culture and the best ideals of ancient Greece and Rome, and it took that culture and those ideals farther than had been possible in the special circumstances of Greece and Rome. It started in Italy, so near to the centre of the classical world. There the medieval cities had accumulated wealth by trade, and they were fortunate in that not only the merchant class wished to indulge a taste for art and beauty but the aristocracy and princes of the Church displayed as violent a desire for lovely and imperishable things as for the kind of activities to be expected of a violent age. Susceptible to the penetration of their medievalism by influences from the East and the Greek Byzantium, cities like Florence, Venice, Milan used the rising standards of living to rise with them. The capture of Constantinople by the Turks in 1453 accelerated the pace of the rescue operation of classical learning.

In literature the Renaissance culminated in the genius of Shakespeare and Marlowe in England, of Boccaccio, Cervantes, Rabelais on the Continent; in music in the beginnings of opera; in painting and sculpture in the works of Leonardo da Vinci, Michaelangelo, Titian, Raphael and, in Northern Europe, Dürer and Holbein; in religion in the Reformation; in personal experience and physical adventure in the geographical discoveries told of in the next chapter.

The great exemplar of all time was Leonardo da Vinci (1452–1519), whose so-called masterpiece, the 'Mona Lisa', is known to every tourist who visits the Louvre. But this item of popular acclaim, together with the equally popular picture of the Last Supper in the refectory of the convent church of S. Maria delle Grazie, by no means represent the sum of his great genius. He was an engineer, inventor, architect, painter, sculptor, philosopher—and an athlete: he was the 'all-round man,' the possessor of a healthy mind in a healthy body, the ideal of the Greeks. His notebooks show the astonishing versatility of his genius; he anticipated Newton's laws of motion; he understood the principle of the lever and the pulley; he arrived at the idea of the wave-motion of light and sound; he improved the mariner's compass; he designed a steam-cannon; he explored the possibilities of propulsion of ships by steam; he dissected human bodies in the cause of the correct representation of the human frame; he wrote a work on bird flight and examined the possibilities of flying machines.

That he 'worked for' patrons, including the designing of machines of war, was an economic necessity with which the great majority of mankind has to come to terms: he was chief engineer to Caesar Borgia. But the rich aristocratic patrons of the Renaissance patronised genius because it was genius, and provided the funds and the means by which genius could carry on its work. What happens in 'democracy' is shown by the example of Rembrandt, whose picture known as *The Night Watch*, painted in 1583, marked the beginning of his fall from public favour: he painted a work of art instead of rendering a photographic representation of the worthy burghers.

5. THE RISE OF SCIENCE

Fascinating as an exploration of the artistic and cultural achievements of the Renaissance would be—and at the moment there are some beautifully produced books on the theme—we must restrict our survey to the more materialistic aspects of the Renaissance movement. By the fifteenth century the necessity for the use of scientific method to arrive at knowledge of the physical world was accepted outside the Church, jealous of its prerogatives and explaining everything by its own decrees.

The Church had approved the Ptolemaic system of the Universe—Ptolemy lived in the second century A.D.—in which the earth was the centre of the Universe, and the planets moved around it in circles. Copernicus (1473–1543) said that the earth moved around the sun; and was so frightened by the probable consequences of his presumption that he did not allow the publication of his work, *On the Revolutions of the Heavenly Bodies*, which he had written in 1520, until the year before his death. He explained the succession of night and day and the precession of the equinoxes.

Copernicus had escaped the fury of the Church, Catholic and Protestant, by not publicising the results of his researches during his life—they were published in Nuremburg in 1542 and only on his death-bed did the author handle his published work. A Dominican monk, Giodarno Bruno, who was a follower of Copernicus and who had suggested that the stars were other suns in the Universe, was not so lucky or circumspect; he was imprisoned by the Inquisition and on his refusal to recant was burned at the stake in 1600.

The Dane, Tycho Brahe (1546–1601), and his assistant and colleague, Johann Kepler (1571–1630) laid the foundations of modern observational and mathematical astronomy. Kepler stated the laws relating to planetary motion. The age was still dark outside the circle of scientific investigation; Kepler had to defend his mother against a charge of witchcraft.

Galileo Galilei (1564–1642) followed on the researches in magnetism of William Gilbert of Colchester (1544–1603), Court Physician to Queen Elizabeth. Galileo, engaged in the study of medicine at the University of Pisa, turned to the study of physics and mechanics. He discovered the fact that the rate of swing of a simple pendulum depends on its length. He became Professor of Mathematics at Pisa, and investigated the behaviour of falling bodies, the Leaning Tower being convenient for this purpose. His use of practical experiment to confound the teachings of the professors steeped in the Aristotelian errors displeased them, and Pisa was made too hot to hold him. Had it been realised that he approved of the Copernican system, his position would have been hotter still.

Galileo found a more congenial climate at Padua and wrote *Concerning the Science of Mechanics*. In this work he founded the study of the forces acting on moving bodies, a foundation on which Isaac Newton was to build. One recollects, with a certain surprise at the nearness of these events, that Newton was born on the day Galileo died.

Galileo improved upon the existing telescopes and observed the larger four moons of Jupiter, the phases of Venus and what were subsequently to be seen as the rings of Saturn. The refusal of the local professors actually to look through Galileo's telescopes may have had something to do with Galileo's decision to leave Padua and take up service with the Duke of Florence, Ferdinand II, to whom he dedicated his *Dialogue on the Ptolemaic and Copernican Systems*. Now he was in trouble with the Inquisition, which summoned him to appear at Rome, and was compelled under threat of torture to abjure his heresies about the movement of the earth around the sun. It is probable that the story of his muttered remark, 'Eppur si muove!' ('Nevertheless it moves!') is apocryphal; but there can be no doubt that he thought it. He was put under observational restraint; but was allowed to receive distinguished visitors when he became blind in 1638.

The study of the theory and practice of medicine was continued by Vesalius, who published in 1543 a work on the structure of the human body. William Harvey (1578–1657) continued his work and discovered the circulation of the blood.

Francis Bacon (1561–1626), Lord Chancellor of England, belied in his life the elevated sentiments of his famous *Essays*, and showed yet another side of his character by writing on the philosophy of science, emphasising the value of observation and deduction.

With Malpighi (1628–94), who observed capillary attraction; Torricelli (1608–47), who made the first barometer; Robert Boyle (1627–91), who discovered that the volume of a gas varies inversely with the pressure at constant temperature, we move out of the period generally regarded as the Renaissance. By this time the scientific method of observation and experiment, the forming of hypotheses, the testing of those hypotheses, and the establishing of laws subject to verification and perhaps revision, had been established.

The age of the great painters was waning a little; the age of Haydn, Mozart and Beethoven had yet to come, and grand opera was yet to delight the many. The spirit of scientific enquiry went steadily on, eventually to transform the Western World into one of machines and power and conquest over physical resources—beyond, indeed, the capacity of the so-called social sciences of Economics and Politics and Sociology to deal with the multitude of facts and human attitudes presented to them. Not until 1776 was Adam Smith to publish his famous *Wealth of Nations*, which inspired a free-trade movement in Britain.

6. NEWTONIAN SCIENCE

In the hands of the scientists, mathematics was being developed to serve more faithfully the needs of the men who were investigating the laws of physical Nature; it had become clear that Science is measurement. John Napier (1550–1617) invented logarithms. Algebraic methods were applied to geometry by René Descartes (1596–1650), a philosopher who was contemporary with Galileo.

In 1675 the Royal Observatory was founded at Greenwich for the purpose of observing the stars, and advances were made in meteorology and clock- and compass-making. The Royal Society (the Royal Society of London for Improving Natural Knowledge) had been founded about 1645; its first charter was granted by Charles II in 1662. Its most famous fellow was Isaac Newton, who was elected in 1671 and whose *Principia* was published with the encouragement of the Society.

Newton (1642–1727) was part-inventor of the calculus (the other was Leibnitz (1646–1716)). Newton's great intellect was applied to the study of gravitation. He did work in optics, inventing the reflecting telescope; in mathematics; and he gave us his Laws of Motion. It is said that his interest in science was evinced only in short periods, and that at times he expressed a distaste for it. With his tremendous intellect went a deep humility. The two characteristics mark him as being in many ways the Leonardo da Vinci of his age: he was no recondite academic theoriser; he showed the aptitude and grasp of a practical man of affairs when in 1698 he was appointed Master of the Mint and forthwith set about putting the chaotic affairs of that institution into order. Newton strove to bring order out of Nature.

The seventeenth century was the age of Newton. His example impressed and inspired; and thereafter the years of the seventeenth and eighteenth centuries are studded with the names of those who strove to follow his light, e.g., that of Christian Huyghens (1629–95), who also engaged in the study of physics and mechanics.

And now it is time to pause in our survey of the achievements of the Renaissance spirit in science and see what developments were taking place in the lives of men and women engaged in the ordinary business of life, making things, trading, gaining a living in the new kind of world that was coming into existence.

CHAPTER V

THE BEGINNINGS OF THE MODERN WORLD

1. THE GREAT GEOGRAPHICAL DISCOVERIES

THOUGH one age moves into another not in jumps but by a process often slow and not readily recognised at the time, one can discern the pattern of the new age after the change has taken place. The 'Middle Ages' were gone; Henry VII, though seemingly a medieval king, was the first of the moderns—he was very far from the gallant, swashbuckling kings who had preceded him. The mailed knight had gone; politically, the birth of the modern English constitution was taking place.

And in the world beyond our shores events were taking place which were directly leading to the shaping of Britain as a 'world power'. We have told how the ships of Europe were sailing the world seas, confined no longer to the practically land-surrounded Mediterranean. Christopher Columbus was trying to find practical support for his idea of reaching the East by sailing westwards; in 1492, his little expedition of eighty-eight men, his trio of tiny ships—the famous *Santa Maria* was only of 100 tons burthen—sailed into unknown seas. A little over two months later Columbus, bearing the royal banner of Spain, landed on what he thought was the coast of India: the islands he discovered were the West Indies, off the shores of the New World. To the day of his death, he was ignorant of the fact that he had brought into the horizon of the people of Western Civilisation a world which may, indeed, have been first discovered by the Northmen of old, but which had been forgotten by the West for centuries.

His success inspired the Portuguese to new efforts; in 1497 Vasco da Gama sailed to India. In 1519 Magellan, a Portuguese in the employment of Spain, passed through the straits which bear his name, sailed across the Pacific Ocean and discovered the Philippines.

So the ships of Spain sailed across to the New World; their captains plundered and destroyed the ancient civilisations of the Aztecs and the Incas in Mexico and Peru, bringing back the gold and silver of Central and South America that enabled Spain to take a dominating but temporary position among the nations of Europe.

In the path of conquest, but as trading nations rather than military powers, came the English, the French and the Dutch. Trading companies seeking monopoly in particular areas came into conflict in India and North America, and economic and political motives were mixed in the wars the European nations waged for power in the New World. Famous trading companies like the East India Company, which received its original charter from Queen Elizabeth I in 1600, were granted charters by the Crown to exploit the resources of the territories they had marked out.

2. THE TRADING COMPANIES

The companies which the growing, powerful class of merchants formed as instruments in their economic activities were of two types, regulated and joint-stock. *Regulated* companies, of which the greatest was the Merchant Adventurers, were associations of merchants who carried out ventures singly or in partnership, the company as a whole possessing a charter to carry on a specified trade. *Joint-stock* companies were associations in which the business was carried on by the company as a whole, the capital being contributed by shareholders among whom the profits were divided.

Companies like the East India Company were granted charters which gave them the monopoly of trade in a certain area. Canada, India, Africa, the great areas 'ripe for development,' were divided out and quarrelled over and fought over by the nations. Such colonies as were founded were regarded by the statesmen of the time merely as exploitation areas providing raw materials and new products for the 'mother country,' and markets for her own goods.

The Mercantilist doctrine had full play, and foreign trade was so regulated as to obtain the greatest advantage to the nation: the most favourable 'balance of trade' and the maximum inflow of precious metals. Navigation Laws were made by the British; these regulations brought them into conflict with the Dutch, who were becoming the Western World's sea-carriers, and who objected to the Navigation Act of 1651, which laid it down that goods imported into England from Asia, Africa or America or the plantations should be carried in English or plantation ships, *i.e.* ships in which the owner, master and the majority of the crew were British; goods from European countries could be brought into England or the colonies only in English ships or in ships of the country of origin. Only English vessels could import certain fish, and foreign vessels were not to engage in the English coasting trade.

The 1660 Navigation Act, amended and added to by various subsequent provisions, laid down the basis of the subsequent regulation of British shipping. During the latter part of the seventeenth century, and throughout the eighteenth century, the volume of English tonnage increased; and it has been argued on the one side that this increase was the result of the Navigation Acts, and on the other side that it would have occurred in spite of them. We cannot enter into this controversy here; but it may be noted that the Baltic trade, at least, was adversely affected, since British ships were not built for the Baltic trade.

Certainly in the case of the American colonies, the mercantilist policy had disastrous results. It has been mentioned that the colonies were regarded as places whence England could obtain raw materials and products she could not produce herself and to which she could export finished goods. Under these circumstances regulation of the colonial trade in the interests of the 'mother country' was considered right and proper—and this regulation in many cases worked to the advantage of the settlers: in tobacco, for example, the colonial enjoyed protection against English competition, and had an assured market with a guaranteed fair price for his goods. But this 'old colonial system' proved increasingly irritating to the expanding colonies, which had built their own ships and wanted to use them as they wished. The restrictions irritated foreign countries, too, and they adopted retaliatory methods of dealing with them. In fact, the early nineteenth century saw the rise of a vigorous free-trade movement, as the principles set out in Adam Smith's *Wealth of Nations* (1776) gained increasing practical support. The Navigation Acts were repealed in 1849 almost entirely; the last remnant of restriction, that relating to the coasting trade, followed in 1854. But by that time the damage, as far as America was concerned, had been done.

3. THE PATTERN OF EXPANDING TRADE

Because the Industrial Revolution grew out of the wealth of the country, and, indeed, was a natural consequence of the commercial revolution that preceded it, it is necessary to look at the pattern of the expanding trade which brought this wealth.

In the Middle Ages the most important commodity was wool. In the reign of Henry III the *Staple* was established. This was a market for the overseas trade in the Staple commodities wool, hides, leather, and tin and lead; taxes on the exports of these commodities provided the Crown with revenue; a circumstance by no means pleasing to Parliament. The place was changed at various times. From 1399 until its loss in 1558, Calais was the Staple. The English merchants who exported the Staple commodities were called the Merchants of the Staple. The Merchants of the Staple came into conflict in the fifteenth century with the Merchant Adventurers, who exported woollen cloth; the latter thus became the rivals of the Merchants of the Staple, who had the right to export wool, which they contended included woollen cloth. In point of fact, the export of wool was declining in favour of woollen cloth.

The Merchant Adventurers also came into conflict with the Hanse merchants, who were German merchants of the Hanseatic League trading in woollen cloth, herrings, furs and tar, and whose London depot was the Steelyard. This struggle ended in 1578, when the Hanse merchants lost their privileges; the Steelyard was closed in 1598.

A certain amount of cloth was exported from England in the thirteenth century. Flemish weavers fleeing from disturbances in the Netherlands were invited by Edward III to settle in England; and their skill helped to develop the woollen and worsted industries of the country. Some of the Flemings were men of means able to employ workmen; and the industry as a whole gradually became capitalistic; by the fifteenth century it was entirely in the hands of capitalists who supplied the raw material and collected the finished article from workers manufacturing the cloth in their own homes. This was the 'domestic system': the system whereby manufacture was carried on in their homes by people as an activity supplementary to agriculture. It must be remembered that right up to the middle of the eighteenth century England was predominantly an agricultural country.

The increasing prosperity of the woollen-cloth trade induced the landlords to enclose lands; and they ejected tenants with little regard to their rights. The hardships thus engendered received the attention of Parliament; and proclamations and statutes in the Tudor period attempted to stem the evils, with little avail: the enclosure movement continued until the end of the sixteenth century.

By the consolidation of the scattered strips and consequent improvements in the methods of farming, some advantages were derived from the enclosure movement; but farming throughout the country was still mainly arable, and open-field cultivation continued on a large scale until late in the seventeenth century. Not until the agrarian revolution of the eighteenth century, when enclosures began again, this time by Act of Parliament and for the purpose of supplying the growing industrial towns with food, were methods in agriculture revolutionised.

The enclosures of the Tudor period took place to supply the woollen industry with raw material; by the end of the seventeenth century about two-thirds of English exports consisted of woollen fabrics. Because of the demands of the home market, the export of wool declined as manufacture grew.

The great port of the sixteenth century was Antwerp, to which England sent for distribution wool, lead, tin, leather and provisions, receiving bullion, precious stones, spices, sugar, cotton, glass, salt, fish and other commodities. But at the end of the sixteenth century Antwerp's position as the entrepôt of Europe passed to London, whose rise was aided by the efforts and skill of the Protestant refugees.

The great discoveries in the East and the New World, and the formation of the trading companies, heralded the rise of Britain as the foremost commercial nation in the world. The greatest of the trading companies was the East India Company. Its forerunners, the Eastland Company and the Turkey Company, failed to fulfil their early promise. The Eastland Company was formed in 1579 to try to secure the Baltic trade carried on by the Hanseatic League. It exported cloth and imported tar, hemp, cordage and naval stores; but the Government came to rely more on the American colonies for naval stores. The Turkey Company was formed in 1581 to deal in the Eastern Mediterranean trade; in 1592 it was merged into a new company, the Levant Company. It suffered from the competition of the Muscovy Company (which for a time monopolised the trade with Russia), and of the East India Company, both of which were engaged in the Persian silk trade.

The East India Company was founded in 1600, becoming at first a company in which joint-stock activity was practised for each voyage and then raising a permanent joint-stock capital in 1657. Initially it tried to build up trade with the Spice Islands in spices, silks, indigo and calico, imports from India much in demand there. The Dutch frustrated this aim; and in consequence the Company turned its attention to the west coast of India. The story of its expansion, its taking on the functions of government and the conflict with the French, is well known. Trade may normally follow the flag, but it would appear that in the case of the East India Company the flag followed trade.

The story was paralleled in Canada. In 1670 Charles II granted a Royal Charter to a group of courtiers and magnates, giving them a monopoly of trade in the lands around the Hudson Bay. The Hudson Bay Company engaged in the fur trade, and from 1690 its young traders explored the interior. Its lands were invaded by the French, who, however, were finally defeated in the political struggle that followed. The company remained in sole control of the huge Canadian area from 1821 until 1869, when it surrendered its monopoly. It now has a retail, wholesale and multiple-store organisation as well as a great fur-trading business. The towns of Western and Central Canada grew up around the company's trading posts. The companies were not merely extending the scope and value of trade; they were opening up continents for exploitation.

Such activities could not help but bring riches to the men who financed and directed them. Public interest in trade and in the profits to be obtained from it grew rapidly in the peace which followed the Treaty of Utrecht (1713), the treaty which concluded the war of the Spanish Succession. Companies were formed to engage in what their members hoped would be profitable enterprises, though some were started by the ignorant and enthusiastic and some by the adventurer type always thrown up by circumstances giving the opportunity to fleece the foolish. One of the most popular companies was the South Sea Company, which was chartered in 1711, and which was granted a monopoly of trade with South America south of the Orinoco in return for loans made to the Government. It gained the right of supplying Negro slaves to Spanish colonies for 30 years; but, this being found less profitable than was expected, it sought to extend its activities, and offered to take over the National Debt in exchange for the monopoly of all extra-European trade. This offer was accepted by the Government, and it seemed to speculators that all their dreams were about to come true. Hundreds of new companies were started, many with the most fantastic objects such as for making salt water fresh, or with no definite objects stated at all. Ruin for many people was inevitable, and the South Sea 'Bubble' was pricked. The South Sea Company itself went back to its former activities; the 'Bubble Act' of 1720 required new companies to obtain a charter from the Crown or to be formed under a special Act of Parliament.

It is evident that there was at that time a fund of money waiting for investment.

4. BANKING AND CREDIT

The development of trade necessitated the introduction of a system of banking and finance. The concentration of the noble classes on fighting, and the preoccupation of the lower classes with the tilling of the soil, had left the work of money-dealing in the hands of the Jews; and for several hundred years before the thirteenth century they were the money-lenders and money-changers of Europe. Usury, the lending out of money for interest, was forbidden by the Christian Church. Towards the end of the thirteenth century, Lombards arrived from Northern Italy; they defied the law about money-lending, and were expelled in the reign of Elizabeth I.

As commerce expanded, merchants built up not only a body of customs relating to the legal aspects of their business but also evolved an instrument by which national and international debts could be settled without the sending of bullion—an instrument, moreover, which could serve as a basis of credit. This was the bill of exchange, by which a debtor trader agreed in writing that he would pay another trader, or anybody else to his order, a certain sum at a fixed future time. The creditor trader could settle *his* debt to a third trader by endorsing the bill in the third trader's favour. The bill could thus be passed from hand to hand, the last holder presenting it for payment to the original debtor trader at the end of the stipulated time.

Certainly the efficacy of such an instrument depended on the credit of the original debtor and on the credit of those who passed on the bill;

in practice, the level of integrity of merchants generally was such that the bill of exchange came, by the sixteenth and seventeenth centuries, to be used extensively in national and international trade.

A great advantage of the bill of exchange, and one that contributed to the spread of commerce and the production of commodities, was that the money for raw materials could be borrowed on the strength of the credit of a merchant, who would arrange to pay after the customer had received the finished commodity. Thus trade, *e.g.* the woollen trade, was financed, and the widening market was able to bear the fact that producer and consumer were often far from one another.

Farmers and manufacturers were able to obtain finance from goldsmiths, clothiers, landlords and other people, who thus engaged in the art of money-lending.

Actual money and bullion was entrusted to scriveners (or financiers) and goldsmiths; the troubles of the Civil War caused merchants to resort more and more to goldsmiths, who had facilities for safeguarding valuables and who issued receipts for the money. Such receipts would be passed from hand to hand, obviating the transference of actual metal, and they became in effect the first bank-notes. Moreover, a client might make an order requiring the goldsmith to pay somebody else a certain sum: this was the beginning of the cheque system. But the cheque did not find favour as an instrument of payment until the nineteenth century, with the rise of the joint-stock banks. The goldsmiths became deposit bankers, lending money on the security of bills of exchange, and lending money also to the Government.

This latter activity involved them in considerable difficulties when the Dutch war depleted the exchequer of the Government. William III obtained a loan of £1,200,000 from business men by agreeing to a plan whereby, in return for the loan, a 'Bank of England' should receive 8% and the privilege of becoming the Government's bank, as well as the privilege of issuing notes to the extent of the loan. The Bank of England was incorporated by Royal Charter in 1694. It met with opposition from the goldsmiths and private bankers, who feared its rivalry; but a bank backed by the Government could not fail to meet such opposition adequately.

In 1708 an Act was passed prohibiting any other chartered bank or partnership consisting of more than six persons from issuing bank-notes. Such importance was attached to this function of note-issuing that for 100 years no other joint-stock banks were established in England, though neither private banks nor joint-stock banks were prohibited. Most banking business was carried on in London; before 1750 there were few banking houses in the provinces, though a good deal of bill discounting (*i.e.* the buying of bills of exchange at a discount) was carried on by shopkeepers and importers. Some merchants, indeed, found bill discounting so profitable that they eventually discarded their merchanting activities and became well-known discounting houses and acceptance houses (*i.e.* they 'accepted' bills of exchange for their clients, making themselves liable to pay—for, of course, a suitable return, and on security).

Thus there was being built up a banking and financial machinery which was to be of especial value when an expanding industry was seeking the means to finance itself and to conduct the multifarious banking transactions which became necessary.

5. THE EVE OF THE INDUSTRIAL REVOLUTION

It has become clear why Britain was so well equipped to take her place as the leading industrial nation. Politically, the country was united under a strong government. Her merchants had built up contacts all over the world. Her geography, her climate, were of the type to stimulate the manufacture and export of the cotton that was to become king in the new kind of world to follow; her resources in coal and iron were waiting for exploitation. Capital had been built up by her foreign trade, and her banking and credit and financial machinery had been developed to a point from which further progress could spring. Circumstances, natural resources, and native energy had made possible a commercial revolution which was the necessary prelude to the Industrial Revolution.

Yet there was no sudden change—at least, on the scale of human life there was no sudden and violent upheaval. It is only when one steps back to survey the long years of quiet, traditional agriculture, of domestic resources supplemented by manufacture within the home, and contrasts them with the period of smoking, humming industry of 60 years later that one realises how quickly the country jumped into modern times.

By the latter half of the eighteenth century England had become a great commercial nation. The most important industry was the manufacture of woollen cloth. In some parts of the country the head of the household was the proprietor of his business: he bought the raw material, worked it up with the aid of members of his family or with the help of journeymen, and sold it. He was not yet divorced from the soil. This was the true domestic system. But in other parts of the country, the handling of the raw materials and finished articles, apart from manufacture, was in the hands of dealers or clothiers, the first of the army of capitalists.

Cotton manufacture was quite unimportant in the early part of the eighteenth century, but it increased in the Lancashire district. Pottery flourished in Staffordshire, hardware in Warwickshire. Coal- and iron-mining were being developed in the north—these were industries which were necessarily capitalistic from the beginning. Birmingham, Sheffield, Manchester, Liverpool, increased their populations. From the five millions of Elizabeth I's time, the population had increased by 1750 to about 6½ millions: increased wealth in the country as a whole, better living conditions for people generally, enabled people more adequately to support children than before.

But the country was still mainly agricultural. About a third of the working-class population consisted of agricultural labourers; the industrial classes were slightly less in numbers. Only about a fifth of the population was concentrated in towns; outside London, only Bristol, engaged in shipbuilding and the American trade, and Norwich, the centre of the Norfolk woollen-manufacturing industry, had over 50,000 in 1700. But Birmingham, Liverpool and Hull were increasing their manufacture and shipbuilding; Leeds had become the centre of the West Riding woollen industry. Iron was being smelted in Sussex and the Forest of Dean; Sheffield was developing her manufacture of cutlery.

The change was beginning; and when it came it continued rapidly. Soon the face of Britain was to be transformed; new social, economic and technical problems were to arise, carrying with the attempts to solve them political implications that were to interact with them and make indeed a new kind of world for the British people.

6. SCIENCE IN THE EIGHTEENTH AND NINETEENTH CENTURIES

The eighteenth century was a period of consolidation of the discoveries in science which had already been made. It was a period of verification and testing of theories; one of slow, steady advance to the point when, in the nineteenth century, the principles were applied and exploited in material production in the spirit of *laissez-faire* and free enterprise.

The scientists themselves, as scientists do, explored the possibilities of control over Nature and the acquisition of human power without taking responsibility for what the private profit-seeker, the exploiter of human skill and energy, would do with this control. Science was to be applied to anthropology and archaeology, and to the more academic aspects of sociology, but not yet to the immediate problems of social and political organisation. That was not to come until wars and devastation and economic misery, made all the more acute because of greater efficiency in the making of weapons and the building of industrial cities which science had made possible, had spread over the world.

In economics, Arthur Marshall, in his *Principles of Economics* was to give a lead in 1890; he defined economics, or political economy, as 'the study of man's actions in the ordinary business of life; it inquires how he gets his income and how he spends it. Thus it is, on the one side, a study of wealth and on the other, a more important side, a part of the study of man.'* But much of the time and effort of those who followed him was taken up in the evolving of academic theories, often expressed in mathematical formulae, of slight consequence to the real industrial world of toiling human beings.

The task of the natural scientists was not handicapped by the intervention in their experiments of human psychology and aspirations and self-centredness; the study of physical phenomena was more amenable to simple discipline. Mathematics in their hands was a tool and not a method of avoiding contact with reality. There were, therefore, steady advances in the control of the physical environment.

In chemistry, Lavoisier (1743–94) followed up the work of Joseph Priestley (1733–1804), who had discovered oxygen in 1774, by establishing a system of the common elements and compounds. His work was cut short by the guillotine in the French Revolution, the President of the Court voicing an eternal principle of 'people's revolutions' by his remark, 'The Republic has no need of savants.' Priestley, before him, had had his house burnt by the mob in Birmingham for his liberal political and theological ideas.

The careful work of Henry Cavendish (1731–1810) enabled him to conclude that water was composed of oxygen and hydrogen; he ascertained the constituents of air and conducted experiments on the density of the earth. He also worked in magnetism, and he and Coulomb, independently, demonstrated the attraction of positive and negative charges of electricity.

The study of electricity and magnetism was enthusiastically pursued during the eighteenth and nineteenth centuries. Humphry Davy (1778–1829), who invented the miner's safety lamp, and his assistant Michael Faraday (1791–1867) applied electrical researches to chemistry. Faraday established the laws of electrolysis; his discovery of the principles of electromagnetic induction was to lead to the dynamo and to modern electrical engineering.

This was indeed the period in which the researches of scientists bore fruit in the invention of machines that were to revolutionise the economy of Britain, of Europe, of the world. In chemistry, John Dalton (1766–1844) brought to practical fulfilment the Greeks' ideas about atoms: he introduced a method of determining the relative weights of the atoms of the elements, a method perfected by the Swede Bergelius (1799–1848) and the Italian Amadeo Avogadro (1776–1856). Atomic science had begun.

Count Rumford (Benjamin Thompson, 1753–1814) was an American who was given his title as Count of the Holy Roman Empire by the Elector of Bavaria; with Sir Joseph Banks he founded the Royal Institu-

* Vol. I, p. 1 (Macmillan & Co.).

tion in 1799. He investigated the transformation of other forms of energy into heat, as did Davy. A pupil of Dalton, James Prescott Joule (1818–89) went farther in this study, and in 1847 stated the principle of the Conservation of Energy.

The application of the results of such studies to the principle of the steam-engine had been investigated by Sadi Carnot, a Frenchman (1796–1832); and already Thomas Newcomen (1663–1729) had invented an 'atmospheric steam-engine' in 1711; it was improved by James Watt (1736–1819), who patented his 'Watt' steam-engine in 1769. The experiments of Rumford and Davy had shown that heat was a form of energy; Joule's work laid the foundation of the internal combustion engine. Thus were begun the advances in mechanical engineering which were to revolutionise power and transport in the Industrial Revolution.

In electrical science, the labours of Hans Christian Oersted (1777–1851) at Copenhagen, of Georg Simon Ohm (1787–1854) at Cologne, of Faraday, of Joseph Henry (1799–1878), of Lord Kelvin (William Thomson, 1824–1917), of Samuel Morse (1791–1872), were to lead to the first telegraph and the first telephone: Alexander Graham Bell (1847–1922) devised the first telephone system in 1876.

The steps taken in the investigation of 'wireless waves' by James Clerk Maxwell (1831–79), Ambrose Fleming (1849–1945), Heinrich Geissler (1814–79), Sir William Crookes (1832–1919) and Wilhelm Konrad Roentgen (1845–1923) were leading inevitably to 'X'-rays and the work of Marie (1867–1934) and Pierre Curie (1859–1906). From the further study of radioactivity were to come great blessings and great means of destruction.

Albert Einstein (1879–1955) continued with the Newtonian tradition and propounded the theory of Relativity; he wrote on peace, but the die was cast: the twentieth century came uneasily to the realisation that the powers of destruction by and of the human race were unlimited —the first atomic bomb was dropped on Hiroshima in 1945.

7. THE DEVELOPMENT OF THE SOCIAL SCIENCES

It might appear strange to an observer unacquainted with the human capacity for self-deception that there could be any connection between biology and geology and the social sciences. The system of classification of plants devised by the Swedish biologist Carl Linnaeus (1707–78) could hardly be described as the first beginnings of such a connection. Yet when Georges Cuvier (1769–1832) mastered comparative anatomy in animals to the extent that he could boast that if he were given a tooth he could reconstruct the whole animal; when Charles Lyell (1797–1875) summarised geological knowledge in his *Principles of Geology* in 1830; when Charles Darwin (1809–82) wrote on the origin of species and formulated with Alfred Russel Wallace (1823–1913) the theory of natural selection, they were really laying the foundation of a change in mental attitudes of Western civilisation that was to be itself a revolution.

Though bloodless in the literal sense, this revolution has had its wars and alarms and strife and conflict. It seemed that a new Renaissance, lacking the patronage of intelligent and cultured princes, was meeting the hostility of reactionary religious bigotry and the alarming intellectual limitations of democracy. Even the work of John Hunter (1728–93), the father of scientific surgery, Louis Pasteur (1822–95) on inoculation, of Edward Jenner (1749–1823) on vaccination, of Lord Lister (1823–1912) on antiseptics, met with criticism and abuse.

The theory of evolution upset the traditional ways of thinking about Man's importance in the Universe. People like T. H. Huxley (1825–95) were involved in verbal brawls with dignitaries of the Church; and those who vehemently attacked the idea of man's slow evolution often by their own conduct evidenced the savage rawness of intolerant, suspicious primitive men.

But science does not justify itself to rank, status, privilege or religious dogmatism; it does not seek to set itself up to be worshipped but seeks only knowledge—including knowledge about Man himself, his ways of thought, his manners, his customs, his beliefs. The study of anthropology pursued its even way, for the most part happily remote from a circle in which its methods and findings would be subject to popular indignation. Anthropologists, at least, could gain some kind of perspective on the question of man's ancestry and achievements. Primitive magic and religion were investigated and commented upon by Sir James Frazer (1864–1941) in *The Golden Bough*.

The experimental method was applied to psychology, and theories of the workings of the human mind and—to the dismay of many unsuspecting people—of the subconscious and unconscious, came from Freud, Jung and Adler: workers whose ideas and conceptions of the motive forces of human behaviour have often suffered from strange misconceptions and distortions at the hands of over-enthusiastic followers and popular writers.

Attempts were made to apply the scientific method—or at least the scientific philosophy—to the study of human institutions. There was born a new 'science': sociology, so broadly based as to attempt a synthesis of the findings of such 'social sciences' as economics, social psychology, ethics. The general results, apart from particular studies of such institutions as marriage, the family, the State, have tended to be philosophy rather than science. The British school has devoted its attention to specific aspects of community life, such as social classes, crime and punishment, the survey and evaluation of codes of morals, in which the work has been closely and necessarily linked with the results of the investigations of such social sciences as social psychology, law and social institutions.

The methods of science have, indeed, proved difficult tools in the hands of investigators themselves heavily influenced by their own upbringing, mental habits, education and social traditions.

More productive have been the less ambitious investigations related to immediate and practical social problems. With the coming of the problems resulting from the Industrial Revolution social investigations have been made leading often to the taking of governmental action. Thus, in 1832, James Kay published *The Moral and Physical Condition of the Working Classes*. In 1842 Edwin Chadwick's *Report on the Sanitary Condition of the Labouring Population* shocked the well-to-do who had not realised under what conditions of filthiness the 'lower classes' lived. Dr Southwood Smith reported in 1844 on the results of overcrowding.

It was the political philosopher Jeremy Bentham (1748–1832) who first applied scientific method to social problems—to such effect as to be directly or indirectly responsible for such reforms as the mitigation of the criminal law, the abolition of transportation, the reform of the poor laws, the protection of inventors, public health legislation. With the publication of Charles Booth's *Life and Labour of the People in London* (1891–1903), B. Seebohm Rowntree's *Poverty: A Study in Town Life* (1900) and *Unemployment* (1911), the study of social phenomena entered upon a phase of private investigation and institutional and governmental investigation that has culminated in the institutions of the Welfare State.

We may now narrow our field of view and go into more detail of the actual circumstances of the men and women who have lived and live in the world of technical change that came from the application of the researches of the natural scientists, those men who, deliberating in such meetings as those of the Lunar Society (founded in the second half of the eighteenth century) on the building of a new world of applied science, could not envisage the vast economic and social changes that would come out of that application.

Period	Political background	Economic background	Commercial and industrial organisation	Science and Technology
Eighteenth Century	Overseas expansion Wars with French in Canada and India Navigation Acts American Declaration of Independence, 1776 British House of Commons unreformed	Britain a great commercial nation Inventions from 1733 (Kay's flying shuttle)	Domestic system in industry Second Enclosure Movement in agriculture; from 1750: application of scientific methods Combination Laws, 1799–1800	*Chemistry:* system of elements and compounds established *Electricity and magnetism:* laws of electrolysis: electro-magnetic induction
Nineteenth Century (to 1914)	Reform Acts, 1832, 1867, 1884 Chartist Movement, 1834–48 Growth of large towns *Laissez-faire* attitude of Government 1833: First effective Factory Act Relief of Poor: 'Speenhamland' System, 1795–1834 *From 1870:* Development of British Empire as a world power 1911: Beginnings of social legislation First World War, 1914–18	Spread of Industrial Revolution; Inventions Rise of Co-operative Movement (1844: 'Rochdale Equitable Pioneers') Transport: Roads, Canals Railways (after 1840); steamships (after 1860) Suez Canal, 1869 Free Trade, 1840–1914 Refrigeration, 1882 *Trade Unionism:* Repeal of Combination Laws, 1824 1834: Grand Consolidated National Trades Union 1850s: 'New Model' Unionism 1880s: 'New' Unionism	Building up of Britain's basic industries; development of private capitalism *Co-operative Movement:* Retail distribution and wholesale distribution Limited Liability, 1858–62 *Factory System* *Combines:* Cartels, Trusts International agreements *Banking:* Private banks 1844: Bank Charter Act 1868: Limited liability applied to banking; great impetus given to joint-stock banks *Agriculture:* Repeal of Corn Laws, 1846 1840–70: Prosperity 1870–1914: Depression	*Chemistry:* Beginning of atomic science *Physics:* Law of conservation of energy (1847) *Electrical science:* first telephone 1876 *Radio technology:* from 1830 *Principles of Geology* (1830)—Lyell *Origin of Species* (1859)—Darwin Rapid advances in mechanical and electrical engineering

CHART 5—*Conspectus of the Eighteenth and Nineteenth Centuries in Britain*

CHAPTER VI

THE INDUSTRIAL REVOLUTION:
I. THE REVOLUTION IN MANUFACTURE

1. THE REVOLUTION IN TEXTILES

The great change, when it came, was heralded by a spate of inventions in the textile industries, and it was in fact the cotton industry that was first revolutionised. The home market for cotton goods was served by an industry which used a linen warp with a cotton weft; the English manufacturers, who had a virtual monopoly of this kind of cloth in the home market, had not succeeded in producing a cotton thread strong enough to serve as a warp. Internal disorder in India, and the Anglo-French struggle there, interrupted the supply of Indian cotton piece-goods for export by British merchants. New markets were being opened up in the colonies and tropics. Cotton-growing was being introduced into the southern states of the United States of America, promising ample supplies of raw material. There arose, then, the technical problem of how to expand British manufacture.

Necessity is the mother of invention; it was necessary for the domestic system to be changed into a factory system designed for large-scale manufacture if advantage was to be taken of these new conditions. The inventions were the result of this necessity, and not vice versa.

Already, in 1733, John Kay of Bury had invented the 'flying shuttle,' which enabled the weaver to weave wider cloth, and weave it more expeditiously than before. This invention made even more acute the problem resulting from the fact that the spinners had been unable to provide sufficient yarn to meet the needs of weavers.

Many attempts were made to meet the situation; and in 1770 James Hargreaves, a weaver of Blackburn, patented a 'spinning jenny,' which increased the number of spindles which could be turned at once.

It would appear that a spinning-machine was invented in the 1730s by John Wyatt, who became associated with a certain Lewis Paul. Wyatt's invention was patented in 1738, and he hoped that several machines would be worked at once by the source of power—the nature of which is obscure. The invention was sold in 1742 to Edward Cave, who set up a workshop at Northampton. But poor administration was responsible for the failure of this factory, and the plant was ultimately sold to Richard Arkwright.

It was with Arkwright's 'water-frame,' patented in 1769, that the

Textiles	Iron, steel and engineering	Coal	Transport and communications
1733: Kay's 'flying shuttle' 1764: Hargreaves' 'spinning jenny' 1769: Arkwright's 'water-frame' 1779: Crompton's 'Mule' 1785: Cartwright's power loom 1790 Cartwright's wool-combing machine *Wool*: Australasian supplies after 1830 *Cotton*: Surpassed wool as chief British export by 1870. Egyptian cotton imported after American Civil War (1861–65). Expansion of cotton trade to 1913 *Organisation in cotton industry*: Individual competing firms; specialisation. *Wool*: concentration in Yorkshire after Industrial Revolution	About 1700–50: Spread of the Abraham Darbys' method of using coal to smelt iron 1780: Cort's puddling process 1856: Henry Bessemer's converter Coal used in furnaces 1868: Siemens–Martin process 1878: Thomas–Gilchrist process Great Britain leading producer of iron and steel until 1890 Development of machine tools and precision engineering *Organisation*: Little combination	Spread of the Abraham Darbys' method of using coal to smelt iron 1720s: Newcomen's pumping engine 1781: Watt's engine using rotary motion 1815: Davy safety lamp 1815: First efficient colliery locomotive Expansion from 1815 *Organisation*: Diversity of units	*Roads*: *Engineers*: Telford (1757–1834); Metcalf (1717–1810); McAdam (1756–1836) *Canals*: 1761: Bridgewater Canal 1773: Manchester–Liverpool 1777: Trent and Mersey Canal End of the eighteenth century: Canal 'mania' *Railways*: 1825: First public line: Stockton and Darlington Railway 1840s: Railway 'mania' Main lines laid down by 1870 *Steamships*: Atlantic first crossed 1819 But sailing ships persisted until 1860s 1875 onwards: steel ships *Other Communications*: 1840: Penny Post 1830s: Telegraphy. Wireless-telegraphy at end of century 1814 onwards: development of power printing

CHART 6—*Technical Inventions and Industrial Organisation in the Eighteenth and Nineteenth Centuries*

new era of factory production was ushered in. Arkwright's invention spun the thread by means of water-driven rollers; the machine could not be worked by hand, and it was too expensive for the home-worker. Arkwright set up a mill on the Derwent at Cromford in Derbyshire, and produced yarn for stockings. It is noteworthy that Arkwright was driven from Lancashire by the resentment of the hand-workers.

In 1779 Samuel Crompton's 'Mule,' so called because the machine combined the principles of the water-frame and the jenny, superseded its predecessors. It produced yarns which were both strong and fine —Arkwright's yarn, though strong and suitable for warp, was coarse —so that muslins (fine cotton cloths) could be produced in England. Many hundreds of spindles could now be turned by one spinner. But the jenny cottage industry did not die a sudden death, and, indeed, it continued to produce yarn for weft; mules could be set up in workers' homes. By the end of the eighteenth century the mules were generally worked by water-power (steam was not in general use in textile factories before the middle of the nineteenth century); and in any case it was more convenient for a capitalist manufacturer to set up jennies and mules together in factories.

These inventions reversed the situation existing between spinners and weavers: the quantity of yarn spun overtook the capacity of the weavers to deal with it. Weavers found themselves in scarce supply, and consequently enjoyed high wages. Naturally enough, inventive capacity was now turned to the weaving problem; and in 1785 Edmund Cartwright invented a power loom. The early model was a clumsy affair; but it was improved, and came into general use after about 1820.

Its introduction was marked by considerable resistance. Kay's 'flying shuttle' was the basis of the weaving industry, and machine-breaking was the inevitable response to an invention that threatened the settled security of workers. But although hand-weaving continued for years, and did not disappear until the middle of the century, power-weaving had come to stay. After 1789 the power-loom was adapted for steam-power.

The humid atmosphere of Lancashire (cotton thread was inclined to break if spun in a dry atmosphere); the fuel supplies in the shape of streams and later of coal; the obvious advantages of Liverpool as a port for the importation of raw materials and the export of finished goods; and the lack of competition from the Clyde valley, which possessed equal advantages but preferred to concentrate on shipbuilding, caused Lancashire to become the most important home of cotton manufacture in Britain. With the opening up of the tropical markets, cotton surpassed wool in importance in Britain, and by 1870 cotton goods comprised the chief British export, woollen goods coming second.

The cotton industry developed rapidly. After Hargreaves' invention the domestic industry expanded quickly, the weavers and their looms increasing at their greatest rate to try to keep up with the spinning jennies in the homes of the spinners. This was perhaps the period of maximum extent of the domestic industry. But in 1785 Arkwright's patent was cancelled, and thereafter the factory system became established. Because of the abundance of water-power, the South Lancashire area became the most important of the cotton-spinning districts. In 1788 there were 41 mills in Lancashire, 17 in Derbyshire and 11 in Yorkshire, these comprising more than half those in the country. Many manufacturers (including Arkwright himself) owned several factories: the new organisation of the cotton industry was necessarily capitalistic. But the old and the new ways lived on together; the 'factory system' as we understand it did not come suddenly. From 1780 Crompton's 'mule' spread through the country, and this machine was adapted for use in the cottages. A modern counterpart lies in the boot and shoe industry: right up to the end of the nineteenth century, when mechanical inventions began to affect the footwear industry, boot manufacture in Norwich was largely in the hands of 'garret masters,' small employers on whose premises some of the work was done, whilst various processes were done in the workers' homes.

In the cotton industry of this time hand- and power-loom weaving existed side by side, and sometimes the raw material and the plant were owned by different people. Not until 1800 could cotton manufacture be said to be a 'factory' industry; and it was to be a decade or so after that before steam-power displaced water-power. The handloom weaver was not finally superseded until the 1860s.

The early 'companies' consisted of partnerships of capitalists; it was the nineteenth century which saw the beginning of the joint-stock enterprises. No doubt it is to the strong individualistic tradition of the cotton manufacturers that the lack of effective combination, which subsequently proved a handicap to the efficient organisation of the British cotton industry, can be traced.

The cotton industry had not to fight against the established practices and traditions of an old-established industry. Invention and reorganisation went on much more slowly in the woollen industry, where, in fact, there was not such great incentive to change. The early woollen industry was carried on in three main districts: Yorkshire, Norfolk and South-west England, though within each area it was diffused, as it was indeed on a smaller scale throughout the country; only in Yorkshire was there a degree of localisation in the West Riding. The industry was a domestic one; John Kay's 'flying shuttle' spread slowly. The weaver owned his raw material and the tools, often owning both spinning- and weaving-machines: the industry could be described as one carried on by a class of small manufacturers, assisted sometimes by a few journeymen, and these manufacturers acted also as merchants of the finished cloth.

But when production outstepped local needs, and it became necessary to produce for a market far afield, the merchant clothier, a capitalist, became of importance. From the first, the merchant had taken charge of the finishing processes. In the south-west of England, particularly, the merchant capitalist bought the raw wool, and saw it through the processes of carding, spinning, weaving, fulling and dressing with the use of his own capital. The weavers might work for several manufacturers and consider themselves independent workers; but by the end of the seventeenth century and beginning of the eighteenth century the process of subordination to a capitalist merchant employer had gathered impetus. In Norfolk, where wool-combing was predominant and needed comparatively large amounts of capital, the best conditions for capitalist organisation existed, and a class of middlemen, the 'master-combers,' arose.

C

These 'merchant clothiers,' who became dominant in the organisation of the woollen industry during the eighteenth century, were often called 'manufacturers,' but they were really merchant employers. The former small producer became a wage-earner, especially in the towns to which he drifted; and when the processes of manufacture became more extended and complicated, specialisation of occupation developed.

The scattered nature of the woollen industry kept it a local one until the end of the eighteenth century. But at that time the industry found its centre in the West Riding of Yorkshire, where water-power was readily available, and where there were rich coal deposits and facilities for importing and exporting. Australasian supplies became available after 1830, and by that date Yorkshire had established itself as the premier wool-manufacturing county. Norfolk (where weaving was introduced by the Dutch and Walloon Protestant immigrants in the later years of the fourteenth century) had no coal; and in the south-west of England the merchant manufacturers were slow to avail themselves of the new technical equipment.

The first worsted mill was established in Yorkshire in 1787. In 1790 Cartwright invented a machine for wool-combing, although it did not come into general use before the end of the first quarter of the nineteenth century. By 1800 spinning and weaving and carding were carried on by machinery, though it was not until the middle of the nineteenth century that hand-weaving was finally displaced. The coming of machinery changed the face of Yorkshire; and wool followed cotton as a mechanised industry, localised in certain parts of the country. Though in the Tweed valley and in the west of England woollen towns existed, and wool was also manufactured in the Scottish lowlands, most worsted production, as distinct from woollen manufacture, became localised around Bradford: the raw material of worsted is merino and fine-quality wools, whilst that of the woollen industry is the medium- and lower-grade short-stapled wool. Geographical specialisation was not so marked as in Lancashire; generally, the north and west concentrated on the production of worsteds, while the south and east produced woollens.

Linen manufacture, far less important in England than the other textiles, was mechanised even later. Belfast and Dundee became the chief centres. The protected silk-manufacturing industry had to face severe competition from French manufactures after 1860, when the duties on imported silk manufactures were abolished.

The Civil War (1861–65) cut off American cotton supplies, and cotton was imported from India and Egypt. The Egyptian long-stapled cotton was, indeed, especially suited to the Lancashire cotton industry.

During the nineteenth century there were changes in both the composition of the cotton trade and the markets. The development of machine spinning on the Continent halted the expansion of yarn exports to Europe; but the export of yarns to India, China, Japan and the Near East increased, until the establishment of spinning-mills in those countries after 1880 halted the expansion. In the early nineteenth century Europe and North and South America were the chief markets for piece-goods; but Europe and the United States set up weaving-mills and protected their industries by tariffs. By 1900 British India was taking nearly 45% of the cotton piece-goods exports, China and Japan about 10%, and South and Central America about 10%.

In general terms, until 1913 there had been a hundred years of expansion in the cotton manufacturing and exporting industry of England, concentrated in Lancashire. Though the British proportion of total world output was declining, this was due to the growth of the industry in other countries, not to an absolute decline. After the disturbance of the First World War there was a demand for cotton goods in Eastern markets, and there was a price boom, which, however, broke in 1920. From 1925 there was a progressive decline in cotton exports, and the Lancashire cotton industry entered on a period of terrible depression; the recovery from this between 1931 and 1939 was only slight.

The depression in cotton was the result mainly of losses in the export trade because of Japanese and other foreign competition. Countries formerly relying on imports set up their own plants; Indian industrialisation was an important factor in the decline.

The modern development of the organisation of the cotton industry was one of specialisation. Raw cotton was imported by Liverpool importing merchants through brokers, who distributed it to spinners. The spinners manufactured the yarn and sold it through agents and brokers to weavers working to the orders of piece-goods merchants. The finishing operations of bleaching, dyeing and packing were done by firms working on commission for the piece-goods merchants.

An important feature of the organisation of the cotton industry was the fact that a large number of independent undertakings were engaged in it, each firm trying to specialise. Not only that, but in Lancashire there was geographical specialisation, the northern towns being generally engaged in weaving, and the southern in spinning. Various processes, e.g. spinning processes, became specialised in certain towns. Though this division of labour carried with it the advantages of such specialisation, the corresponding disadvantages were keenly felt in time of depression. Whereas in Japan most of the raw cotton was imported by a few large undertakings which also controlled the greater part of the yarn and piece-goods exports, in England there were numerous importers and piece-goods merchants.

Japanese industrialists not only had the advantages of cheaper raw material and lower labour costs; they used more up-to-date machinery and better methods of organisation and marketing.

The rugged individualism of the manufacturers of the north of England wavered under the threat of the deposition of 'King Cotton.' The depression of the twenties was met ineffectually by a policy of 'organised short time' advocated by the Provisional Emergency Cotton Committee, formed by a number of spinners in 1922, to supplement more effective centralised control of selling. In 1927 an attempt was made to form a cartel to regulate prices and output and the grading of yarns: the American Cotton Yarn Association, with capital subscribed by spinners. Undercutting of prices by firms outside the cartel caused its failure. In 1928 a Joint Committee of Cotton Trade Organisations was formed to co-ordinate the sections of the cotton industry, and it rather belatedly recommended large-scale amalgamations so as to secure the economies resulting from standardisation and bulk buying and selling. The Lancashire Cotton Corporation was created: a combine which attempted to recondition mills, scrap obsolete plant and organise production of standardised yarns and cloths.

But the depression pursued its inexorable way: in 1932–33 the annual average export of piece-goods amounted to only 33% of that of 1910–13; Japan's exports had caught up to Britain's.

The excessive specialisation which in many ways proved the undoing of the Lancashire cotton industry seems to have begun about the 1870s. In weaving, particularly, the private firm was prominent, constituting about one-third of the total before the First World War; in spinning the joint-stock form of organisation predominated.

On the outbreak of the Second World War the Government took over the bulk buying of cotton. Preoccupation with what the shape of the cotton industry was likely to be after the war inspired a Cotton Textile Mission to the United States, led by Sir Frank Platt, the Cotton Controller, to survey the American cotton industry and advise on changes of method which the mission considered might fruitfully be adopted in this country. The American cotton industry was more efficient than the British; the mission was sent to find out why. It came back with the answer that the superior productive efficiency of the Americans was the result almost solely of greater mechanical efficiency in the United States. It recommended a 'major operation' in the Lancashire cotton industry, necessitating greater mechanisation and modernisation. The basic objects of the Mission's recommendations were the attainments of a higher degree of standardisation and specialisation so as to give bulk production; an improvement in the standard of technical equipment and working conditions; greater co-operation between spinners and weavers; more scientific management; the raising of labour productivity and greater economy in production costs; and the raising of wages by the application of scientific methods to the processes and plant utilisation of the industry. A 'vital requirement' of the British cotton industry was a modification of the methods of distribution.*

In March 1946 the House of Commons approved the Government's decision to continue permanently the system of bulk purchase by the State, instead of reopening the Liverpool cotton market. A system of centralised control was not to be rigidly applied; in a number of cases the responsibility for importing raw cotton had already been handed back to private enterprise. But the Raw Cotton Commission gained little affection in the cotton industry. With a change to a government of freer-enterprise principles, a process of 'unscrambling' began; by 1952 spinning-mills consuming about one-third of cotton imports had used their option and decided to buy privately. In May 1954 the Liverpool cotton 'futures' market was reopened.

The story of Lancashire cotton is an outstanding example of the way in which weaknesses in organisation due to an exaggerated individualism can result in dire consequences to an industry. Lancashire was still living in the mental atmosphere of the early nineteenth century when a new environment surrounded her.

A characteristic of cotton is that it is easily graded—ten distinct grades of cotton were recognised by the Liverpool Cotton Association —and this enabled 'futures' dealings to take place, *i.e.* dealings in which the commodity is bought and sold for future delivery at prices determined at the time of the contract. A certain amount of speculation arose in the cotton market by people who merely bought and sold without any intention of taking or making delivery; but it was argued that such speculation was legitimate and indeed useful to the community when its result was to 'iron out' prices and so prevent disastrous fluctuations.

Wool is far less easily graded; wool has been generally disposed of by auctions, the chief European centre for the sale of imported wool being the London Wool Exchange. Bradford became the commercial centre of the wool industry; the Bradford merchant not merely buying and selling but directing the nature of the manufacture and finishing processes.

The woollen trade was affected by the depression as the cotton industry was. The Far East markets were lost, and the competition of Germany and other countries became serious. The lighter and finer fabrics attracted a greater demand than the heavier; the hosiery trade grew in the years following the First World War. The woollen manufacturers therefore concentrated their attention on the clothing factories; while the worsted spinners turned more to the hosiery markets.

The textile industry, the revolution in which heralded the Industrial

---

* Report of the Cotton Textile Mission to the United States of America, March–April, 1944 (H.M.S.O., 1944).

Revolution as a whole, has itself been the subject of a technical revolution by the introduction of 'man-made fibres.' These artificial fibres are of two kinds; regenerated fibres derived from vegetable or animal materials and processed chemically or physically; and synthetic fibres, wholly man-made from chemical or mineral constituents.

The idea of making an artificial fibre had occurred in 1664 to Robert Hooke (1635–1703), who had worked with Robert Boyle and whose accomplishments included the making of such diverse appliances as an air-pump, the marine barometer and the balance-spring of watches, and who first described plant cells. The idea lay dormant for 200 years until Louis Schwabe, an English weaver, invented a machine which forced molten glass through holes and made artificial filaments. These filaments were, however, not suitable for making textile materials; and attention was directed towards using the natural cellulose such as is found in cotton and flax.

In 1846 nitrocellulose fibres which were strong and flexible were produced by treating cellulose with nitric acid; but they were highly inflammable. In 1883 Sir Joseph Swan, who made the first successful incandescent filament electric lamp in 1879, patented a process for making these filaments harmless; and in 1885 he exhibited textiles made of what he called 'artificial silk.'

Other experiments followed in France; and eventually a viscose regenerated cellulose fibre was produced. The term 'rayon' has been applied to fibres of the regenerated cellulose type. By 1957 rayon formed 19% of the total world consumption of cotton, wool, and man-made fibres (compared with wool, 10%; cotton, 68%).

Synthetic fibres are quite a modern development. Not until the 1930s, after chemists had become interested, in the early years of the twentieth century, in plastics, was real progress made. In the branch of chemistry known as polymer chemistry, a synthetic fibre known as nylon was produced. Nylon had such great advantages, including strength and elasticity, that during and after the Second World War it superseded silk as the textile most used in hosiery. By 1957, 3% of the world consumption of cotton, wool and man-made fibres such as nylon and 'terylene' was of synthetic fibres.

The *Ministry of Labour Gazette* for August 1966 shows that of 767,400 persons employed in Textiles in June 1965, 46,300 were employed in the production of man-made fibres.

The traditional distinction between the cotton and woollen textiles industries can no longer be maintained: there is an increasing consumption of mixtures of rayon with either wool or cotton. Thus the chemical and textile industries had co-operated to produce new materials—a foretaste of a new world which is taking place in the evolution of modern industrial organisation.

2. THE REVOLUTION IN IRON

In order that the machines for the manufacture of textiles could be made, it was necessary that there should be advances in the technique of iron production. Iron of a sort had been produced in this country from earliest times—iron-smelting was carried on by the Romans. Iron was needed for the chain and plate armour of the knights and fighting-men of the Middle Ages; and on the introduction of cannon the demand was greatly stimulated.

The iron was smelted by charcoal produced from the timber of the forests of the country, which was used so lavishly that by the beginning of the eighteenth century there was a shortage of timber. In 1700 the iron-smelting centres were in the Weald of Sussex and the Forest of Dean in Gloucestershire, where guns were made. Coal was considered as a substitute for charcoal when the timber famine became acute; but a difficulty was that sulphur from the coal combined with the iron and caused it to be brittle.

By the beginning of the eighteenth century the iron industry was in decline. The ironworks were declining in Sussex and in the Forest of Dean; the few round Birmingham and Sheffield, where ironmongery and cutlery, respectively, were made (the district had the advantage of the presence of millstone grit and the streams of the Pennines), were not able to meet the demands of these towns for iron, and Swedish iron was imported through Hull. Throughout the country generally there were many small centres of production of such articles as knives, general cutlery, hammers, files and tools of various kinds.

The general organisation of the iron industry was in the hands of mining companies and trading companies; in contrast, the coal-mines were owned generally by private persons. In the metal-working industries small specialised workshops prevailed; it was only by the middle of the eighteenth century that there came a tendency towards capitalist manufacture.

Early in the eighteenth century Abraham Darby of Coalbrookdale invented, or at least employed, a method of using coke from coal for smelting iron; and his son Abraham Darby carried on the process, knowledge of which spread after 1750. The result was that iron production left the forest clearings and became established on the coalfields of South Wales, the Clyde valley, Yorkshire and the Black Country.

The 'ironmaster' of this age used the opportunities that had become available now that the old dependence on wood had disappeared. The Darbys developed their ironmastering activities over three generations. The Wilkinsons were another family renowned in the history of ironmastery: in 1775 John Wilkinson ordered a steam engine from

Boulton and Watt—the first to be used for a purpose other than merely pumping.

Coal, iron and water-power were present in South Wales, but the lack of good road communications with the rest of the country tended to isolate this area. Nevertheless, works were set up there by the 1780s, and also in the Scottish lowlands: John Roebuck founded the Carron works in 1760. The Rotherham foundries in Yorkshire were founded by Samuel Walker in 1741; by 1796 (Walker having acquired by dubious means the secret of making tempered steel first discovered by Benjamin Huntsman in 1750), the Rotherham works had £200,000 worth of capital invested in them. Although large amounts of capital were required in the organisation of such ironworks as these, it was found by small groups of men working as partners. It is to this fact that one may ascribe the tradition of individualism that existed in the British iron industry as it did in the textile industries.

In 1780 Henry Cort invented a process of puddling the iron to get rid of impurities and rolling to produce malleable iron. By 1800 Watt's steam-engine was superseding water-power for the blast for furnaces and for power in rolling mills; and in 1828 Neilson invented a hot-blast furnace, by which air was heated before being forced into the furnace, thus economising fuel and accelerating the smelting process. Neilson's process gave rise to the Scottish industry.

Imported pig-iron, freer from impurities than the British, had been imported from Sweden and Russia for the hardware industries springing up in the Midlands. Towards the end of the eighteenth century, heavy duties were imposed on the importation of this iron. They were reduced in 1825 and subsequently abolished, but by that time the iron industry had become well established.

In 1839 Nasmyth invented a steam hammer for use in forging iron, and his design was put into practice a few years later.

In 1851 an iron-field was discovered in the Cleveland district of Yorkshire; and Middlesbrough and Tees-side developed rapidly.

Steel is an alloy of iron and carbon, a fact which has been known or at least acted upon from early times, but the amount of carbon could not be controlled. In 1856 Henry Bessemer used a converter which oxidised the impurities and added the correct amount of hardening material, so that molten iron could be readily converted into steel. The steel produced by Bessemer was more malleable, stronger and cheaper than the malleable iron formerly used for such commodities as rails and girders; and his steel could be produced in greater quantities. A result was that the existing ironworks became obsolete and had to be replaced by steelworks.

A fault with the Bessemer converter was that it failed to remove phosphorus from the iron, and most British ores contain phosphorus; so that for the production of non-phosphoric steel, ores had to be imported from Spain and Sweden. In 1868 the Siemens-Martin open-hearth process, using iron and steel scrap instead of iron ore, also came into use. In 1878 both these processes could be used for the production of steel from phosphoric iron ores through the invention of the Thomas–Gilchrist process, which consisted of lining the converters and open hearths with basic materials which absorbed phosphorus.

So it was that more iron ores could be used in the production of steel—and a great German steel industry could be built up with the ores of Lorraine and Luxembourg. Greater quantities of steel could now be produced at cheaper prices, and transport and engineering and building projects received the advantage of strong, cheap materials; in addition, armaments could be produced in great quantities.

Until 1890 Great Britain was the leading producer of iron and steel. Then her output was exceeded by that of the United States, and Germany succeeded in surpassing Britain's output in 1903. In 1913 Great Britain was producing 10 million tons of pig-iron, the United States 30 million tons and Germany 16 million tons.

These developments were reflected in the export trade. British pig-iron exports ceased to expand after 1870; the finished iron exports declined, whilst the export of sheets, tin-plates and tubes increased. Britain was concentrating on high-grade steel and developing a trade in steel bars and sections. This trade was based on imports of semi-manufactured steel, for the Continental makers of cheap basic steel were able to undersell the British manufacturers.

British costs were comparatively high: as in the case of textiles the strongly individualistic character of British organisation in the steel industry led to only a limited degree of combination and prevented co-ordinated planning of the industry as a whole. The main trade associations, or 'conferences', were affiliated to the Iron and Steel Federation; they were concerned with eleven branches of production: pig-iron; steel; steel sheets; tin-plates; hot finished tubes; wire and wire rods; heavy forgings and railway tyres, axles, solid wheels and disc-wheel centres; alloy and stainless steel; crucible and high-speed steel; light rolled-steel products; and bolts, nuts, screws and rivets.

Before the First World War the larger proportion of sales at home and abroad was made by merchant houses; after the war, when the decline in the export trade occurred, the tendency was for manufacturers to market their own products by contract and to set up associations to control prices and allocations of orders.

The Second World War set up, of course, unprecedented demands for steel. The coming of a Labour Government at the conclusion of the war resulted in the nationalisation of the steel industry—a 'doctrinal' move dictated by the current Socialist preoccupation with nationalisation as a panacea for all economic ills. The see-saw of politics resulted in a Conservative Government in 1951; and the Government, following a view held not merely by its own supporters but also privately by many Labour adherents, proceeded to 'unscramble' steel in 1953. The Iron and Steel Act, 1953, set up an Iron and Steel Board, appointed by the Minister of Supply, to exercise a general supervision over the iron and steel industry with a view to promoting the efficient, economic and adequate supply under competitive conditions of iron and steel products; and it had certain powers to determine the maximum prices to be charged by producers in the United Kingdom for iron and steel products.

Since 1939 many firms took part in an arrangement known as the Industry Fund by which the excess cost above home prices of imported pig-iron, scrap, semi-finished steel and finished steel was spread over the cost of steel production. The Industry Fund was fed by levies determined by the Iron and Steel Federation, an organisation comprising the majority of iron and steel producers.

By 1958 the attitude of some trade-union leaders suggested that a re-nationalisation of the steel industry should be accomplished with a minimum of derangement: the companies could be left with their existing names and individualities, but their shares could be transferred to the State, and the Board's powers to control and co-ordinate policy on prices, production, development and exports could be strengthened. As a gesture towards the left-wing section of the Labour movement, the Labour Government of 1964 accepted the inevitability of steel re-nationalisation, but reluctantly. It was not until its re-election in 1966 that the Labour Government made any positive move towards re-nationalisation.

3. THE RISE OF ENGINEERING

The Machine Age has necessitated the development of precision engineering; indeed, the Industrial Revolution as we know it could hardly have occurred without the coming of machine tools by which textile and other machines could be mass-produced. In the eighteenth century a machine could not be introduced into a factory with confidence that it would run without constant attention and frequent breakdowns. By the middle of the nineteenth century the development of accurate machine tools enabled textile and other machinery to be mass-produced, and so made possible the mounting tempo of a true industrial revolution.

In the application of steam-power to industry the development of engineering techniques was especially necessary. Water-power had previously been used to turn wheels working flour-mills; and in the late eighteenth century it was used to drive textile machinery. But water-power is unreliable, and necessitates the siting of the factories on the banks of streams. As coal came more into use as a source of power, the working of deeper seams called for pumping machinery to pump the water out of the mines. A steam-pump invented by Thomas Savery in 1698 was unsatisfactory. In the early eighteenth century an engine invented by Thomas Newcomen was used, but proved wasteful and unreliable. In the last quarter of the eighteenth century James Watt devised a steam-engine working on the rotatory principle, and with a tubular boiler and a steam-jacket around the cylinder. Watt's partner in the firm of Boulton and Watt, Matthew Boulton, succeeded in boring cylinders accurately.

The application of steam to industry took place only slowly. There were only a few undertakings producing steam-engines under the licences of Boulton and Watt, who held the patents; and there was an absence of skilled engineers. But it was not long before the ironmasters seized the opportunity to equip their factories with the new source of motive power. The alliance between the metal-works and steam-power began. By the middle of the nineteenth century steam was in general use in the textile factories. It was applied, too, to flour-mills, malt-mills, flint-mills and in the sugar-cane crushing mills. Indeed, Watt himself, with the aid of John Rennie, arranged the equipment for the Albion flour-mills, which were built in 1786.

The first public railway line to use locomotives, the Stockton and Darlington Railway, was opened in 1825. Steam paddle-ships were being used on inland waterways in the opening years of the nineteenth century; in 1819 the *Savannah* crossed the Atlantic with much assistance from her sails, and in 1838 the *Great Western* crossed under steam-power alone.

The precision steam-engine enabled the factory system to be set up on the coal-fields and iron-fields of the country; it made possible the development of rail transport, so that the country was covered with a network of railways. Engineering skills branching out from this basic technique have resulted in the establishment of a multitude of trades: *e.g.* agricultural machinery; textile machinery; locomotive and shipping machinery; and the great diversity of trades grouped under the phrase 'motor industry.' There is a corresponding diversity of methods of production and distribution. It has become difficult to define the term 'engineering'; and standardisation and the application of research in related or distantly related trades and techniques have made for greater and greater precision in machines and specialisation of product. The diversity of products has made combination difficult, especially in selling.

The nineteenth century, especially the last quarter of it, was an age of expansion of 'engineering.' As we have seen, the textile machinery first began to be produced towards the close of the eighteenth century. Industries producing locomotives, rolling stock and railway equipment arose with the railway era of the 1830s. The small metal-working undertakings which had been handicraft trades turned over to mechanical means of production and began to make machine tools. The production of gas-engines began in the 1870s. During the next decade electrical engineering and the cycle trade reached a position of importance. Then came the motor industry in the nineties; and during and after the First World War the aircraft industry expanded. The growth of radio and television production is within the personal knowledge of present-day readers.

The internal-combustion engine was first invented as a gas-engine by Lenoir in 1860; and Lenoir later produced a road vehicle driven by coal gas. This method of propulsion by road raised the problem of fuel supply. But soon after the middle of the nineteenth century, large oil-fields were discovered in the United States; and the use of petrol was developed. Successive improvements in petrol-driven engines were made by Markus in 1865, Otto in 1875, Benz in 1878 Daimler in 1883. Daimler began the production of motor-cars in Germany; and in 1889 the manufacturing rights in the Daimler engine were acquired by the Panhard company, which began to produce vehicles in France. The English Daimler Motor Company was founded in 1896.

Dunlop took out a patent for pneumatic tyres in 1888, when the bicycle was becoming a popular means of transport. The principle was applied to the motor-car. The necessity for lightness of weight in proportion to power in the motor-car engine led to developments in alloy steels. After the 1880s efficient electrical ignition devices were available.

The principle of standardisation of parts was, however, not followed in this country to the extent that it has been followed in the United States and Germany. Because Great Britain has had to cater for a large number of different foreign markets and for a home market smaller and less uniform than that of the United States and Germany, the engineering industry, apart from the heavy equipment production, became extremely diversified. The west Midlands in particular became the chief centre of the light-engineering industry. Coventry, Birmingham and Wolverhampton became known for cycle and later motor-car manufacture. But the British manufacturers' failure to organise for standardisation and mass-production lost them the lead in motor-car manufacture to the United States, where the size of the manufacturing firms expanded. The Ford Motor Company began to concentrate on the production of a cheap standardised car in 1908; and by 1915 three-quarters of American car production consisted of such cars. In contrast, the British firms remained small in size and many in number.

For thirty years before the First World War, the British engineering industries were expanding; in 1909–13 the exports of machinery were three times as great as they had been in 1880–84. In 1913 about 1¼ millions were employed in engineering occupations, including shipbuilding.

After the post-war boom there were more people employed in engineering than the industry had the power to absorb permanently. When the time of the depression came, about 1920, there were many unemployed. The pattern of the branches of the industry changed, too. The 'heavy' industries of the north and east declined, and the 'light' industries—radio, sewing-machines, electric appliances, etc.— increased in importance, being attracted to the south-east counties, where there was a large market for their products, and not being tied to the coal-fields for fuel and power.

In the world markets, Britain lost her lead to the United States and Germany. With some exceptions, such as Vickers-Armstrong, John Brown, Cammell Laird, Britain's engineering industries followed the same pattern of individualised small manufacturing firms as in textiles; and in selling their technique was well behind that of Germany and the United States.

So matters stood until the outbreak of war in 1939 once more re-set the stage for a further phase of the Industrial Revolution; and science was applied even more ingeniously and meticulously to the fashioning of engines of war.

In 1941 the first jet aircraft flew—the Gloster–Whittle E.28. Invented by Sir Frank Whittle, the jet-engine has been one of the triumphs of modern engineering, making possible not only a more efficient military weapon, but also air travel of a scale and range not known before.

After the Second World War, a new word of tremendous implications came into the language: automation, comprising the process by which work is carried on in factories by automatically planned supervision.

Automation does not mean merely mechanisation, which in essence is only the substitution of mechanical power for human muscle. 'Automation' implies the *supervision* of the machine, so that errors and defects are 'reported' and rectified, a result obtained by means of electronic devices. In the gas industry, for example, measurements such as pressures, levels and speeds are checked and recorded. Up to the present, automation has been most fully developed in Britain in chemical engineering.

4. COAL

In contrast to metal mines, such as copper-mines, which were worked by companies of varying importance, coal-mines were nearly always worked by private persons, sometimes the owners themselves

—for example, the Duke of Bridgewater, who built the Worsley canal to ship his coal to Manchester—but more often by contractors, who paid a royalty on the coal they extracted.

During the Middle Ages coal mined from deposits on or near the coast was used in towns; it came mainly from Newcastle. Coal was introduced into such industries as brickmaking, brewing and dyeing by the beginning of the seventeenth century; and the deforestation of the country, which had so alarmed the Tudor monarchs and threatened the early iron industry, turned the attention of ironworkers to coal. But lack of knowledge to overcome the impurities inherent in coal as a fuel for iron-making led to the neglect of the immense deposits of the country, while charcoal became scarcer and dearer. It was only when the Darbys invented a method of using coal for iron-making in the early years of the eighteenth century that the problem was solved.

The use of the steam-pump made possible the working of deeper seams. In 1815 the Davy safety lamp was invented, and the result was an increase in production because the more dangerous seams could then be worked. In 1815, too, Stephenson manufactured the first efficient colliery locomotive. By the middle of the nineteenth century steam could be applied to wind the coal up the shafts; and by the middle of the century, too, railway transport became available for coal, and the slower canal traffic was superseded. Coal-cutting machinery worked by compressed air was introduced soon after the middle of the century.

From about 1815 the coal industry expanded, so that by 1860 the output of the country's industry had risen to about 80 million tons per annum. In 1913 the output was 287 million tons; one-tenth of the whole occupied male population of the country was then engaged in coal-mining.

Coal, indeed, was the basis of Britain's prosperity. It provided the fuel for her expanding iron and steel and engineering industries; it was sold to countries undergoing the process of industrialisation, these exports thus avoiding the sending out of British ships in ballast and so keeping the freight rates and prices of imported goods, and therefore manufacturing costs, low; it satisfied the demand arising from the introduction of steel ships.

But this expansion was obtained at a price—the exhaustion of the more accessible seams. Coal is a factor of production in 'inelastic supply'; the cost of production in the industry was rising. The average annual output per head reached a maximum, indeed, in the last quarter of the nineteenth century. The Coal Mines Regulation Act of 1908 reduced the length of the working day, and this made for a further decline in output.

The First World War accentuated the changes that deeply depressed the British coal industry. Output fell to 208 million tons by 1933;

numbers employed, including salaried persons, fell from 1,127,000 in 1913 to 797,000 in 1933. There was a brief stimulus to British coal output in 1922 and 1923, owing to a sixteen-weeks' strike in the United States in 1922 and the French occupation of the Ruhr in 1923. But the real seriousness of the coal position could not be long obscured. The Government control of the war period and afterwards, with its fixing of prices at home at a low level and the licensing of exports, had after-effects when depression came and prices were forced down.

The post-war depression hit the coal industry very severely, for other factors came into play to make conditions worse. Improvements in boiler and furnace design and technique reduced demand abroad; in industry and transport, electricity and oil became powerful rival fuels; the use of oil for ships reduced the demand for coal; foreign coal-producers reaped the benefit of British experience, and could produce at lower costs; road transport, using the internal-combustion petrol engine, became a great rival to rail transport.

The British coal industry lacked up-to-date equipment; and the costs of marketing and distribution were high. And once again the same story is told of coal as of other industries: there were many producing units of the most diverse nature, with a lack of co-ordination between them. From August 1925 to May 1926 the Government subsidised the coal-owners; and this was merely a putting off of the evil hour of reckoning. The seven-months' strike in 1926 had no other effect than the worsening of the position of all concerned.

The Royal Commission on the Coal Industry of 1925 had pointed to the bewildering variety of producing units with their differing costs of production, size, scope of operations, organisation and degree of business prosperity. In 1924 there were 2480 mines belonging to 1400 separate undertakings; and these undertakings ranged from those owning small pits employing a dozen miners to large companies controlling several mines and employing thousands of men. Ninety-eight per cent of the total production in 1923 came from 715 undertakings each employing over 100 persons. The average age of mines employing 500 persons or over was 51 years; more than 78,000 miners were working in mines more than 100 years old. The Commission found that output per man-shift rose with the increase in size of the undertaking, whilst costs fell. On the other hand, proceeds per ton were generally higher with the small mine because of its nearness to the market or the higher quality of the coal mined. In general, the balance of advantage seemed to lie with the larger groupings.

Statistics indicate that the percentage of coal cut by machinery was 42% in 1933 as compared with 8% in 1913. In 1929, 75% of the bituminous coal from United States mines was mechanically mined. But it has to be mentioned that much of the coal of this country lies in inclined seams and is unsuitable for mechanical cutting. Nevertheless, the British coal industry was slow in adopting mechanical methods where these were possible.

The rising costs of distribution were another feature commented on by the 1925 Commission: there was a wide gap between the prices paid at the pit-head and those paid by consumers. In the home market the coal was and is still distributed by three main agencies: the wholesalers or factors, buying coal direct from the collieries and selling it to merchants and/or directly to consumers, both householders and industrial users; the coal merchants, who buy their coal from wholesalers or sometimes direct from the collieries for resale to householders and some small industrial undertakings; and the small retailers, who buy from wholesalers or merchants for resale to householders. Lack of standardisation in the transport system increased the transport charges: the ownership of wagons was divided between the private owners and the railways.

The Commission recommended an extension of co-operative trading, the consolidation of the agencies engaged in distribution, increased municipal trading, and the establishment of marketing organisations by the collieries themselves.

The variation in efficiency among the mines did not encourage vertical combination, but the necessity to introduce some sort of order into prices led to horizontal combination in the form of pools or cartels. Some such attempt had been made in the nineteenth century by the Newcastle Coal Vend, which controlled the sales of coal sent by sea to London from the north-east; it broke down when it had to face the competition of coal sent by rail to London. Before the war, too, there had been some combinations formed in the South Wales anthracite area.

By means of quotas of output and subsidies on exports, attempts were made to meet competition in the contracted markets—schemes for this purpose were begun in South Wales and Scotland; and the 'Five Counties Scheme,' which came into operation in the Midlands in 1929, was an attempt to meet inland competition by means of a subsidy on exports raised by a levy on the coal mined.

The Coal Mines Act, 1930, imposed on the industry Government control in the form of the regulation of production and the controlling of minimum district prices—the latter being a difficult task because of the variety of coal produced and the number and variety of markets. Part II of the Act established a Coal Mines Reorganisation Commission empowered to promote colliery amalgamations; in point of fact, between 1926 and 1933 38 amalgamations, covering 369 pits and 240,000 workers, were carried through.

Nationalisation of the coal industry seemed to be the only adequate and ultimate measure. Under an Act of 1938 a Coal Commission was established to take over the ownership of all coal and certain associated minerals as from 1st July 1942, and to promote amalgamations of colliery undertakings where the efficient working, treating or disposing of coal required it.

The Reid Technical Advisory Committee recommended (1945) the reorganisation of the industry on a coal-field or area basis, and the creation of a central authority with statutory powers to ensure the formation of such units and stimulate reorganisation plans.

The Coal Industry Nationalisation Act, 1946, completed this phase of the story by establishing public ownership and control of the coal-mining industry; and the National Coal Board became the entrepreneurs acting on behalf of the nation. Whatever views are held by those of varying political creeds on the necessity or expediency of nationalising iron and steel and related industries, the nationalisation of the coal industry, with its multitude of competing undertakings and the variations in efficiency and scale of production, has been generally regarded as an inevitable and necessary step.

There was a fuel crisis in 1947 and coal was imported into Britain; but after 1957 exports exceeded imports and the annual output of coal increased to over 200 million tons. Most of the increase has gone to industry; coal still remains the main supplier of the needs of the country in fuel and power. But the methods of distribution to merchants, small industrial firms and householders remain archaic.

CHAPTER VII

THE INDUSTRIAL REVOLUTION:
II. THE REVOLUTION IN AGRICULTURE

1. THE ENCLOSURE MOVEMENTS

Agriculture is the oldest of our industries, and though the developments in the manufacturing and constructional industries loom so large in the history of our nation, the necessity for a balanced way of life of the nation and for a source of food in time of direst need makes its study of the utmost importance. The problems of modern agriculture will be best appreciated in the setting of the historical background of the industry.

There has been more than one revolution in agriculture. A certain amount of enclosing of the land for sheep-rearing had taken place after the Black Death of 1348–49, when there occurred an acute shortage of labour. The process of commutation and the abandonment of their holdings by the serfs when commutation was refused by the lords tended to mitigate any hardship which might otherwise have been caused by enclosures. But by the middle of the fifteenth-century landlords wishing to take advantage of the profits to be derived from satisfying the demands of the cloth trade often carried out enclosures of land by plain seizure. In Henry VII's time Parliament was forced to take notice of the hardships suffered by the poorer classes. Enclosures and the disbanding of the retinues of the barons at the close of the Wars of the Roses; the rise in rents due to rises in prices, helped by the debasement of the coinage by Henry VIII; the dissolution of the monasteries, and consequently the destruction of an important source of the relief of destitution, were the causes of the pauperism which gave expression to its resentment in such revolts as Kett's Rebellion in Norfolk in 1549.

The Tudors passed laws intended to check the enclosure movement, but as ever, economic forces proved stronger than enactments; especially since the Justices of the Peace, whose duty it was to enforce legislation against enclosures, belonged to the class of landed gentry, and the interests of this class lay in the opposite direction.

The enclosures were not entirely disadvantageous to the country as a whole. It is true that there was a certain amount of depopulation and unemployment as a result; but to the extent that the open fields

1066 onwards	OPEN-FIELD SYSTEM
Fourteenth century	Export of Wool to Continent
	1348–49: Black Death—intensified ENCLOSURES
Fifteenth century	Expansion of WOOLLEN CLOTH INDUSTRY
	WOOLLEN INDUSTRY in hands of capitalist employers
Sixteenth century	ENCLOSURES
	IMPROVED CULTIVATION
Eighteenth century	SECOND ENCLOSURE MOVEMENT
	FOOD PRODUCTION FOR TOWNS
	AGRARIAN REVOLUTION—Application of Science to Agriculture
	1750: Jethro Tull—Seed drill, horse hoe
Nineteenth century	Lord Townshend—Norfolk four-course rotation of crops
	Thomas Coke—Estate improvement
	Robert Bakewell—Improvement of stock
	1795–1833: 'Speenhamland' System
	1816: Corn Laws
	1846: Repeal of Corn Laws
	1840–70: PROSPERITY
Twentieth century	1870–1914: DEPRESSION—Competition from America and Australasia
	1914–18: FIRST WORLD WAR
	Depression—Government efforts to help agriculture
	1930s: Marketing Schemes
	1939–45: SECOND WORLD WAR

CHART 7—*Agriculture from 1066*

were enclosed and consolidated, and farming methods were improved, especially by the new owners of the previously monastery-held land, the new order was a transition from medieval to modern farming. But the open-field system still largely prevailed at the end of the sixteenth century: one must not exaggerate the extent and nature of the 'agrarian revolution' of that time.

During the next century and a half, indeed, there was little progress. The Stuarts opposed enclosures as the Tudors had done, but the general trend of public opinion was in favour of replacing the old, wasteful methods of cultivation. On the large enclosed farms experiments were made by leaseholders trying to get the best return for the rents they paid. Efforts at scientific breeding, manuring, drainage, and the growing of potatoes, hops, clover and turnips, were made; the Earl of Bedford converted a large area of England into corn and pasture-land by draining.

It was in the eighteenth century that the second enclosure movement took place; it occurred as the result of the pressure of economic forces, and this time it had the authority of the State behind it. The enclosures that took place during the eighteenth and nineteenth centuries constituted an agricultural revolution comparable with that in industry; improved techniques were required not only of agriculture in general but also of the small peasant in particular, for the latter's duality of occupation was coming to an end. As the factories grew, home weaving declined.

The scattered strips which constituted an agricultural holding in the early eighteenth century were a feature of the organisation of agriculture throughout the country. The open fields were also 'common' fields in the sense that the land so designated was in the hands of several owners, some being freeholders, some copyholders, who occupied it on perpetual or very long lease. There were also 'common' wastes and 'common' pastures in the other sense of the word; but, legally, these belonged to the lord of the manor, though the land-owners of the village would have rights of pasture or waste—rights regulated generally by the extent of land-ownership. Actual 'common' cultivation in the sense of communal cultivation had disappeared by the eighteenth century.

The movement that was to sweep away the inconveniences of the 'open-field' system began, indeed, in the fifteenth century. The turn-ing of ploughland into pasture, the increase of personal estates, the partition of the open fields and the seizure of common lands were really continued throughout the sixteenth century, and they slackened in the seventeenth century. The eighteenth century enclosures, often described as the second enclosure movement, may perhaps be discerned as the continuation of the first, after the seventeenth-century interval, with the difference that the second enclosure movement had the support of Parliament.

Parliament consisted of the representatives of the great landed interests, to whom the open fields were an obstacle in their schemes for the reorganisation of the country's agriculture. The petitioners for a Bill of Enclosure were the great landowning classes; they could afford the hiring of lawyers and the bearing of legal costs much better than the small men; and the commissioners to whom was entrusted the task of redistributing the land of the country were nominated by the petitioners. Not until 1801 was an Act passed to prevent the abuses to which this method of operation was obviously open.

The consolidation of the great estates effected by Enclosure Acts was carried a stage farther when the small yeomen farmers were induced to sell their properties through becoming discouraged at the results of these measures, or by succumbing to the lures held out by the large landowners. There is no justification for blaming the factory system for the disappearance of the small yeoman. Often engrossing (*i.e.* the joining of small holdings on an estate into large farms) fol-lowed enclosure.

The picture of the effect of all these events on his native village has been painted for posterity in Oliver Goldsmith's immortal poem, *The Deserted Village.*

In the middle of the eighteenth century the open-field system still existed in about half the manors in the country. But the enclosure movement went on rapidly during the latter half of the century; and by the end of the century one-third of the arable land had been enclosed.

Between 1760 and 1820 Parliament approved over 3000 Enclosure Bills, authorising the enclosure of about 6 million acres. In 1830–37 (the reign of William IV) the amount of enclosure was only about 250,000 acres, mainly because by that time there was little land left to enclose.

Macaulay, in the famous third chapter of his *History*, says:

> The progress of this great change can nowhere be more clearly traced than in the Statute Book. The number of enclosure acts passed since King George the Second came to the throne exceeds four thousand. The area enclosed under the authority of those acts exceeds, on a moderate calculation, ten thousand square miles. How many square miles, which were formerly uncultivated or ill cultivated, have, during the same period, been fenced and carefully tilled by the proprietors, without any application to the legislature, can only be conjectured. But it seems highly probable that a fourth part of England has been, in the course of little more than a century, turned from a wild into a garden.

George II reigned from 1727 to 1760; the first two volumes of Macaulay's *History* appeared in 1848.

By enclosure, the peasant lost his woodland and grazing rights; he gained a little consolidated holding (by paying his share of the legal charges) and was faced with the expense of fencing—the provision of those fences and hedges which go to make up the appearance of the English countryside today. Sometimes he was only too glad to sell out to one of the new middle class: the rising wealthy industrialist needed land worth £600 per annum to become a county Member of Parliament and land worth £300 per annum to become a borough member, and needed, too, the prestige that went with land-holding. Some peasants moved to industrial towns and became town labourers; some stayed where they were to become landless country labourers. Some used their capital wisely to become tenant farmers of a few hundred acres; some used their capital in the new manufacturing opportunities.

But the class of 'old English yeomen' disappeared; the new social grading was: landowner or squire, tenant farmer, farm labourer. It has been estimated that at the end of the seventeenth century there were 180,000 freeholders in England; Arthur Young (1741–1820), who travelled extensively over the country in his study of agricultural methods and became Secretary to the Board of Agriculture, saw with regret 'their lands now in the hands of monopolising lords.'

The picture is in contrast to the Danish scene: in Denmark enclosures were carried out by the Government in the interests of all classes of the community.

2. THE INTRODUCTION OF SCIENTIFIC MANAGEMENT
IN AGRICULTURE

Improved farming methods came as a revolution in agriculture, necessitating enclosures, proceeding concurrently with them and in some respects resulting from enclosures, since it was necessary to cultivate intensively to meet the expenses of enclosure. The pioneer work was done in the eighteenth century, and the nineteenth century saw the adoption, application and development of 'scientific management' in agriculture: a term which means merely using one's resources to the best advantage, so that the organiser plans his work and applies his factors of production in order to obtain the maximum return.

The pioneers were landlords who pursued a policy of enlightened self-interest: higher rents became possible as a result of increased production; and the landlords responsible for the increase naturally claimed the reward of their skill and enterprise. Already, in 1750, Jethro Tull had invented a seed-drill and had used a horse-hoe. The Norfolk farmers enthusiastically turned their attention to better production; Lord Townshend ('Turnip' Townshend) introduced the Norfolk four-course rotation of crops—wheat, clover, barley, turnips —providing winter food for cattle and eliminating the fallow year. Thomas Coke, squire of Holkham, who became Earl of Leicester, invested half a million pounds in the improvement of his estate, and his farm became a model throughout Western Europe. He died in 1842 when over 90 years of age, full of honour and wealth. He believed in manure; he applied the theoretical knowledge dispensed by Arthur Young. George III ('Farmer' George) established a model farm at Windsor, and gave his support to the new methods. Robert Bakewell improved the breed of stock. Threshing, reaping and haymaking machines were invented; artificial fertilisers were developed after 1850; drainage of land with pipes was undertaken.

So fruitful was the application of these scientific methods that agriculture was able successfully to withstand the repeal of the Corn Laws in 1846. The Corn Laws were passed in 1816 after the Napoleonic Wars in order to keep up the price of corn by imposing a heavy duty on imports. The landlords thrived on their high rents, but the mass of the people was in sore distress, for the pressure of the industrial population on food supplies was against their interests but in favour of that of the farmers. The antagonism between Town and Country, to be discerned so clearly in our own day, was in being.

By 1815 the large enclosed farm had become the normal unit of organisation in British agriculture. The wars had hastened the disappearance of the smallholders. A series of bad years at the close of the eighteenth and at the beginning of the nineteenth century caused a problem aggravated by the conditions of the war. Marginal land was brought into cultivation in response to the rise in prices. But the wages of labourers remained low; the Speenhamland system, by which relief was granted to the distressed agricultural labourers to supplement their income, was a scheme leading to the pauperisation of the agricultural labourer, for the relief depended upon the price of wheat and the size of the labourer's family. Between 1795 and 1833 this vicious system spread throughout England and Wales; it came to an end only as the result of the investigations of the Poor Law Commission of 1834.

The new middle classes, the industrialists, supported the anti-Corn-Law agitation, not so much because they loved the workers—they were soon to join forces with the landlord-aristocratic class in forming a new class of wealth and power in the political field—but because they did not relish the idea of paying high wages to enable the workers the better to support life. By the efforts of liberal-minded people like Cobden, the Corn Laws were repealed.

The lowness of the wages of agricultural labourers was a factor in the sustaining of the prosperity of British agriculture in spite of the repeal of the Corn Laws. To a great extent, this prosperity was due to the increased efficiency resulting from the application of science to agriculture and to the high demand for the products of the industry; but the low wages of the labourers were a factor in the low costs. In point of fact, the Corn Laws kept up the rents of farms—rents which many farmers could not feel justified in paying if their farming was to be anything more than a speculator's gamble. The nation was not getting the food which was the *raison d'être* of the farming industry, and a wise Prime Minister, Sir Robert Peel, repealed the Corn Laws in 1846 in spite of the fact that his Ministry was in favour of protection; after resigning on the matter he was once more called upon to take up office, and thereupon took the step so necessary to the country's welfare. By this time the railways were opening up markets at home and making it easier for the farmer to obtain tools and machines and raw materials.

3. The Nineteenth-Century Depression in Agriculture

It was the improvement in means of communication and the application of engineering to agriculture which, indeed, led to the end of the 30 golden years British agriculture enjoyed after 1840. The great wide open spaces of America became transformed into vast wheat-producing areas; agriculture on a large scale, and with correspondingly low costs, resulted in British farming feeling the cold draught of competition: wheat prices were reduced by 60%. Cheap wheat came from the

United States in the seventies and from Canada in the eighties; and it came also from Australia, Argentina, India and Russia. The invention of refrigerating processes enabled the Argentine to send Britain chilled beef, and Australia and New Zealand to send frozen mutton. The British farmers, too, suffered from poor harvests in the last quarter of the century; and disease among the stock was so alarming as to call forth legislation in the form of the Contagious Diseases (Animals) Act of 1878.

Prices fell—to some extent aided by a fall in the value of silver relative to gold, so that Indian produce could be obtained more cheaply. Rents fell; many farmers became bankrupt; land went out of cultivation. Many of the best agricultural labourers migrated to the towns. The labourers who remained demanded higher wages through the Agricultural Labourers' Union, founded in 1872 by Joseph Arch.

Royal Commissions considered the problem presented to the agricultural industry; the Eversley Commission of 1893–97 thought that the best hope of the farmers lay in the direction of market gardening and dairy farming, fruit and flower growing. Farmers took the hint, or had already taken it. British farming adapted itself to the new conditions; the British climate is suited to dairy farming, and the markets for the products of market gardening lay in the large towns. Farmers raised pedigree cattle and sold them profitably to the Argentine, and English meat was regarded as superior to imported meat. But labour continued to be scarce—the 'rural exodus' continued.

In an attempt to revive a class of small cultivators, in 1892 the Government empowered county councils to provide small holdings on advantageous terms, and compelled them to do so under the Small Holdings and Allotments Act of 1908, the Board of Agriculture being given powers to intervene if the county councils proved recalcitrant. But these efforts met with little success; some thousands of small holdings (10–50 acres) were in fact provided; but less than one-third of the holders was drawn from those formerly employed in agriculture —the exodus of farm labourers to the towns continued. Up to the outbreak of the First World War in 1914 British agriculture continued to remain in the doldrums.

4. British Agriculture from 1914

The outbreak of war brought with it, of course, the menace of a shortage of food: a menace which was met by the negative method of seeking decreased consumption and the positive method of encouraging the growing of more food. The Corn Production Act, 1917, guaranteed a minimum price for wheat and oats and a minimum rate for agricultural wages. But the weakness of the British economy in its agricultural aspect was emphasised by the war; in spite of the British command of the seas—threatened, but by no means defeated, by the unrestricted U-boat warfare waged by the Germans—the food shortage remained acute. The call back to the land was an unsuccessful one. In the light of history the Small Holdings and Allotments Acts, 1908 to 1926, the Corn Production Acts, 1917 and 1920, the Agricultural Wages (Regulation) Act, 1924, seem faintly reminiscent of the legislation designed to keep the peasants on the manors in the Middle Ages, and of the laws directed against the first enclosures. Depression began in 1922 and reached a critical stage in 1927, when the acreage of ploughland in England and Wales had declined by some 700,000 acres and in Scotland by 20,000 acres since 1914.

The Government tried to meet the situation by giving agricultural credits. The Agricultural Credits Act, 1923, empowered the Ministry of Agriculture to form agricultural credit societies having as their object the making of advances to members for approved agricultural purposes. The Agricultural Credits Act, 1928, provided for the making of loans on the security of farming assets through a company formed out of public funds, the resources of which were increased by the Agricultural Development Act, 1939.

Subsequent legislation guaranteed prices and assured markets to farmers, to such a degree in recent years as to arouse some resentment on the part of the non-farming community. The gap between the prices paid to farmers for produce and the prices paid by the consumer has been a topic of perennial comment.

The marketing side of agricultural activity has, indeed, been the subject of important legislation. Although the aim of the State was to encourage producers to form their own organisations rather than to compel them to submit to Government direction, nevertheless the passing of the Agricultural Marketing Acts, 1931 and 1933, marked a stage of direct and comprehensive State intervention.

The 1931 Act gave producers powers to draw up marketing schemes and impose them on all producers concerned if a majority of two-thirds of registered producers accepted the proposals. A Hops Marketing Scheme, started in 1932, replaced selling by individual growers to brewers by a scheme of centralised selling by a Hops Marketing Board, which was given a complete monopoly of sales. Protection by a tariff ensured a success to the hops scheme not shared by schemes for other commodities.

The 1933 Act went farther than the 1931 Act. The State took powers to control output and imports; and the development of home production, where desirable, was encouraged. Marketing schemes were to be drawn up for particular products, either by the State or by the producers themselves.

An original scheme for milk marketing drawn up by the Reorganisation Commission of 1932 differed in many respects from that subsequently adopted: a Milk Marketing Board was formed representing all registered producers, and the milk produced became the property of the Board, which fixed prices paid by the distributors, though the latter were allowed to arrange their own contracts with the producers. The country was divided into eleven districts, the total sum realised by the sale of milk in each district being credited to a 'regional Pool' and divided among the producers at the pool price for the district. Milk sold to manufacturers and for other than liquid consumption was sold at a lower price than that of liquid milk.

In 1954 Government control of the Milk Marketing Board came to an end. The production of milk was then 1650 million gallons (80% sold for liquid consumption) as compared with 1100 million gallons before the Second World War.

A Pigs and Bacon Marketing Scheme came into operation in 1933; a Pigs Board, representative of producers, and a Bacon Board, representative of curers, together fixed the price to be paid for bacon pigs. Imports were restricted, and the prices of fixed supplies to curers from the home market were controlled. The output of pigs exceeded the estimate, so that imports were further restricted; the British public persisted in preferring Danish bacon to British. By the time the Second World War broke out the Scheme had succeeded in increasing the home supply of bacon from one-seventh to one-quarter of the total consumption, at the cost of a higher price for imported bacon and ham.

A Potato Marketing Scheme came into operation in 1934, and proved a considerable success, especially in preventing large fluctuations in supply and in maintaining prices. Production and supplies were regulated by a Potato Marketing Board; imports were restricted, and the size of potatoes placed upon the market was regulated. Producers and merchants were registered: only registered producers and merchants could deal with one another.

Eggs and Poultry Schemes and Cattle and Sugar Beet Schemes were in preparation when the Second World War broke out. It was then that the serious state of British agriculture was again thrown into prominence. It has been estimated that before the war the British people were using the produce of two and a quarter acres per person. To feed 50 million people, about 30 million acres of crops and grassland were available, with about 17 million acres of 'rough grazing.' In 1939 an era of cheap imported food ended; former agricultural countries were becoming industrialised, and wanted their own produce to feed their growing industrial populations. On the outbreak of war the Government instituted a form of general direction of British agriculture, based on local self-government by agricultural committees, which has been continued into peace conditions. A National Agricultural Advisory

Service was set up, giving farmers free advice. By 1951 the farmers had increased their output by 40% above the pre-war figures.

Self-sufficiency in food production in Britain has not and cannot be attained, having regard to the large population of the country. But agriculture still remains Britain's largest single industry, with an annual turnover of about £1500 million.

Mechanisation and improved methods of organisation have enabled British farmers to increase output by about 70% since 1959. By a system of guaranteed prices and deficiency payments to make up falls in market prices and by production grants, the Government has protected agriculture, at a cost to the British taxpayer of about £350 million a year. In May 1963 the policy was introduced of controlling imports or import prices for meat and cereals—which account for the greater part of the Government's deficiency payments—and the system of 'standard quantities' was applied to these products, the guarantee being related to a given quantity of home production.

In 1966 the Wise Committee's Report on Smallholdings suggested that the average size of the smallholdings administered by county councils should be increased from 44 to 80 acres—it is very difficult, short of increasing prices very greatly, to get holdings smaller than 80 acres to pay their way. The Report also suggested the use of smallholdings as a means of training young entrants to agriculture.

CHAPTER VIII

THE INDUSTRIAL REVOLUTION:
III. THE REVOLUTION IN TRANSPORT
AND COMMUNICATIONS

1. ROADS

The Romans had made good roads in Britain; but when they left the country the road system was neglected. Not much attention was paid to road-making or repair during the Middle Ages, and it was not until 1555 that the authorities realised that it was necessary to do something about public highways. In that year the Government of Mary Tudor passed a law declaring the parishes to be responsible for the roads lying within their boundaries; two surveyors appointed by the parishioners were to see that the repairs necessary were carried out. The law was only perfunctorily observed; and right up to the end of the seventeenth century the highroads continued to be unfenced tracks, impassable because of mud in wet weather, deeply rutted in summer. It was easier to travel by river; improvements in river facilities were in fact begun about 1650.

In the seventeenth century turnpike trusts came into existence. These were created with the idea that users of roads should pay for their upkeep: stretches of roads were controlled privately, and tolls were charged to those passing upon them. The system received a great impetus from the march of the Jacobites on London in 1745; after this alarm there was considerable activity in road construction for strategic reasons. The by-roads continued to be neglected; but by the end of the eighteenth century large towns were linked by main roads.

The end of the eighteenth century and the beginning of the nineteenth produced three great road engineers, who built up the technical knowledge so lacking in earlier times. Thomas Telford (1757–1834) demonstrated the importance of a good foundation; besides achievements in canal-making and bridge-building (*e.g.* the Menai Suspension Bridge), he built many hundreds of miles of road in Scotland and the north of England. John Metcalf (1717–1810), called 'Blind Jack of Knaresborough,' also built stretches of road in the north of England. John McAdam (1756–1836) gave the language the word 'macadamise'; he used rough angular fragments of stone of approximately equal size as a surface for the repair of roads; the slight camber caused wear and tear to be confined to the middle, so obviating the tendency to form ruts which the traffic tended to wear in the old, steeper-cambered roads.

In 1784 Palmer organised services of mail coaches for letters and passengers; and in the early nineteenth century posting-houses and the system of horse relays enabled a fast mail-coach, averaging about twelve miles an hour, to travel from, *e.g.*, London to Bath in one day. Between 1827 and 1840 steam road-carriages were in use, but the heavy tolls discouraged them. In the thirties the railways provided serious competition.

The Local Government Act of 1888 made the local authorities (the county councils and county boroughs) the responsible authorities for roads. The Local Government Act of 1929 divided the roads into 'county roads' and 'ordinary highways' and into 'classified' and 'unclassified' roads, and transferred the functions of Government Departments concerning roads to the Minister of Transport. The Trunk Roads Act of 1936 introduced the category of 'trunk roads,' comprising the principal roads in Britain except for roads within the County of London or within any county borough, and the Ministry of Transport became responsible for them. The total mileage of trunk roads in Britain is now about 6000, and the total mileage of public roads generally is over 170,000, about 71,000 being classified by the Ministry of Transport in Classes I, II and III. In 1914–15 the cost of new constructions, repair and improvement was nearly £19 million; in 1938 the figure was £68 million. The habit on the part of successive Governments of dipping into the fund produced by the road tax for the purposes of meeting general Government expenditure has contributed to the present unsatisfactory state of the roads in Britain. In Germany *autobahnen* were constructed for motor transport, in long stretches and with specially designed crossings. In the United States trunk roads designed to carry heavy, fast-moving traffic have been developed.

The roads of Britain belonged, in fact, to an earlier if pleasanter age; nevertheless, the coming of road transport provided the railways with a pretty problem. In the 1930s the competition of road-transport services was causing them such acute uneasiness that they obtained powers to run road-transport undertakings and to acquire financial interests in omnibus undertakings. In 1933 the four main lines had acquired a controlling interest in Carter Patersons and Pickfords, the two great road-haulage firms; and by 1935 the railways had invested over £8 million in omnibus undertakings.

The losses in traffic receipts due to road competition led the railways to agitate for a 'square deal.' In 1932 the Salter Committee on Rail and Road Transport was appointed, and the recommendations of this Committee were largely followed in the framing of the Road and

Rail Traffic Act, 1933. Part I of the Act dealt with road transport: in future licences (additional to the Road Fund licences) were to be obtained by persons using a mechanically driven vehicle to carry goods by road; particulars of an applicant's business and rates charged were to be given to the Ministry of Transport, which was also empowered to regulate the hours of work of employees and to inspect vehicles to see that they were kept in a fit and serviceable condition; licence-holders were obliged to keep a record of hours of work of employees and of journeys done. Part II of the Act extended the powers of the railways to quote competitive rates; Part III provided for the setting up of a Transport Advisory Council to advise the Minister of Transport in the co-ordination of transport facilities. The general effect of the Act was to strengthen the position of the railways as against the road-transport undertakings.

The Transport Act of 1947, which nationalised the railways, also nationalised British long-distance road-haulage services. But the Transport Act, 1953, had as its main provision the denationalisation of the road-haulage business conducted by the British Transport Commission through the Road Haulage Executive by virtue of the Transport Act, 1947. By the 1953 Act the British Transport Commission was required to dispose by sale of its road-haulage property held through the Road Haulage Executive. The Commission was still left free to provide, continue and develop services for road carriage otherwise than as a part of the operation of the existing road-haulage undertaking.

The 1953 Act provided, also, as from the end of 1954, for the repeal of Section 52 of the Transport Act, 1947, restricting the use of goods vehicles more than 25 miles from the operating centre. This provision of the 1947 Act had been greatly resented by private enterprise.

Attempts to sell the road-haulage property of the British Transport Commission were not very successful. In the upshot, certain trunk services were retained by the British Transport Commission; and the situation has become one in which British Road Services operate in competition with private enterprise.

The roads themselves were by 1953 in sad need of repair and extension. They had been starved of capital expenditure: between 1948 and 1953 the roads were allocated only about £40 million, compared with the railways' £200 million, the £1000 million of electricity, gas and coal, and the £2200 million of the manufacturing industries. Road accidents cost the country £150 million a year; and it has been estimated that the inadequacies of the road system cost industry £60 million a year.

Plans for road improvements announced by the Government in December 1953 were denounced generally as inadequate. In February 1955 the Government authorised a four-year road-improvement plan at a cost of £147 million; in July 1955 it was announced that 345 miles of modern motorways would be built in the next five to eight years, at an estimated cost of £85 million, or a quarter of a million pounds per mile; the actual cost has averaged about £530,000 per mile.

In September 1955 plans were published showing the proposed line of the first 53 miles of the London–Yorkshire motorway, the first British *autobahn*, for the exclusive use of motor traffic. This stretch of M1 was opened in 1959. Subsequently other motorways were built; 286 miles were in use by 1 April, 1964.

By the early 1960s, the number of vehicles in use in Britain reached 10 million, and it was estimated that the number would reach 40 million by the year 2100. The state of congestion in the towns, already severe, would be appalling. The problem was examined in the Buchanan Report, *Traffic in Towns*, 1963.

2. CANALS, INLAND WATERWAYS AND PORTS

In the early years of the Industrial Revolution the possibilities of canals and inland waterways were not overlooked by those seeking means of distributing goods and obtaining raw materials: a horse pulls about 40 tons by water as compared with 2 tons by road. Work on the improvement of rivers, by the provision of locks and weirs and towpaths, began about 1650; and by the middle of the eighteenth century all the main rivers had been made navigable for considerable distances: *e.g.* the Severn to Welshpool, the rivers of Yorkshire to Ripon and Leeds.

In 1759–61 the Bridgewater Canal to carry coal from Worsley to Manchester was constructed as a result of the application of the genius of Brindley, the engineer; the success of this venture resulted in the halving of the price of coal in Manchester. A second canal was constructed by Brindley in 1773 to carry the Manchester, Runcorn and Liverpool traffic. The Duke of Bridgewater had to go to London for his funds, and the scheme cost £220,000; but by 1792 it was paying over 35% in dividends, and the transport rate was 6s. per ton as compared with 12s. per ton by river.

There followed a great era in canal-building with the improvement of waterways and the linking of river to river by canal. In 1777 Brindley constructed the Trent and Mersey Canal, giving 'trunk' navigation from Hull to Liverpool, and assisting in the development of the Potteries district; transport costs were reduced by about three-quarters.

For a few years at the end of the eighteenth century, there was a 'canal mania.' Canals were made all over the country. Many of them were useful aids in the development of the Industrial Revolution of the eighteenth century. Many others were promoted at the instance of the ever-present scourge—the unscrupulous and predatory speculative promoter; many were planned as the result of misplaced and unforseeing enthusiasm. The spirit of independence and sturdy if misjudged self-reliance which has characterised so much of British industry resulted in the building of numerous unco-ordinated canals, without facilities for transference. They suffered from congestion at some times and lack of cargoes to make up loads at others; inadequate protection of goods from pilfering; an excessive number of locks; and a too narrow gauge, resulting in too slow a speed.

It is not to be wondered that these defects of the canals made the competing railways more attractive to merchants and industrialists. When the railways came, the railway companies bought up many canals, and in effect closed them. In non-industrial districts one comes across neglected canals blossoming with water-loving flowers, the haunts of water-fowl.

Of the total canal mileage of 3639 in England and Wales, 183 in Scotland and 848 in Ireland, 1360 miles were controlled by the railways before nationalisation; of the 17 million tons carried by the canals in 1938, $1\frac{1}{2}$ million tons were carried by the railway-owned canals; of the other canals, the Manchester Ship Canal carried over 6 million tons, the Aire and Calder and Birmingham carried over 2 million tons each, and the Grand Union, the Lea Navigation, the Leeds and Liverpool and the Bridgewater over a million tons each.

About 2500 miles of canals are still in use. During the Second World War a Central Canal Committee was set up by the Minister of War Transport to advise him on questions of policy regarding inland waters and to co-ordinate the work of six Regional Canal Committees which were reconstituted in order to ensure the most efficient operation of the canals. Under the Transport Act of 1947, management of docks and canals was allocated to a Docks and Inland Waterways Executive, one of the six executives appointed by the Minister of Transport in consultation with the British Transport Commission. The canals were organised into five areas, excluding the Manchester Ship Canal, the Bridgewater and the Thames Conservancy.

In 1959 the Government announced the setting up of a Canal Advisory Committee; the Committee proposed the linking of the north-east and south-west of England and of the north-west and south-east by an 'X' system. Under the provisions of the Transport Act, 1962, the British Transport Commission was dissolved, and a statutory body, the British Waterways Board, was formed.

The administration of ports and docks were placed by the Transport Act, 1962, under the authority of a Docks Board. The situation at that time was that of Britain's 300 ports, fifteen handled about 70% of the country's imports and exports and about 60% of the coastal traffic. A committee was set up under the chairmanship of Lord Rochdale to consider the working of Britain's docks and harbours. In its report of September 1962* the Committee urged the establishment of a National Ports Council and the formulation of a national plan. The Council was formed, and in an 'Interim Plan for Port Development' published in July 1965 the National Ports Council recommended development schemes for fourteen of the major ports with renovation schemes for others. The Devlin Committee formed to investigate dock labour questions reported in August, 1965, recommended that regular employment should replace the casual labour system.

3. RAILWAYS

Britain's leadership in the Industrial Revolution entailed the disadvantage that the country had to feel its way by trial and error and make mistakes which were necessarily costly, and which could be avoided by other countries following the more pleasing method of profiting by somebody else's experience. This was especially true of railways: the surveys; the submission of evidence to Parliamentary Committees; the purchase of land; the lack of Government co-ordination and the discouragement of amalgamation; the building of duplicate rival lines; all helped to make the cost of building British railways extremely high, and it has been estimated that the cost of preliminary proceedings alone was as much as £4000 per mile of line built. Britain paid about £55,000 per mile in all, as against £22,000 in Germany and even less in the United States.

In the initial stages of development the design of railways and locomotives was not co-ordinated. Wooden and then iron tramways were used in the early years of the nineteenth century to link collieries with towns and canals, the trucks being drawn by horses. Murdock, Trevithick and others made locomotives for use on the roads. In 1825 the first public line intended for use with locomotives was opened: the Stockton and Darlington Railway; but the passenger-coaches were to be drawn by horses. Coal shipments at Stockton increased from under 11,000 to 1½ million tons; and the possibilities of the new means of transport became apparent. In 1830 the Liverpool and Manchester Railway was opened; it was the first railway to enter into direct competition with the canals, which had proved themselves inadequate for the traffic. Stephenson's 'Rocket' reached 35 m.p.h.; the cost of transport between Liverpool and Manchester was reduced by one-third, and the time saved was very considerable.

The canal companies and turnpike trusts viewed this new rivalry with apprehension; but theirs was not the only opposition. The conviction that railways spelt ruination of their estates, combined with

* Report of the Committee of Inquiry into the Major Ports of Great Britain (Cmd. 1824).

D

natural cupidity, induced the landlords to charge exorbitant prices for their land. Fear of the admittedly fearsome monsters which the railway companies proposed to let loose on the country, together with the innate conservatism of most people, resulted in opposition from the public. One beneficent result of the public apprehension was that the railway companies constructed the tracks with special attention to safety, but this increased the cost, as did the efforts of Parliament,

1825	First public line—STOCKTON AND DARLINGTON RAILWAY
1830	LIVERPOOL AND MANCHESTER RAILWAY—the first railway to enter into direct competition with the CANALS
1840s	RAILWAY 'MANIA'
	George Hudson—the 'Railway King'
1847	Establishment of Railway Clearing House (Amalgamations)
1854	Cardwell's Act
	MAIN LINES LAID DOWN BY 1870
	DEVELOPMENT OF STATE CONTROL
1873	Establishment of Railway and Canal Commission—reconstituted 1888
1890s	Movement towards Nationalisation
1911	Railway Strike
1913	Formation of National Union of Railwaymen
1914–18	FIRST WORLD WAR
1919	Establishment of Ministry of Transport
1921	Railways Act—RAILWAYS COMBINED INTO FOUR GROUPS
	COMPETITION OF ROAD TRANSPORT
1932	Salter Committee
1933	Road and Rail Traffic Act
1939–45	SECOND WORLD WAR
1947	TRANSPORT ACT—Nationalisation of Railways
1953	TRANSPORT ACT—Reorganisation of railways
1962	TRANSPORT ACT—Dissolution of British Transport Commission; Railways Board established

CHART 8—*Landmarks in British Railway History*

which controlled without encouraging: it was necessary to bring a Bill before Parliament in promoting a railway.

By 1840 the methods of future development had been worked out; it had been discovered that the original plan of providing the track and charging a toll to the users for permission to place a vehicle upon it was not workable. Neither was the idea that horse-drawn and locomotive-drawn traffic could share the same track. The extent of the demand for passenger transport was, too, a pleasant surprise; indeed, for some years the greater part of the revenue was drawn from passenger traffic, the canals continuing to carry the bulky raw material.

So profitable did the new means of transport appear that a 'railway mania' occurred in the 1840s: a mania with which the name of George Hudson, the 'Railway King,' is associated. The economies of large-scale amalgamation were too obvious to be ignored. In 1847 a Railway Clearing House was established for the adjustment of claims between companies relating to the use of one another's lines and the interchange of traffic. In 1846 Parliament directed that a standard gauge (the distance between the rails) should be adopted. Over-enthusiasm and desire to make money brought about a crisis in 1847–48 which brought Hudson down.

The trend towards amalgamation was viewed by Parliament with considerable alarm; this was the era of *laissez-faire*. Nevertheless, it must be conceded that Parliament was also concerned with the question of the power which would be attained by unrestrained giant combines controlling the transport ways of the country. Commissions of enquiry were instituted. In 1854 Cardwell's Act (the Railway and Canal Traffic Act) directed the railways to provide facilities for through traffic, and forbade the giving of undue preferences, *i.e.* the preferring of one customer to another; already, in 1845, Parliament had fixed maximum rates for the carriage of goods.

But stronger action was needed if real control was to be effected. The companies could fix what rates they liked, subject to the maxima imposed, and preferences could be given in various devious ways. The *laissez-faire* system of ideas competed with the realisation that if control was to be undertaken by Parliament at all, it had to be effective. In 1873 a Railway and Canal Commission was established; and this was reconstituted and made permanent in 1888. Its functions were to determine reasonable rates, to examine proposed amalgamations and sanction the buying up of canals, and to enforce the law regarding preferences.

The main lines of the country's railways had been laid a quarter of a century before; by 1870 13,000 miles had been built; and after 1885, when the mileage was 16,700, the additions were mainly branch lines. The maintenance of the *laissez-faire* attitude and the reluctance to sanction amalgamations were, therefore, the contributory factors in a situation where any planning the Government felt called upon to do had to be done in the face of an accomplished fact which it was exceedingly hard to change—there are few things so little susceptible to political manipulation as a complete railway system.

The Government did its best. In 1888 the Railway and Canal Traffic Act provided for a revised and uniform classification of rates; and a new schedule came into operation in 1893. Thereupon, the companies raised their rates to the permitted maximum. Parliament retaliated by passing, in 1894, an Act which limited the rates to those in force in 1892. This begins the era, continued to our own day, when increases in rates stated to be necessary to maintain solvency have provoked a public outcry, followed by protestations on the part of the railway authorities that increases are necessary. The position in 1894 was that traders were able to appeal to the Railway and Canal Commission against increases they regarded as unreasonable. The companies therefore found it difficult to raise their rates; but they were also wary of lowering them, since it might be held that subsequent increases were unnecessary and unreasonable.

Improvements in passengers' comfort now became the basis of competition between the companies, and their working costs rose. The inevitable result was a more pronounced tendency towards amalgamations and working agreements. Parliament was still distrustful of this movement; and, in 1909, refused to sanction a combine of the Great Northern, Great Eastern and Great Central Railways: the answer of the railways was, of course, informal agreements. The general public again began to be apprehensive of the formation of a great railway monopoly. So were the railway employees, who found the Conciliation Boards, set up by the Board of Trade after unrest in 1907, unsatisfactory; there was a strike in 1911, and the National Union of Railwaymen was formed in 1913.

Nationalisation was a remedy suggested in many quarters, but the Government seemed reluctant to take this step. The outbreak of the First World War in 1914 forced the Government's hand: the Government took control of the railways and guaranteed dividends.

After the war, in 1919, a Ministry of Transport, with extensive powers over the regulation of rates and charges, was set up. It was believed by some people that the time was now ripe for nationalisation; but still the Government held its hand: a compromise was in fact effected. By the Railways Act of 1921 the Government handed back the railways to private control; but the 121 railway companies, apart from the London electric and underground railways, were combined into four groups: the Southern; the Great Western; the London, Midland and Scottish; and the London and North Eastern Railways. The Minister of Transport was given powers to enforce measures leading to the standardisation of ways, plant and equipment; a Railway Rates Tribunal was set up to fix fares, rates and charges; and permanent wages boards were established. The Railway Rates Tribunal sanctioned rates which came into operation on 1st January 1928; the General Railway Classification of Merchandise set out the standard schedules of charges for the carriage of commodities.

The story of the increasing competition of road transport has already been told. Meantime, arrangements were being made to deal with the possibility of industrial disputes in the railway scene. Failure to reach agreement in a dispute was to result in a reference to a Central Wages Board, composed of representatives of the companies, the National Union of Railwaymen, the Amalgamated Society of Locomotive Engineers and Firemen, and the Railway Clerks' Association. An appeal could be made to the National Wages Board, containing representatives of the companies, the unions and the users, e.g. the Association of British Chambers of Commerce; an independent chairman was to be nominated by the Minister of Labour. In 1935 the Railway Staff National Council, consisting of representatives of the companies and the unions, superseded the Central Wages Board; a reference on any point not agreed upon was to be referred to a Railway Staff National Tribunal, whose decision was not to be legally binding; but the decision could hold up a strike or lock-out until the Tribunal investigated the matter.

The coming of the Second World War meant that the Government again took charge of the railways; the Government paid a fixed rental to the companies of about £43½ million. The peak revenue year of the war period was in 1942, when the Government's share of the revenue pool was about £66 million. By 1945 there was a considerable drop.

The prospect of nationalisation was not looked upon very favourably by the boards of the companies. The request for a 'square deal' in relation to road transport was brought up again. By this time the railways had substantial holdings in motor-omnibus and carrier companies, and were showing a considerable interest in air-transport development. The four main-line companies had interests in sixteen air companies, five of them operating services; and they appointed an air adviser in 1943. The war years naturally caused rapid depreciation of railway assets; by the time peace came it was estimated that about £100 million would be required for deferred maintenance and renewals alone.

It was perhaps inevitable that when a Labour Government came into power in 1945 the railways should be nationalised. The Transport Act, 1947, gave power over all forms of inland transport, except air transport, to the British Transport Commission, responsible to the Minister of Transport. The management of the various forms of transport was entrusted to Executives appointed to run: (1) railways; (2) docks and canals; (3) road-haulage undertakings, except for certain short-distance undertakings; (4) London passenger transport; (5) railway hotels. To the Railway Executive passed, on 1st January 1948, responsibility for the administration, maintenance and operation of British Railways, the Railway Executive having the status of a public authority dealing with the public, employing the staff and entering into contracts. The members of the Railway Executive were to be appointed by the Minister of Transport in consultation with the Transport Commission. A Transport Tribunal took the place of the Railway Rates Tribunal.

The Transport Act, 1953, required the reorganisation of the railways. The British Transport Commission was required to submit to the Minister a scheme for the reorganisation of the railways, providing for the abolition of the Railway Executive and for the delegation of functions to new area authorities.

The Act amended the powers and duties of the Commission in certain important respects. Its general duty, as laid down in the Act, was to provide or secure the provision of 'an adequate and properly co-ordinated system of passenger transport for the London Passenger Transport Area, to provide in such places and to such extent as may appear to them to be expedient, other transport services, facilities for traffic on inland waterways, and port facilities (if in such places they were, on 1st July 1952, either providing port facilities or were specifically empowered to so do), due regard being had to efficiency, economy and safety of operation and to the needs of the public, agriculture, commerce and industry.'*

Those sections of the Transport Act, 1947, which provided for the making of schemes for road-passenger transport services were repealed, so that the eventual nationalisation of municipal passenger transport was no longer envisaged. The Commission was not required to provide port facilities where it was not already doing so or had power to do so.

The organisation of British rail transport is in process of modification to meet modern conditions. In January 1955 the British Transport Commission published a fifteen-year plan estimated to cost £1200 million, but since reassessed at £1500 owing to rising price levels. The main features of the plan included electrification of certain main lines; the building of diesel locomotives and multiple-coach diesel units for branch and cross-country lines; the improvement of track and signalling to allow main line speeds of up to 100 miles per hour; the speeding of goods trains, with improved safety devices; the rebuilding of stations; and the cleaning-up of carriages. A great extension of suburban electrification was envisaged. A reappraisal of the programme was completed in 1959, and published as a Government White Paper (Cmd. 813). As a result, modernisation is being accelerated to improve railway finances as quickly as possible.

The Transport Act, 1962, dissolved the British Transport Commission and replaced it by five statutory bodies. Four Boards for Railways, London Transport, Docks and Inland Waterways, respectively, were established; a Holding Company was formed for the remaining activities of the British Transport Commission: the road services and the shipping freight services. The hotels formerly managed by the B.T.C. came under the control of a company under the Railways Board. The railways came under the administration of the British Railways Board and six Regional Boards with delegated management functions.

* Statement by the British Transport Commission.

In 1963 the Beeching Report envisaged a reorganisation of the railway system by which unprofitable lines would be eliminated and closer integration with the economic life of the country achieved.

4. SEA AND AIR TRANSPORT

The repeal of the Navigation Acts in 1849 and the freeing of the coastal trade in 1854 have already been commented upon.* In the early nineteenth century the first engines for water travel made their appearance—the Atlantic was crossed by a steamship, the *Savannah,* in 1819. The earliest steamships were sailing vessels fitted with engines and paddle-wheels; and, indeed, sailing ships formed the great bulk of British shipping right up to the 1860s. Iron replaced wood, and soon after the middle of the nineteenth century the clipper ships which raced one another across the seas with cargoes from China and Australia were fitted with iron hulls, which were lighter than wood because of their comparative thinness, and which were stronger, cheaper to build, more watertight and gave more cargo space. In the last quarter of the century steel began to replace iron; the advances in the techniques of production enabled steel to be produced much more cheaply. Thus steel ships took the place of iron ones.

It was in the 1850s that steamships began seriously to compete with sailing vessels; the inventions of the screw, the compound engine with tubular boilers, gave more power for less fuel. Engines were improved; the steam-turbine engine, using the principle of the pressure of a steam jet on blades of the propeller, was invented by Sir Charles Parsons in 1884. The opening of the Suez Canal in 1869 gave a decisive advantage to the steamships; coaling-stations were set up at Port Said and Aden, shortening the Far East route, with consequent saving of time and fuel.

Britain built up the largest mercantile marine in the world. The American supplies of coal and iron were not so conveniently situated for iron and steel shipbuilding; and in the Civil War of 1861–65 the Americans lost a considerable amount of merchant shipping. The payments for shipping services earned by the British mercantile fleet helped to make up the deficit on the visible trade balance of Britain with the rest of the world; the net national shipping income just before the outbreak of the Second World War was about £100 million.

Private enterprise built up Britain's shipping as it had built up Britain's industrial supremacy; but it brought with it the consequences of that selfishness and ruthlessness which inevitably give rise to State control. Vessels were sent to sea in an unseaworthy condition, undermanned, a danger to the crew. Samuel Plimsoll, a Member of Parliament, devoted his energies to an attack on the evil of the 'coffin ships.'

* See p. 40.

The Board of Trade, already conducting examinations for Master's and Mate's certificates by the middle of the century, had inadequate powers. A Royal Commission was appointed, but the Government was not over-eager to act until public opinion, roused by Plimsoll's activities, forced it to do so. The Merchant Shipping Acts of 1875 and 1876 imposed penalties on shipowners who sent their ships to sea in an unseaworthy condition, limited deck cargoes, and established a load-line—the 'Plimsoll Line.' The Merchant Shipping Act, 1894, amended by subsequent legislation, codified the law relating to the liability of shipowners. After the loss of the *Titanic* in 1912 the regulations relating to the safety of crew and passengers at sea were tightened.

The British Merchant Navy expanded from 4 million tons in the middle of the nineteenth century to 12 million tons by 1913; and British overseas trade expanded correspondingly. The advantages which Great Britain enjoyed—her diversified industrial activities, her cheap coal, her already sound establishment as a world carrier, the policy of Free Trade which enabled her shipbuilders to obtain materials cheaply—combined to cause her to outstrip the Continental countries and the United States. In 1892–94 she was building four-fifths of the total gross tonnage of merchant shipping launched; at this time iron had been superseded by steel in ship construction, and Britain's supremacy in metallurgical science was enjoying full play. Subsidised foreign competition then began to affect British interests adversely, so that the proportion of shipping built by Britain declined; but in the years immediately before the First World War, the tonnage built by Britain had recovered to 61% of the world total.

In the last quarter of the nineteenth century the shipping companies, faced with depression and competition, formed combinations. Depression had come about through the building of tonnage in excess of that required for world trade; it was met, in some cases, by amalgamations; in others, by 'conferences'; the latter were associations of companies laying down tariffs of freights and agreeing upon 'territories' for their liners. The monopolistic nature of such conferences caused legislative action to be taken against them when they were adopted in the United States and Australia. Another device was the deferred rebate system, by which individual shippers promised loyalty to companies in return for rebates.

Britain lost 8 million gross tons of shipping through enemy action during the First World War; and the depression of 1929–32 reduced her proportion of world tonnage to 32% by 1935. After the war the shipping of other nations was heavily subsidised. The consequence of the unequal struggle was that British earnings for shipping services declined rapidly, and many companies were faced not merely with a low yield for the capital invested but also with actual losses. By 1932 the volume of British shipping lying idle was over 2 million tons, a figure subsequently reduced by sales for breaking-up and by sales to foreign buyers—the latter hardly a method of reducing foreign competition.

The British Government met subsidy by subsidy—an annual subsidy, of a maximum of £2 million for 1934, being promised to the tramp-shipping industry on condition that it evolved a scheme to prevent the dissipation of the subsidy through domestic competition, and to ensure the greater employment of British shipping. A scheme was evolved by the British Tramp Shipping Committee; and an International Committee was formed in 1935. This Committee put into operation a scheme of minimum freight rates; rates began to rise in 1936, and eventually again reached the 1929 level; the subsidy was renewed each year up to 1937.

In spite of the difficulties experienced, British ships were carrying in 1939 over 40% of the world's overseas trade, between 60% and 70% of the trade between the United Kingdom and the rest of the world, and over 90% of the trade between the United Kingdom and the British Empire.

During the Second World War the British Government took over merchant shipping, paying a rental which did not include a contribution for replacement or obsolescence. In the war over 11 million gross tons (to 1945) were lost to the British Empire by enemy action; by 1948, however, these losses had been replaced: Britain then possessed 22% (18 million) of world tonnage, coming second to the United States, which possessed 36% (nearly 30 million tons). Britain's tonnage, indeed, was higher than in 1939; but the United States had increased her tonnage in much greater proportion. In 1958 Britain's share was 25%.

In the 1940s the shipping concerns were not anxious to receive subsidies from the Government; and they certainly were not in favour of nationalisation; the Annual Report of the Liverpool Steam Ship Owners' Association for 1943 pointed out that experiments in nationalised shipping made in the United States and in Australia had ended disastrously.

It can be argued that the variety of changing conditions in the shipping industry calls for individual enterprise rather than State organisation. The constant need for close supervision in home and foreign ports, and the selection of the right type of vessel for a given cargo in a given trade are, it is held, qualities which the State type of enterprise cannot provide.

However this may be, the State has acted with alacrity in acquiring control in the modern and contrasting industry of air transport. The First World War, with its research and development of fighting weapons, gave an impetus to aviation; and between 1919 and 1936 the mileage of world air routes grew from 3200 to 305,200. In 1925 Imperial Airways, Ltd., was formed; it was granted a Government subsidy to develop British air routes overseas. Its air-transport undertakings were acquired on 1st April 1940 by British Overseas Airways Corporation, one of the three statutory Corporations established to operate: (1) the United Kingdom–Commonwealth, United States and Far East routes (British Overseas Airways); (2) the internal and United Kingdom–Continent routes (British European Airways); (3) the United Kingdom–South America and West Indies routes (British South American Airways; the England–South America services were later abandoned).

The privately owned American companies have apparently run their lines more economically than the British corporations. The British, like other nations, have operated aircraft services for prestige rather than purely commercial purposes, and have conducted costly experiments. It must be added, however, that recent developments in European services have enabled passenger fares to come down to a level comparing not unfavourably with railway fares.

The variety of considerations involved, including those of design and development for other than commercial reasons, and the rapid march of progress in air transport in modern times, including the use of jet aircraft, make the evaluation of air transport in relation to other forms of transport a difficult one.

It is difficult, also, to evaluate the value of space-travel research which has proceeded so vigorously during the 1960s. Apart from strategic and prestige considerations, the research and development of apparatus which has gone on in space research have been applied also to the details of other technologies such as aircraft and motor-car construction.

5. COMMUNICATIONS

Postal services were in operation in most European countries by the beginning of the eighteenth century; but the services were necessarily slow and costly. In 1666–67 it took 30 hours for mail to pass between London and Bristol; and between London and Edinburgh the time taken was up to 100 hours. It was in 1837 that Rowland Hill, appreciating that distance added little to the cost of sending letters, proposed a standard charge, and the Penny Post came into being in 1840. In 1875 an International Postal Convention was signed at Berne; and it is now possible to send letters all over the world by merely affixing the necessary stamps.

Telegraphy became a practical proposition in the 1830s, and wireless-telegraphy at the end of the century. Ships were equipped with wireless apparatus; the public imagination was fired when, in 1910, a murderer, Dr Crippen, was apprehended in America by detectives apprised of his identity by the captain of the ship in which he was travelling from England.

The transmission of speech was successfully accomplished before the end of the First World War. The British Broadcasting Company, Ltd., was formed in 1922, and the British Broadcasting Corporation in 1927. And so began the era of the babble of voices in the ether, the strenuous propaganda and counter-propaganda of nations and the onset of commercial advertising. Television came to the fore; and in 1953 much controversy was raised in Britain by the Government's proposals to establish an alternative television programme to that conducted by the B.B.C.

Printing in Britain remained a handicraft from the time William Caxton started work in London in 1476 until the nineteenth century. In 1814 *The Times* initiated power printing. Thereafter, power printing developed rapidly, and printing techniques interacted with the social revoluion caused by the implementing of the Education Act of 1870, making elementary education compulsory. Alfred Harmsworth, later Lord Northcliffe, was the founder of the 'new journalism' of the closing years of the nineteenth century and the opening years of the twentieth; in 1896 he launched the *Daily Mail*; in 1904, by which time the opinions of women in political and current affairs had come to matter to the wielders of power, he began the *Daily Mirror* as a cheap women's paper. Soon a large part of the London and provincial Press had become the property of several large combines, which endeavoured, often with success, to influence popular thought.

In a characteristic phrase, H. G. Wells once referred to the popular newspapers as those 'wildly flapping caricatures of contemporary thought.' It would appear that beyond the more serious journals (themselves often ponderous, precious and lacking in the saving grace of humour directed at themselves), the bulk of the Press set out not to elevate and instruct but to amuse. What could have become a tremendous power to enrich the education provided by a paternal State became in the hands of the worst sections of the writing and publishing community an evil thing, taking the greatest advantage from the relaxing of the laws relating to obscenity.

In television, the division of the nation into 'two Nations' in a sense not perhaps realisable by Disraeli became apparent, with B.B.C. 1 catering for the masses, and B.B.C. 2 for those regarded as of more fastidious taste and power of artistic appreciation; commercial television, beyond some spasmodic attempts at 'culture,' frankly provided entertainment. Even the new communications satellite, Telstar (1962), was pressed into service not worthy of the technological achievement.

Here was a way to take up the great force of communications, and forge it into a means of avoiding those tendencies leading to a mentally and psychically stratified world community such as that forecast by Aldous Huxley in his *Brave New World*.*

Yet the way is still there; and we may be lacking in a sense of perspective if we regard too seriously what may well be mere passing phases in the life of our society.

The opportunities for commercial advertising in the popular Press are too well known to require more than a passing comment in this work. It must not be forgotten, however, that advertising may be good or bad; and that the same forces making for harmful influence are equally available to make known the products of responsible undertakings and to render possible the production of comparatively cheap but worthwhile literature. Modern industrial organisation, with its special departments devoted to publicity, depends for its own existence ultimately on the efficiency of communication not only for distributing products and obtaining raw material but also for disseminating information whereby consumers are made aware of specific firms, their products and the suggested suitability of these products to consumers' special needs. Ultimately, too, the power of the Press is reducible to the power of the members of the community willing to support it: that power partakes of the quality of the individual persons who possess it.

* Chatto and Windus, 1932.

CHAPTER IX

FINANCIAL ORGANISATION AND THE REVOLUTION IN BANKING

1. THE RISE OF THE JOINT-STOCK LIMITED LIABILITY COMPANY

IT has been stated that the pricking of the 'South Sea Bubble' led to the 'Bubble Act' of 1720 by which new companies had to obtain a charter from the Crown or be formed under a special Act of Parliament.* This Act was repealed in 1825; and in 1844 incorporation of a company without a charter or special Act was made possible.

The expansion of the opportunities for profitable investment, the large amounts of capital accumulated through commercial enterprise, the new techniques calling for the use of a considerable amount of loan capital, made inevitable the invention of financial machinery to enable those who had money to invest without possessing technical knowledge, and those who had the technical knowledge and business ability, to pool their resources to the advantage of both. The possibility of finding himself liable for the whole debts of a business undertaking, the working of which he had but a hazy understanding, could not fail to deter anybody interested in the apparently limitless possibilities of industrial development displayed as the Industrial Revolution proceeded.

In the earlier common-law joint-stock companies the members were responsible for the debts of the company as a whole. They were unincorporated, and the liability of the members was unlimited. Not until 1855 did Parliament pass an Act legalising the principle of limited liability; in that year limited liability was introduced for shares of not less than £10. In 1862 this limit was removed.

The principle of limited liability has been of the utmost importance in the evolution of modern industrial organisation. Limited liability means that the liability of an individual member of a joint-stock limited-liability company is limited to the amount of share capital which he has undertaken to subscribe: a person who takes up shares of the value of £50 is liable only for this amount; and once his shares are fully paid up, he cannot be called upon to contribute more in the paying-off of a company's debts if the company goes into liquidation. The company is a corporate body, *i.e.* it is a legal entity in the eyes

* See p. 43.

of the law, separate and distinct from the members who compose it, able to hold property and make contracts and sue and be sued just like an ordinary natural person, and with perpetual succession, so that although individual members may die or transfer their shares to somebody else, the company goes on. A public limited company may be formed with as few as seven members, and the public may be invited to subscribe for shares or debentures of the company.

It thus became possible for the general public to invest money in industry without fear of becoming involved in large debts; and the number of companies formed increased rapidly. The returns of the Registrar of Companies showed that over 5000 new companies were registered every year. By 1944 there were over 13,000 public companies in existence, with a total paid-up capital of over £3800 million.

Previous legislation relating to companies was consolidated in the

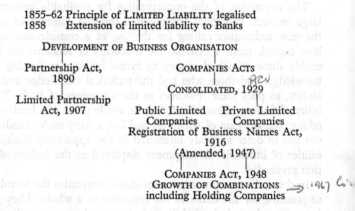

1720. 'South Sea Bubble'

Companies formed by Charter or Act of Parliament

1855–62 Principle of LIMITED LIABILITY legalised
1858   Extension of limited liability to Banks

DEVELOPMENT OF BUSINESS ORGANISATION

Partnership Act, 1890   COMPANIES ACTS

Limited Partnership Act, 1907   CONSOLIDATED, 1929

Public Limited Companies   Private Limited Companies
Registration of Business Names Act, 1916
(Amended, 1947)

COMPANIES ACT, 1948
GROWTH OF COMBINATIONS
including Holding Companies

CHART 9—*The Development of Legal Forms in Business Organisation*

Companies Act, 1929. The Companies Act, 1948, consolidated the Companies Acts, 1929 and 1947 (other than the provisions of the 1947 Act relating to the registration of business names, bankruptcy and the prevention of fraud in connection with unit trusts).

The principle of limited liability was applied to partnerships by the Limited Partnership Act, 1907 (legislation applied to ordinary partnerships had been codified in the Partnership Act, 1890). The 1907 Act created the limited partner, one whose liability extends only to the amount he has contributed to the partnership, but who is subject to various restrictions, of which the most important is that he is not allowed to take any active part in the conduct of the business; there must be one or more general partners, liable for all the debts of the firm, in a limited partnership. A limited partnership must be registered with the Registrar of Companies, or the firm will be regarded as an ordinary partnership in the eyes of the law. The disadvantages of a limited partnership have resulted in this type of organisation not being popular in Britain. All the advantages of a limited partnership, with none of the disadvantages, may be obtained by the formation of a private limited company, the minimum number of members of which is two, and the maximum 50 (excluding persons in the employment of the company and persons who have been formerly in the employment of the company, who were members while in that employment and who have continued to be members after the termination of their employment with the company).

A private limited company enjoys certain exemptions from obligations imposed by law on public limited companies; but it prohibits any invitation to the public to subscribe for shares or debentures of the company, and it restricts the right to transfer its shares.

To compare the growth of private limited companies with that of public limited companies: in 1944 there were 169,205 private companies with a total paid-up capital of £1,935 million. In 1951 took place the 500,000th company registration in England and Wales since the coming into operation of the 1862 Act. In 1954, of the quarter of a million companies, only about 4% were public companies, but together they owned two-thirds of the total capital. At the end of 1964 there were 15,251 public companies and 420,264 private companies. There were 10,886 public companies with a share capital; their issued capital amounted to £11,098,000,000.

It is evident that the creation of such machinery for the legal organisation of business undertakings also created opportunities for unscrupulous and clever people to conduct activities of doubtful moral integrity while keeping within the letter of the law: there is, for example, the question of the 'one-man' company. The Cohen Committee was set up to consider the question of company law amendment, and reported in 1945. The Companies Act, 1948, embodied some of the recommendations of this report.

A recent development is one by which the small investor may spread his investments over a large number of different securities, thus spreading his risk. This is done through an investment trust, a financial institution which divides its capital into units, each one of which, held as a share, represents investment in many companies. An American idea, coming to this country in the 1930s, was the fixed trust, which invests its capital in a definite group of shares, e.g. brewery or mining.

By such means industry is able to make use of small amounts of capital—small in themselves, but collectively forming a stream of loan capital which is of the utmost importance when joined with management, labour, fixed capital and enterprise. The nature of such small investment may be gauged from the information given in an advertisement in 1953 in a national newspaper, addressed to the small investor: the unit trust advertising offered an opportunity to those investing as little as £20 to spread the risk over 25 'high-class companies' covering Shipping and Motors, Oil and Fuel, Stores, Textiles, Breweries and Distilleries, Tobacco, Gold Mines, Building and other industries.

The buying and selling of industrial securities is conducted in this country on the London Stock Exchange and twenty-two provincial Stock Exchanges, working in co-operation with the London Stock Exchange. The London Stock Exchange was founded before the close of the eighteenth century. The original deed of settlement, laying down the constitution of the Stock Exchange, was made in 1802, and was superseded by a deed of settlement of 1875. Until 1945 there was a 'dual-control' system of control, the building and finances being controlled by nine elected members called the trustees and managers, while the conduct of business, such as the admission of members, was in the hands of a committee for general purposes. On 1st April 1945 the dual-control system was abolished, the two bodies being merged into the Council of the Stock Exchange.

The general social changes of the past few years have had their effect on the Stock Exchange. Nationalisation, the disappearance of large foreign investments, the taxation of the rich, the redistribution of wealth among the community, with a subsidiary effect of diverting money from share purchases to football pools and similar speculations, the diversion of small private savings into savings certificates, bank deposits and buildings societies, are factors which have brought down the 'normal' business dealing figure from 13,000–18,000 share dealings a day to under 12,000 a day. The effect on the flow of entries to the Stock Exchange has been such that whereas the total cost of becoming a member used to be about £3000, the total cost is now less than £1000. A Public Gallery was opened in 1953.

In 1961 over 9000 different securities, valued at £50,000 million, were quoted on the London Stock Exchange. A growing share of Stock Exchange business is now done on behalf of the smaller investors.

2. THE CO-OPERATIVE MOVEMENT IN BRITAIN

The co-operative idea was tried out in Britain as early as the eighteenth century, but it was not until the nineteenth century that the movement developed its real strength. French revolutionary doctrines; the distress and unemployment following in the wake of the changes brought about by the beginnings of the Industrial Revolution; the unrest at the close of the Napoleonic Wars; all had their influence in fostering the growth of the idea of co-operative ownership of the means of production and distribution.

Producers' co-operative societies did not flourish in England; a group of such societies was indeed founded at Leicester, but they were concerned with the standard of craftsmanship rather than with volume of production. It was in agriculture, in the Scandinavian countries, that productive co-operation met with success.

Robert Owen (1771–1858), the manufacturer–reformer, pioneer of scientific management and humanitarian teacher, inspired the founding of productive co-operative groups; but these groups lacked adequate capital and suffered from severe competition. They failed; but, as in so many other instances in history, they were but the individual casualties in a struggle that was to have widespread and far-reaching results in the field of business organisation.

It was in distributive co-operation that the success of the British co-operative movement was founded. In 1844 a small group of weavers in Rochdale, the 'Rochdale Equitable Pioneers,' formed a co-operative group, and founded a distributive store. Each of the 28 members subscribed one pound, and was to receive a share of the profits in proportion to the amount of his purchases. The movement spread, particularly in the north of England and Scotland. The Industrial and Provident Societies Acts of 1852 and 1862 provided legal protection: the liability of the members was limited to the amount of their shares. The Industrial and Provident Societies Act of 1952 limited the amount of share capital any member might possess to £500.

In 1863 a federation of co-operative societies was founded, called the English Wholesale Society; it became not merely a wholesale society but a combine producing staple commodities, owning factories and steamships. In 1869 a central propagandist body, the Co-operative Union, was founded, and set up a co-operative college: a residential college for adult education. In 1869, too, the Scottish Wholesale Society was formed.

A few years later, in 1876, the Co-operative Bank was founded; it applied its profits to the reduction of interest charged for loans, and to the increase of interest given for deposits, and in many respects became more of a savings bank than a deposit bank in the ordinary sense.

By 1937 the number of members in the consumers' societies reached 8 millions; and the turnover was over £250 million. In the 1940s the number of co-operative retail societies passed 1100, the numbers of members varying from a few hundred to some thousands: the membership of the original Rochdale Equitable Pioneers expanded to 15,000.

The retail societies are independent of one another. They are members of the Co-operative Wholesale Society (C.W.S.), and receive dividends in proportion to their purchases from that organisation. But not

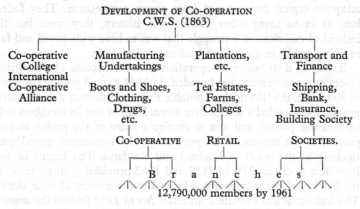

Producers' Co-operation
ROBERT OWEN (1771–1858)

DISTRIBUTIVE CO-OPERATION

1844 'The Rochdale Equitable Pioneers'
1852 ⎰ The Industrial and Provident Societies Acts (now superseded by the
1862 ⎱   Industrial and Provident Societies Acts, 1893–1954)
1876 Amount of a member's share capital limited to £200
1863 English Wholesale Society
1869 Co-operative Union Founded
1869 Scottish Wholesale Society
1876 Founding of Co-operative Bank

DEVELOPMENT OF CO-OPERATION
C.W.S. (1863)

Co-operative	Manufacturing	Plantations,	Transport and
College	Undertakings	etc.	Finance
International			
Co-operative	Boots and Shoes,	Tea Estates,	Shipping,
Alliance	Clothing,	Farms,	Bank,
	Drugs,	Colleges	Insurance,
	etc.		Building Society
	CO-OPERATIVE	RETAIL	SOCIETIES.

B r a n c h e s
12,790,000 members by 1961

CHART 10—*The Story of Co-operation in Britain*

all the commodities in which they trade are obtained through the
C.W.S.

In goods not requiring expert, detailed knowledge and a high level
of entrepreneurship, the Co-operative system attained a strong position
in British trade: in 1939 the Co-operative Union handled 14·1%
of the nation's retail trade in groceries, particularly foodstuffs, nearly
14% of the trade in coal, and over 9% of the trade in boots and shoes.

Perhaps because of the levelling of incomes, the Co-operative movement attracted many middle-class and professional members. The low
percentage of attendance of members at meetings of the retail societies,
particularly in the south and west, indicates that its supporters have
been more interested in dividends than in social movements; before
the Second World War the average dividend was about 1s. 6d. in the
£1, while today it is about 9d.

The movement has strong links with the Labour Party; at one time
it put forward Co-operative candidates for Parliament. Linking the
movement internationally is the International Co-operative Alliance.

By 1958 it was found that the retail co-operative stores were facing severe competition from the supermarkets and self-service stores—it was ironic that the Co-operative movement had initiated self-service stores in Britain. A supermarket style of retailing was adopted by many grocery branches. In 1962 the amalgamation of the separate whole-saling, productive and advisory sections of the Co-operative movement was proposed.

The general conclusion would seem to be that the return of monetary dividends to customers, the original principle of the Co-operative move-ment with its idea of the customers as owners, has been sacrificed to the idea of the supermarket and self-service stores gaining profit from its customers, on the principle of 'If you can't beat them, join them.'

3. THE DEVELOPMENT OF BANKING

The growth of England's industry and trade during the nineteenth century attracted foreign traders dealing in such staple commodities as cotton, wool and timber. So high a reputation did many of these foreign and British traders attain that their signature on a bill of ex-change carried with it an excellent guarantee; and they made it an important part of their functions to accept bills of exchange for other traders. This extension of their normal business activities became very profitable, and eventually many of them became merchant bankers, *i.e.* bankers not in the technical sense of being deposit bankers or note-issuing bankers, but accepting and discounting houses, financing trade by putting into circulation bills of exchange. They later became joint-stock companies—*e.g.* in 1920 C. and J. Hambro and Sons amalgamated with the British Bank of Northern Commerce to form Hambros Bank, Ltd.

The connections of the acceptance houses with their associations on the Continent were disorganised by the First World War, and a pro-cedure was developed by which credits abroad were granted only with the guarantee of foreign banks and through them as intermediaries; a consequence was that English, American and foreign deposit banks entered into competition with the accepting houses. Since the First World War, too, the volume of Treasury Bills (promissory notes fin-ancing Government borrowing) has greatly exceeded that of com-mercial bills of exchange. It is held by many economists that not until the return of the commercial bill of exchange drawn on London to the position of the prime financial instrument in international trade can this country regain its strength in finance.

Another line of development, and one of supreme significance to this country, where the cheque system has prevailed to a much greater extent than on the Continent, was the establishment of joint-stock deposit banking. A joint-stock deposit bank is a bank whose main functions are the receipt of customers' deposits, the issue of cheques

Sixteenth and Seventeenth Centuries: Development of use of bill of exchange. The Goldsmiths—safeguarders of valuables. Beginning of use of 'cheques' and 'bank-notes.' Beginning of private banks.

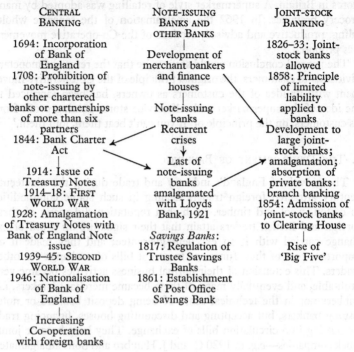

CENTRAL BANKING	NOTE-ISSUING BANKS AND OTHER BANKS	JOINT-STOCK BANKING
1694: Incorporation of Bank of England	Development of merchant bankers and finance houses	1826–33: Joint-stock banks allowed
1708: Prohibition of note-issuing by other chartered banks or partnerships of more than six partners	Note-issuing banks Recurrent crises	1858: Principle of limited liability applied to banks Development to large joint-stock banks; amalgamation; absorption of private banks: branch banking
1844: Bank Charter Act	Last of note-issuing banks amalgamated with Lloyds Bank, 1921	1854: Admission of joint-stock banks to Clearing House
1914: Issue of Treasury Notes 1914–18: FIRST WORLD WAR 1928: Amalgamation of Treasury Notes with Bank of England Note issue 1939–45: SECOND WORLD WAR 1946: Nationalisation of Bank of England	*Savings Banks:* 1817: Regulation of Trustee Savings Banks 1861: Establishment of Post Office Savings Bank	Rise of 'Big Five'
Increasing Co-operation with foreign banks		

CHART 11—*The Development of Banking in England and Wales*

as a safe and prompt method of payment, and the granting of loans to customers on security.

As we have seen in Chapter V,* after the establishment of the Bank of England, an Act was passed in 1708 prohibiting any other chartered bank or partnership consisting of more than six persons from issuing bank-notes. The small country banks continued to issue notes, but their tendency to issue notes beyond their capacity to meet them in a crisis involved them in frequent failures. The situation became so serious that government intervention became inevitable, and two schools of thought on the future of bank-note issuing arose, one of which, the currency school, held that all notes issued should be backed by an equivalent amount of gold, while the other, the banking school, thought that the volume of notes issued by banks should depend upon the latters' estimates of the requirements of trade. Doubtless because the Government thought that the bankers had demonstrated their ability

* See p. 44.

in this direction only too clearly, the currency school of thought prevailed, and the Bank Charter Act, 1844, was passed. This Act prohibited an increase in the note issues of the private banks, and provided that, in the event of bankruptcy or amalgamation, the right to issue notes should be lost and the Bank of England could issue notes to the extent of two-thirds of the lapsed issues. As a result of the operation of this Act, and the absorption of the note-issuing private banks by the growing joint-stock banks, the Fiduciary Issue of the Bank of England (*i.e.* the issue of notes not backed by gold or silver) reached £18,450,000 by 1914. In 1921 the last of the private note-issuing banks, Fox, Fowler and Co., amalgamated with Lloyds Bank; and the Bank of England became the sole note-issuing bank in England and Wales.

In the meantime banking had reached out in another direction. In 1826 an Act was passed allowing the establishment of joint-stock banks with power to issue notes so long as they were farther than 65 miles from London. In 1833 joint-stock banks were allowed inside London, but not with note-issuing power. It was in 1858 that a great impetus was given to joint-stock banking: the principle of limited liability was extended to banks. In 1879 unlimited companies formed before the 1862 Act, which allowed limited-liability joint-stock companies to be formed, were allowed to adopt limited liability; and practically all the joint-stock banks availed themselves of the opportunity.

The way was thus open for the founding of large joint-stock banks, and a process of absorption of the small private banks (the last private country bank, Gunner and Co., was bought up by Barclays in 1953) and the establishment of branches began, and culminated in the bulk of the deposit-banking business of the country becoming concentrated in the hands of the 'clearing banks,' the members of the London Clearing House the 'big five': Barclays, Lloyds, Midland, National Provincial and Westminster; Martins, the District Bank, the National Bank (an Irish bank), Glyn, Mills & Co. and Williams Deacon's Bank (owned by the Royal Bank of Scotland), and Coutts & Co. (owned by the National Provincial Bank).

Besides their main functions—the receipt of customers' deposits, the provision of the cheque system and the granting of loans to customers —the joint-stock banks have carried on other functions: discounting and accepting bills of exchange; acting as agents for investments; trustee and executorship business. They became an integral part of the money market, centring on the City of London and the Bank of England, that intricate machinery for the borrowing and lending of money and for investment in industry and government and municipal loans: it comprises the commercial banks; acceptance and discounting houses; bill-brokers (dealing in bills of exchange); the foreign-exchange market; issuing houses (which arrange for the issue of shares); investment trusts, and finance houses. It was the establishment and maintenance of this financial machinery which made London the financial centre of the world—a position she held until the rise of the United States as the great creditor nation after the First World War transferred the world's financial centre of gravity to New York.

Another line of development has been the establishment of savings banks. Trustee Savings Banks were begun early in the nineteenth century; there were 78 such banks already in existence in 1817, when they were first regulated. By the 1940s there were over 700 offices of Trustee Savings Banks in the country, with over $3\frac{1}{2}$ million accounts and over £450 million due to depositors. The Trustee Savings Banks work under Government guarantee.

The Post Office Savings Bank was established in 1861; by the 1940s over £1000 million was due to depositors.

4. CENTRAL BANKING; MONEY AND PRICES

The Bank Charter Act of 1844 fixed the Fiduciary Issue at some £14 million; the lapsed note issues of private banks stood before the 1914-18 war at £7,435,000. The legal limit of the Fiduciary Issue was £19$\frac{3}{4}$ million.

The Act provided for the division of the Bank of England into two departments: the Issue Department, which issued notes, and the Banking Department, which conducted banking business.

As the financial machinery of the country took shape in the nineteenth and twentieth centuries, the Bank of England developed its functions as a central bank:

(1) It regulates the money of the country, controlling the note issue in England and Wales and issuing the token coinage on behalf of the Royal Mint; it safeguards the gold reserves of the nation, and controls the Fiduciary Issue.

(2) It acts as the Government's banker, keeping the Consolidated Fund, the Government's banking account; and it manages the National Debt.

The Bank of England Act, 1946, nationalised the Bank of England; but this was to a great extent merely a 'practice' move on the part of the Labour Government, for the first time in full power: the Bank of England was to all intents and purposes nationalised already.

(3) It acts as the bankers' bank, holding the cash reserves of the other banks. A bankers' clearing house had been established as early as 1775; the joint-stock banks were admitted to the clearing house in 1854. 'Clearing' of cheques results in the indebtedness on balance of one bank to another: the debtor bank settles its indebtedness by drawing a cheque on the Bank of England in favour of the creditor bank.

(4) It controls the credit of the country. The joint-stock banks formerly maintained a ratio of 10% of cash in hand and at the Bank of England to deposits. It was reduced in 1946 to 8%. If a loan is made to a customer, the amount of the banks' deposits rises by that amount, and the ratio is reduced. If the Bank considers that a contraction of credit is desirable, it will, by 'open market operations,' reduce the commercial banks' capacity to lend; it offers securities for sale, and customers who buy such securities will pay for them by withdrawing money from their accounts. The Bank may also raise the Bank Rate, and a rise in the Bank Rate is followed by a raising of other rates in the Money Market, so that the rate of interest on loans is increased; this will discourage borrowers.

The Bank of England, too, co-operates with other Central Banks and with such institutions as the Bank for International Settlements, the International Bank for Reconstruction and Development (the World Bank) and the International Monetary Fund. In Scotland the development of banking went along somewhat different lines; there is no Central Bank for Scotland, this function being carried on by the Bank of England. Virtually five Scottish banks issue notes, and Bank of England notes circulate in Scotland; the two systems work closely together.

Before the Second World War the delicately adjusted machinery for control of credit and the maintenance of an adequate supply of currency worked fairly well. But the Bank Charter Act was not able to prevent the recurrence of financial crises—which were met, indeed, by the suspension of the Act, enabling the Bank to issue notes in excess of the Fiduciary Issue. A crisis in 1847 occurred as a consequence of a combination of factors: tremendous spending on railway construction, speculation, a succession of failures of the potato crop in Ireland, bad harvests in England, a short cotton crop in America, the dearness of raw materials, the importation of grain on the repeal of the Corn Laws in 1846, a drain of gold, a sudden fall in wheat prices, the onset of unemployment. Other crises followed in 1857 and 1866, the latter year seeing the overwhelming of the great and respected house of Overend, Gurney & Co. The nineteenth century, indeed, was a century of crisis occurring with such seeming regularity that the expression 'trade cycle' was applied to the succession of booms and slumps which occurred.

The granting of credit and dealing on credit must eventually involve the provision of currency to meet the needs of the people. On the outbreak of war in 1914, with the rising of wages and salaries and the demands for currency, the Government issued Treasury Notes through the Bank of England, the issue being authorised by the Currency and Bank Notes Act, 1914. These Treasury Notes were for

£1 and 10s.; there was, therefore, a dual system of currency notes in operation, the Bank of England issuing notes for £5 and upwards. The Currency and Bank Notes Act, 1914, authorised the Bank of England to increase its Fiduciary Issue beyond the figure of £19¾ million, its hitherto legal limit. The Gold Standard, under which notes were freely convertible into gold and *vice versa*, disappeared throughout Europe.

By the end of the war there were £98 million bank-notes in circulation and £323 million of Treasury notes. The rising prices were a

Pre-1914	The Gold Standard
1914–18	FIRST WORLD WAR. 10s. and £1 Treasury Notes
	Rise in prices. Inflation
1918	Cunliffe Committee
1920–25	Deflation. Fall in prices. Unemployment
1925	Restoration of Gold Standard—Gold Bullion Standard
	Fall in world prices. Trade improvement
1928	Amalgamation of 10s. and £1 Treasury Notes with Bank of England issue
1928–29	Stock Market boom in the United States. Flow of capital to the United States. Accumulation of gold in the United States and France
1929	Wall Street crash
	Contraction of trade. Fall in prices. Unemployment
	The United States now the great creditor nation
	Beginning of depression
1931	Macmillan report
	Britain abandoned gold standard
1932	Exchange Equalisation Fund
1933	World Economic Conference—failed
1933–39	Stimulus given to prices by rearmament
1939–45	SECOND WORLD WAR
	Inflation. Lend-Lease arrangements with the United States
	Fiduciary Issue now over £1,000,000,000
1944	Bretton Woods Conference
1945	Creation of Finance Corporation for Industry, Ltd., and Industrial and Commerical Finance Corporation, Ltd
	Appointment of Development Areas Treasury Advisory Committee
1946	The United States lent Britain £1,100,000,000
	Canada lent Britain £281,000,000
1947	Marshall Aid—European Recovery Programme
	Continued Inflation
	The International Monetary Fund and the International Bank for Reconstruction and Development began to operate
1948	General Agreement on Tariffs and Trade
1949	Devaluation of British pound sterling from 4·03 U.S. dollars to £1 to 2·80 dollars to £1
1950	European Payments Union
1951	Suspension of Marshall Aid—merging into general defence contribution
1959	Radcliffe Committee Report
	Rising Prices
1962	National Incomes Commission
1965	National Board for Prices and Incomes

CHART 12—*Money and Prices since 1914*

warning that inflation was in existence; and in 1918 the Cunliffe Committee was appointed. It recommended that a limit be fixed to the Fiduciary Issue and that the Treasury Note issues and Bank of England note issues should be amalgamated. This latter recommendation was carried out in 1928 under the provisions of the Currency and Bank Notes Act, the Bank of England being then empowered to issue notes for £1 and 10s. The Fiduciary Issue was fixed at £260 million. In 1945 Bank of England notes of £10 and upwards were withdrawn from circulation.

The Gold Standard was restored in 1925, but was abandoned again in 1931. The onset of depression caused the appointment in 1929 of a Committee on Finance and Industry, the Macmillan Committee, to investigate the causes of the depression and to recommend measures which would enable the banking and financial system to promote the development of trade and commerce. The Committee reported in 1931 that the Bank of England should be the authority for a managed currency system, in which the supply of currency should be managed to meet the needs of trade and industry; the division of the Bank into two departments should be abolished; the proper use of gold was not to back notes but for international payment: more elasticity was required in the control of the note issues by the Bank.

The main recommendations of the Macmillan Report were not implemented; the State certainly adopted a managed currency, but did not manage it very well. The Report recommended an extension of the commercial-bill business; in fact, the Government continued to borrow money on a huge scale through the medium of Treasury Bills, the management of which does not demand very much in the way of financial knowledge, and little in the way of entrepreneurship or commercial risk-taking, which has been the foundation of Britain's prosperity. While stating that Bank Rate policy was a necessity for the sound management of a monetary system, the Report pointed out that it was a means of maintaining the stability of the exchanges rather than the stability of business. Opinions on the efficacy of the 'open market operations' and Bank Rate policy are still divided; it would seem that these instruments of the Central Bank serve merely to indicate the trend of events to commerce and industry rather than to initiate events.

In Britain the banking system generally has not been so intimately connected with industrial organisation and development as in the United States and Germany. The British banks have followed the tradition of keeping themselves aloof from speculative enterprise—perhaps a wise policy, but not making for co-ordination in the State's industrial structure. The banks receive subscriptions, but do not vouch for the issues of shares of undertakings. In the United States financial undertakings had a great deal to do with the development of American railways and other industries. The German banks provided financial assistance and advice to industry, issued credit, and, in fact, assumed a definite responsibility in the control of industry. The German banks made the German industrial revolution possible. In France the banks made nearly all the issues in industrial undertakings, and certain powerful banks developed into *banques d'affaires*, intimately connected with industry both at home and abroad.

The Macmillan Report did not sympathise with the idea that the banks should manage industry but stated the view that there should exist a closer connection with the City of London and industry, and that while the industrialists themselves should be responsible for the business and general management of a company, the banker should be the adviser in matters of finance.

The Second World War initiated another period of rapid inflation; and after the Fall of France in 1940 the era of sweet reasonableness in respect of wage-increase demands gave way to an era of wages and prices chasing each other in an ever-increasing spiral. The Fiduciary Issue soon reached over £1000 million: the time of 'astronomical' figures in the issue of notes not backed by gold had begun.* On the outbreak of the Second World War the resources of gold held by the Exchange Equalisation Fund (this was established in 1932 in order to 'iron out' violent fluctuations in the exchange rates by taking up the demand for sterling or buying sterling when large amounts were offered) amounted to about £510 million, and these were depleted during the war. Exchange restrictions were imposed and tightened. Lend-lease arrangements were made with the United States to enable Britain to import goods from her after Britain's dollar resources had become exhausted. The financial chaos resulting from the war induced the calling of the United Nations Monetary and Financial Conference at Bretton Woods. A scheme for setting up an international monetary system was formulated but subsequently abandoned; but it was agreed to set up an International Monetary Fund to promote international trade and to set up an International Bank for Reconstruction and Development—the World Bank.

It is evident that 'central banking' has been developed during the past century to mean something far more than the close-knit, quasi-private proceedings of the commercial banks in relation to the Bank of England that obtained in the era of the Bank Charter Act, 1844. A closer system of connection with industrial organisation has been attained—a process greatly accelerated by the exigencies and effects of two world wars upsetting the delicately adjusted machinery of international finance and necessitating State control on a far wider scale and of a more direct nature than could have been imagined in the *laissez-faire* period of the early nineteenth century.

---

* On 7th March 1962 the Fiduciary Issue was £2,375 million; the notes in circulation were £2,311·7 million.

The importance of this closer connection between industry and the State in the evolution of modern industrial organisation cannot be exaggerated. Though our situation in the middle of events makes it difficult for us to estimate its full significance in the development of industrial organisation in relation to future trends, a survey of the past industrial and commercial background such as we have undertaken in this work is valuable in helping us to contrast the modern position with that of past times. Industrial organisation in the nineteenth century developed to some extent apart from the organisation of the financial system, in contrast to the interlinked processes of the Continent and the United States. To a large degree, this made for the financial strength and international reputation of the British system: the great joint-stock banks concentrated their attention on financial soundness, and accommodation to industrial undertakings was given on adequate security. It was doubtless for this fundamental reason that Britain avoided such a crash as shook Wall Street in 1931. But the dependence of Britain on international trade made inevitable the spreading to this country of a depression abroad; and the profound changes in international economic relationships caused by two world wars have caused equally profound changes in the relationships between the State and industrial organisation.

The problem of controlling inflation inspired the British Government to appoint a Committee on the Working of the Monetary System. This Committee, the Radcliffe Committee, published its Report in August, 1959.*

The Radcliffe Committee Report agreed with the Macmillan Committee Report in expressing doubts about the efficacy of the Bank Rate as a means of ensuring business stability; monetary measures alone, said the Radcliffe Committee, cannot be effective in keeping the economy of the country in balance. As to monetary measures themselves, the Report stated that the major regulators were control of international capital, control of hire purchase credit, and control over lending by financial institutions other than the banks, e.g. in house purchase finance. The Government should know all the sources from which individuals and institutions get their money, and be able to control them: the key to monetary management was 'liquidity.' By gaining detailed knowledge of these matters and of the effects of monetary measures, and by taking the public into its confidence and gaining co-operation from the public, a 'credit squeeze' could effectively deal with inflation.

It fell to the lot of a Labour Government, elected in 1964 and re-elected in 1966, to put this somewhat painful doctrine into operation.

To counter inflation and make the 'credit squeeze' more effective, a 'Special Deposit Account' system was imposed at intervals from

* Cmd. 827, 15s. net.

1958 onwards, requiring the British joint-stock banks to deposit with the Bank of England a percentage of their deposits, thus diminishing their lending resources.

Our story of modern industrial organisation from now on will show the characteristic of an ever-widening and embracing State control and regulation; and where not control and regulation, State influence, extending not merely to the regulation of conditions in factories and workshops and the relationships between employers and employed in wages structure, but to the siting of industry itself, to the activities of combines, to the contemplation and limitation of restrictive practices. The State has itself entered the field of large-scale industrial organisation in the creation of great public corporations and has sometimes replaced private enterprise by State enterprise. The State, in fact from the advent of a Labour Government in 1964, entered upon a course of direct planning of the economy, a policy advocated by Lord Beveridge in his book, *Full Employment in a Free Society,** published in 1944, twenty years before.

Such movements and influences can be understood only by reference to the general background of financial and economic organisation of the resources of the nation generally; and it is to a survey of this background that we must now turn our attention.

* Allen & Unwin, Ltd.

CHAPTER X

THE MANAGERIAL REVOLUTION

1. COMBINATIONS, MONOPOLIES AND RESTRICTIVE PRACTICES

As is so often the case in historical development, the beginnings of significant features of modern Western civilisation are to be found early in our history. Capitalism began with the gilds; it started to be significant at the time of the rise of the merchant class; and reached its culminating point in the gathering of vast resources and the hiring for wages of large numbers of people by comparatively small groups of wealthy people during the Industrial Revolution. Quite apart from the question of technical advances, it is the problem of the relation between economic and political and social power which should be of greatest moment to the modern historian, whose concern is more with people than with individual rulers or social abstractions.

The necessity for the control of large amounts of capital and for the restriction of competition, so far as possible, led to combination and monopoly in business organisation; though pure monopoly, in which an undertaking has full control over the production and distribution of a commodity *and its substitutes*, is very rare. A modern approach to this type of organisation has been the Coffee Institute of Brazil.

Two main lines of development were followed: vertical combination, or trusts, in which control is secured of the various stages of production of a commodity, from the raw material to the finished product; and horizontal combination, or combination of undertakings agreeing on prices or 'territories'; its most complete form is the cartel, in which a separate company is formed to market the products of the individual producers—a good example is the Imperial Tobacco Company (of Great Britain and Ireland), Ltd. In practice, combination has proceeded along both lines together, the resulting organisation often being called a 'combine' (though terminology varies), such devices as amalgamations, interlocking directorates, and holding and subsidiary companies being used; a holding company is one which holds more than 50% of the shares of the other, or subsidiary, companies.

It was thus that J. & P. Coates, Ltd., by 1890 controlled one-third of the cotton-thread trade of the United Kingdom and attained a virtual monopoly of the world's cotton-thread industry, and that Lever Brothers, the giant soap firm, amalgamated with the Margarine Union,

Great Britain	Europe	U.S.A.
1890: Cotton thread: Soap, etc. (Lever Bros.)	Germany, 1870s: Chemical Cartels 1890s: Coal Syndicate 1890s: Dynamite Trust 1904: Rail-making Cartel 1913–28: Kreuger Match Combine Germany, 1904: Krupp Organisation (Steel)	1882: Standard Oil Trust, followed by Whisky, Tobacco and Sugar Trusts 1890: Trusts declared illegal 1901: U.S. Steel Corporation 1900–10: Enforcement of Anti-Trust Legislation

1914–18: FIRST WORLD WAR

1934: British Iron and Steel Federation	1927: France—chemical combine Germany — Development of Hugo Stinnes and Thyssen organisations (Steel)	

INTERNATIONAL AGREEMENTS IN RUBBER (Natural and Synthetic),
CHEMICALS, STEEL

1939–45: SECOND WORLD WAR
1939: German chemical interests seized by British Alien Property Custodian

U.K.—1946: fforde Committee on Cement Costs
Simon Committee on the Distribution of Building Materials and Components
1947: Lloyd Jacob Committee on Resale Price Maintenance
1948: Monopolies and Restrictive Practices (Inquiry and Control) Act: established a MONOPOLIES AND RESTRICTIVE PRACTICES COMMISSION
1956: Restrictive Trade Practices Act

CHART 13—*Some Landmarks in the History of Combinations, Monopolies and Restrictive Practices*

to form Unilever, Ltd., a gigantic concern with 140 subsidiaries, whose activities ranged from fishing, whaling and sealing to the production and sale of candles, jam and cocoa. The Margarine Union was the result of the amalgamation of two Dutch companies controlling the margarine and soap trade of the Continent. The formation of this combine illustrates how the trusts and cartels of the late nineteenth and early twentieth centuries spread across international frontiers.

By 1914 there were international agreements to control the sale of aluminium, electric bulbs, calcium carbide, plate glass, bottles and enamelware. In chemicals three great combinations, Du Pont in the United States, I.C.I. in Great Britain and I. G. Farben in Germany, each with ramifications abroad, were formed; in steel an international steel cartel formed in 1926 was joined by England in 1935. The First World War interrupted these conglomerations of capital, business 'acumen' and financial wizardry; but between the two Wars the inter-weaving of interests went on. In the 1920s electrical generation and appliances, wood pulp, rayon and non-ferrous metals were the chief industries concerned in the international manipulations of undertak-ings. 'Napoleons' of industry sprang up, as George Hudson had done, to control and direct and build—sometimes too giddily for their ability. Ivar Kreuger, for example, a Swedish 'match king', who built up an organisation controlling factories in 43 countries, producing 80% of the world's matches, outran the limits of his ability and ended as a sordid suicide in a Paris hotel bedroom. Hermann Goering formed in 1939 a Steelworks Union; yet another Napoleon ended his life in circumstances lower than those of his victims, this time by self-administered poison in 1946 in preference to the gallows. One hesitates to estimate the nature and scope of the exploitation to which the ordinary man was subjected in those days. The Second World War saw the breaking up of many such vast organisations.

In Britain, as we have seen, the troubles in the iron and steel and textile industries arose largely from the British industrialists' reluctance to combine. Nevertheless, though unification in the British iron and steel industry reached nothing like the stage attained in Germany, France, Belgium and the United States, the formation of combines did occur. In 1929 a combine owning steel furnaces, rolling mills and forges was formed by the acquiring of interests in various steel firms by the English Steel Corporation; in 1930 the British (Guest, Keen and Baldwin) Iron and Steel Company was formed, controlling the entire output of heavy steel products in South Wales and Monmouth-shire. Among firms producing heavy steel in the North-east, Scotland, Lancashire, South Yorkshire and Lincolnshire there was also some combination. But the attempt in 1933 to set up an Iron and Steel Corporation of Great Britain proved abortive; and a less comprehen-sive plan was adopted in 1934, with the formation of a British Iron and Steel Federation.

In cotton, the combine movement in the closing years of the nine-teenth century was confined to the fine-spinning, sewing-thread and finishing trades. After the First World War two combines were formed in spinning; the sewing-cotton firm of J. & P. Coates had amalgamated with its four rivals in 1895–96.

The subsequent story of the organisation of the British great industries, steel, cotton, coal, has already been told.

Besides combination in large-scale industrial organisation, there took place also the development of trade associations: associations of producers and distributors to regulate the machinery or prices, output and distribution—to this extent adopting the basic feature of cartels—and also to improve production methods, undertake research, exchange information, conduct national advertising campaigns, and appoint representatives to discuss matters of common concern with other associations and with Government departments. They began at the end of the nineteenth century, and the First World War gave them a great impetus, for the Government needed to establish means by which Government policy could be discussed with representatives of the various industries; at the end of the war they numbered about 500. There was a tendency towards their disintegration in the 1920s; but the need for combination to counteract import competition in the 1930s revived them, and the Second World War gave them a new impetus, as the First World War had done. By the middle of the century the number of trade associations had increased to over 2000.

The weapons of the trade association were resale price maintenance —recalcitrant dealers were put on a 'stop list' circulated to producers, who would refuse supplies; restriction of output; and, so the accusation runs, deliberately keeping quality low, often by buying up and refusing to use inventions which would make for durability in articles of common consumption. Ladderless stockings, everlasting matches, electric lamps of very long life are, it has been claimed, included among such inventions, but it is not clear how much truth there is in such claims.

Corresponding to the restrictive practices of workmen—*e.g.* going slow, the forbidding of overtime by union action, the attempt to enforce employers to employ only union men—there have thus grown up restrictive practices on the part of employing undertakings, which would all appear to be to the detriment of the general public, of whom the employers and workmen form a part.

Nevertheless, in industry generally during the inter-war years those industries which were most criticised for monopolistic and restrictive tendencies were amongst the most successful and progressive: monopoly is not necessarily to the disadvantage of the consumer, a point made in the Coalition Government's White Paper on Employment Policy in 1944.

In 1946 the Ministry of Works initiated two enquiries: the fforde Committee on Cement Costs, and the Simon Committee on the Distribution of Building Materials and Components. The fforde Committee on Cement Costs found no evidence of the restriction of production and the elimination of competition in order to increase prices; but the Simon Committee on the Distribution of Building Materials and Components found that the system of price maintenance and the practice of exclusive trading and loyalty rebates were not in the public interest.

The Monopolies and Restrictive Practices (Inquiry and Control) Act, 1948, established a Monopolies and Restrictive Practices Commission to consider cases referred to it by the Board of Trade; subject to the control of Parliament, the recommendations of the Commission may be implemented by an order of a Minister declaring restrictive practices, either involving agreements to withhold supplies or to give preferences, or relating to conditional sales, to be unlawful.

The Commission lost little time in getting to work. In July 1951 an Order was made following its recommendation to prohibit certain practices in the distribution of dental goods. Certain practices were disapproved of in its report upon the activities of the Electric Lamp Manufacturers' Association.

The Commission issued reports on, among other things, dental goods, electric lamps, electric wires and cables, insulin, matches and match-making machinery, imported timber and calico printing. In July 1955, following a Press report that ten tenders alike to a penny at £57,517 1s. 8d. for steelwork were sent to the London County Council, an enquiry into steelwork prices was begun by the Monopolies Commission.

Faced with the prospect of an investigation, certain trades adjusted their practices voluntarily so as to conform with the Commission's recommendations.

In 1947 the Government set up a committee to consider resale price maintenance, the practice by which minimum wholesale and retail prices or margins for the resale of goods were fixed by producers. This committee, the Lloyd Jacob Committee, reported in 1949. It estimated that resale price maintenance applied to about 30% of the total amount spent on goods by private consumers; it applied usually to branded goods. The Committee considered the advantages of resale price maintenance to manufacturers, distributors and consumers. They considered also the collective sanctions imposed by associations on traders, and declared that in their view they were an unreasonable interference with the freedom of distributors. The Committee recommended that the application of collective sanctions should be made illegal, and that the Government should consult with industry to ensure the unimpeded distribution of goods and the protection of the public against measures likely to deprive it of improvements.

The Monopolies and Restrictive Practices Commission issued its twelfth Report in June, 1955.* It aroused considerable public interest, probably because it was the first Report of the Commission dealing with the problem generally and because the Press had been reporting recent instances of the 'trying' of recalcitrant traders by private trade association tribunals.

The majority of the Commissioners condemned resale price maintenance agreements, and favoured the legal prohibition of private trade courts. A minority thought that a general legal prohibition would be too inflexible; but there was general acceptance of the view that there

*Cmd. 9504, H.M.S.O., 3s. 6d.

E

should be compulsory registration and publication of the restrictive agreements.

Under the Restrictive Trade Practices Act, 1956, the Government appointed a Registrar of Restrictive Trade Agreements with power to compile a list of illegal trade practices and to take cases before the Restrictive Practices Court. The Act had a moderate success; but in 1964 the Government introduced a Bill to abolish resale price maintenance altogether, providing for exceptions in cases not against the public interest. The Bill was passed as the Resale Prices Act, 1964. A White Paper issued in March 1964 proposed the appointment of a Registrar of Monopolies and the giving of greater powers to the Monopolies Commission (as it now became).*

In 1961, as a result of the proposals of the Departmental Committee on Consumer Protection, the Molony Committee, appointed in 1959, the Consumer Protection Act was passed: the Government was empowered to prohibit the manufacture, importation or sale of unsafe goods. The final Report of the Committee was presented in 1962. In 1963 a Consumer Council was established to investigate consumers' problems and to determine what action should be taken on their behalf. The Council advocated the abolition of resale price maintenance.

The Consumers' Association, Ltd., a non-profit-making body, was and is testing products and reporting to its readers in its publication, *Which?*

It is a relevant comment on the relation between manufacturers' interests and those of the general public that only after five children had been burned to death was legislation passed to require minimum safety standards for drip-feed oil heaters—after a campaign conducted by the indefatigable M.P., Sir Gerald Nabarro.

The protection of consumers was increased when the Hire Purchase Act, 1964, was passed: it embodied a provision for a period during which a hirer who had incontinently signed an agreement under sales pressure might change his mind.

Thus, the managers of industry were themselves being managed by a State which was responding to the need to protect the ordinary public against the worst effects of unrestricted private enterprise, a stage in the dealing with the complex problem of 'social priorities' which Lord Beveridge had postulated in 1944.

2. THE RISE OF SCIENTIFIC MANAGEMENT

There have been three main problems in the management of undertakings since the Industrial Revolution enlarged the scope and scale of industry, and raised new industrial classes: the efficient organisation

* *Monopolies, Mergers and Restrictive Practices* (Cmd. 2299, H.M S.O., 1s.).

and management of large-scale organisations; the concentration of industry generally to assist in this efficient organisation and management on a national scale; and the harmonious and fruitful conduct of relations between employers and employed. The term 'scientific management' has been variously applied to activity related to all three problems, though mainly used in relation to the first; it often includes the third, which is customarily treated as a special branch of managerial activity of its own and called 'personnel management.'

The story has been told of the broad development of unplanned and unco-ordinated industry in this country. The individualism practised in the cotton industry, the breeding of an excessive number of units in the coal industry, and the circumstances which forced some measure of combination and co-ordination in the British basic industries, have been described. Of the entry of the State into the industrial field as supreme manager and co-ordinator, something will be said in the next Section. It is our present task to examine the development of 'scientific management' as the movement has affected the organisation of individual business concerns and the conduct of relations between employers and employed—the two aspects form part of one whole, since a business undertaking cannot be wholly efficient without tolerable management.

It has already been shown that 'scientific management' had already been practised long before the modern developments of the idea. Robert Owen had demonstrated how to make a profit while conducting business on humane and enlightened lines, somewhat to the disgust of his fellow-manufacturers, over a hundred years before the twentieth-century application in England of the ideas of the modern apostle of 'scientific management,' F. W. Taylor. The early application of such ideas was, indeed, more concerned with efficiency of technical operation than with the conception of a business undertaking as a necessary means of economic production, not of value for its own sake as one of the Absolutes, but a machine involving the efforts of men and women whose welfare is of importance in the life of the community as a whole.

A Cambridge professor of mathematics, Charles Babbage, who was visiting factories in England and on the Continent in connection with his invention, a calculating machine, was led to study management and 'those principles of generalisation to which my pursuits had naturally given rise'; and he published his treatise, *On the Economy of Machinery and Manufactures* in 1832. But it was not until the 1880s that the 'scientific management' movement was really begun by a group of American engineers in the United States. The outstanding figure in the movement was F. W. Taylor (1856–1915), an engineer and inventor, who expounded his views in his *Principles of Scientific Management* and *Shop Management* in the early 1900s. Taylor's ideas began to be publicised in 1910–11, when the railroads were seeking to justify an increase in rates; the opposition showed how costs could be reduced by the application of Taylor's ideas.

In essentials, Taylor's body of ideas consists of the planning of work in advance; selecting the best men for particular jobs; determining standard times for the performance of given pieces of work; standardising tools and equipment; the elimination of unnecessary movements; adequate cost accounting; and wages payment on a bonus system.

The workers, faced with efficiency 'drives,' suspected exploitation; and certainly the 'stop-watch' methods, which were pioneered in time-and-motion study by men like F. W. Taylor and F. B. Gilbreth, were often undertaken by their followers with more enthusiasm than humanity. Taylor's quality of mind may be gauged by the fact that in high-speed steel research he conducted 40,000 experiments: a notable achievement in scientific method but indicative of a type of mind which may not prove too happy in human relations. Frank Bunker Gilbreth (1868–1924) pursued his search of the 'one best way to do work' with more humour and with more understanding than Taylor of the fact that man does not live for work alone. The third member of a trio often regarded as the founders of 'scientific management' was H. L. Gantt (1861–1919), who evolved a number of charts: his graphical representations were designed to assist the planning of production.

In France French engineers like Charles de Freminville and H. le Chatelier took up Taylor's ideas; and contemporary with F. W. Taylor, Henri Fayol (1841–1925) was also pursuing the subject. Fayol, a mining engineer, analysed business operations into six groups: technical, commercial, financial, security, accounting and administrative; he emphasised the value of training for management.

In America, Mary Parker Follett (1865–1933), a political scientist and philosopher, supplied the philosophical and humanist background in business organisation so lacking in the work of the engineers. She was much concerned with the conflicts that arise in the conduct of industry. She paid a visit to England in 1926, came again in 1928 and continued to live in England until her death. Her *Creative Experience* was published in 1924.

The doctrines of 'scientific management,' as expounded by the Americans, spread more slowly in England than they did in the United States. The resources of a powerful mind allied to a warm humanity were brought to the consideration of the problems of industrial organisation, especially as they affected human relations in industry, by B. Seebohm Rowntree (1871–1954), who directed the Industrial Welfare Department established at the Ministry of Munitions during the First World War; from this Department sprang the Industrial Welfare

Society. The cocoa works at York, of which Rowntree was a director, became well known as a model organisation. No narrow 'captain of industry,' Rowntree interested himself in social problems, particularly those related to poverty and unemployment; and it is in this field that he is even better known to the student of social affairs.

The enthusiasm with which ideas relating to 'scientific management' have been taken up in recent years by many industrialists both in the United States and in this country has given rise to much writing on the subject of business organisation (much of it marred by verbosity and irritating business jargon). The role of the manager in industry has indeed been elevated by some writers nearly to that of the ruling class depicted in Aldous Huxley's *Brave New World,* a savagely satirical comment on the possible direction of human progress. An American philosopher, James Burnham, wrote a book, *The Managerial Revolution,* first published in the U.S.A. in 1941 and in England in 1942,* putting forward the thesis that the control of the world was passing into the hands of the managers. The failure of the capitalist system to work would result not in socialism, but in the rule of the administrators.

Certainly the tendency of modern industrial and government organisation is to demand a high degree of ability, technical qualifications and training in its administrators. The Administrative Staff College at Henley-on-Thames, supported by funds from business firms and individual persons, was founded in 1946, providing courses in the principles and techniques of organisation and administration. In 1963 the Centre for Administrative Studies was opened for the training of civil servants; its studies include courses in Management Techniques. The Treasury Organisation and Methods Division was enlarged in the re-organisation of 1962 and re-named the Management Services Division.

Among the various aspects of the managerial revolution which have come into prominence in recent years, production control has received recognition as a valuable tool of business organisation. It is the lineal descendant of the older 'efficiency' methods; it is a system whereby it is intended to achieve a smooth, co-ordinated flow of work within a factory so that, by planning and control of all the productive operations in the stages of manufacture of an article, the final product is completed in accordance with the plans laid down.

The twentieth century has seen considerable advances in industrial psychology. On the foundation of what has been solidly established in psychology, as opposed to fads and misrepresentations of the imperfectly understood research of original thinkers like Freud, the industrial psychologist investigates such matters as the training and selection of workers, incentives, the posture and movements of workers, their

* Penguin Books, 1945.

material environmental conditions, such as lighting, heating and ventilation, and the psychological relations between labour and management.
In Britain the National Institute of Industrial Psychology was formed
in 1919 as a non-profit-making body for promoting the study of the
'human aspects' of business.

Arising out of these investigations, and receiving an impetus from
the outbreak of war in 1939, came the modern developments in personnel management. The need for an exceptional production effort
impelled Mr Ernest Bevin, the Minister of Labour, to introduce in
1940 the Factories Medical and Welfare Order. His successor, Mr
George Isaacs, associated himself with the work of the Industrial
Welfare Society; and Sir Stafford Cripps, when Minister of Aircraft
Production, established personnel departments in the factories he
controlled.

Many undertakings found that the addition of personnel departments
was of such value that they retained them as a permanent part of their
organisation; and personnel officers, or personnel managers, or welfare
officers, today perform such functions as the keeping of employee
records, recruitment and employment, the provision of welfare services,
the supervision of health and safety measures, where these are not
adequately served by special officers, the conduct of joint consultation
relations, and the supervision of the education and training of young
employees.

Another modern development has been Training Within Industry,
a Government-initiated scheme whereby foremen, supervisors and
executives learn the best way to perform the training duties with which
they are entrusted as part of their functions.

The broader aspects of management training were considered in a
report of a special committee appointed by the Minister of Education
in 1945. The Committee consisted of representatives of professional
bodies concerned with the part-time study of management in technical
and commercial colleges, to consider whether action could be taken to
co-ordinate their requirements. The Committee's Report, *Education
for Management*, was published in 1947; it contained proposals for
courses of study in management subjects. The subsequent formation
of the British Institute of Management in 1947 was a further step in
the co-ordination of management study; the Institute of Industrial
Administration, with which the British Institute of Management was
integrated in 1957, had been founded in 1920. Since then, there has
been much 'literature' on Management—some of it incorporating a
good deal of elaboration of the obvious.

3. THE STATE AS MANAGER

The story of the evolution of industrial organisation, as we have followed it, has shown an increasing participation by the State in the organisation of industry as a whole, particularly on the part of such 'economic' departments as the Treasury, the Board of Trade, the Ministry of Transport, the Ministry of Agriculture, Fisheries and Food, and the Ministry of Labour. In industrial conditions, through such legislation as Factories Acts and Truck Acts; in industrial relations through the negotiating machinery set up; in wage regulation; in social insurance, such as the National Insurance (Industrial Injuries) Act, 1946, superseding the Workmen's Compensation Act; in providing information to and insurance facilities for exporters—in all these the State has directly concerned itself with the organisation and direction of industry. The Board of Trade has been actively associated with the Working Party Reports which have reviewed the practical conditions of industry; and the nationalised industries are represented on the British Productivity Council, the successor to the United Kingdom section of the Anglo-American Productivity Council, which has published numerous reports relating to the investigations of productivity teams and specialist teams in production methods in British industries.

But the State has done more than that. It has itself adopted the role of manager. In the seventeenth century it had established a General Post Office, and in the course of 300 years this Government machine (scheduled to become a public corporation) has developed into a huge technical and commercial concern.

Early experiments in public control were conducted by municipal authorities rather than by the State; but in the inter-war years the Central Government began to create public undertakings which were of such a nature as to involve the public interest intimately and on a large scale. Here came about the true managerial revolution: a revolution in which a new tool was being formed in the administration of public affairs. This tool is the public corporation: it is a new conception in the story of the evolution of industrial organisation, and it is still in process of being fashioned; as yet, no satisfactory means has been discovered of controlling the new autonomous monopolies by Parliamentary action.

In 1926 the Central Electricity Board was established to promote and control the bulk generation of electricity and the distribution lines, functions formerly carried out by a number of independent units. In 1948 the electricity industry, comprising 541 supply undertakings, 60% of which were publicly owned, passed under the control of the British Electricity Authority by an Act of 1947. The British Electricity Authority became responsible to the Minister of Fuel and Power for the generation of electric current and its distribution to fourteen Area Boards. The British Electricity Authority was renamed the Central Electricity Authority in 1955.

Following the Herbert Committee Report, 1956,* the Central Electricity Authority was dissolved in 1958 and its assets and executive functions concerned with the generation and bulk transmission of electricity were taken over by a Central Electricity Generating Board.

The establishment of the British Broadcasting Corporation in 1927 and the experiment of the Agricultural Marketing Boards, out of the direct line of the formation of corporations, have already been mentioned. In 1933 a significant chapter came with the creation of the London Passenger Transport Board, the board, the responsibility of Appointing Trustees, comprising people of wide experience in financial, transport, industrial or commercial matters—a method of appointment designed to avoid the risk of political interference.

The British Sugar Corporation was established in 1936; it was formed by the amalgamation of the existing fifteen sugar-beet companies. Then, in 1939, came the British Overseas Airways Corporation; the subsequent establishment of British European Airways and British South American Airways has already been mentioned.

In the twelve years before the Second World War four major public corporations were established. After the war the process of the creation of these corporations to control vast sections of the nation's industrial organisation was continued and accelerated. The Bank of England was nationalised in 1946—though, as has been explained, the Bank was virtually a nationalised body already. It was in 1946 that a major industry was brought under Government control and ownership by the Coal Industry Nationalisation Act of 1946. The Cable and Wireless Act of the same year transferred all shares in Cable and Wireless, Ltd., to Treasury nominees, though the company remained in existence and operated under the Companies Act; the Act provided for the transfer of the assets to the Post Office by 1949: a process of gradual nationalisation. The Gas Act, 1948, nationalised the gas industry.

Cotton control and bulk buying became a fruitful field for controversy; controversy was less vehement in the nationalisation of transport by the Transport Act, 1947; but the nationalisation of steel in 1951 provoked hot arguments, often founded more on political ideologies than on sincere opinion regarding the best methods of developing the nation's steel resources.

In colonial development, too, the State was acting, setting up funds for colonial development; in a grandiose groundnut scheme of 1947–49, in Tanganyika, colonial development was pursued with more

* *Report of the Committee of Enquiry into the Electricity Supply Industry,* January 1956. Cmd (H.M.S.O., 6s. 6d. net).

enthusiasm for the spending of public money than care in the application of the principles of sound management. Under the Overseas Resources Development Act, 1948, the Colonial Development Corporation was established with power to spend large sums of money on the development of the Colonies.

The setting up of the United Kingdom Atomic Energy Authority in 1954 was an unusual experiment in organisation: the structure adopted was partly that of a Government Department, partly that of an industrial undertaking. Besides the undertaking of research, the Authority's functions include the designing of nuclear power stations to be operated by the Electricity authority and British industry.

Though the setting up of organisations such as public corporations does not involve the State in direct control of management, their conception and creation and the degree of Ministerial responsibility concerned do make the State a general reviewer of their policy, with a consequent responsibility of the Government to Parliament, somewhat vague though this responsibility may be. Recognition of that responsibility may induce a certain reluctance on the part of a Government to allocate to itself any more of that responsibility than it can help. The work of the Select Committee on Nationalised Industries, established in 1956 and consisting of thirteen members of the House of Commons drawn from all Parties in proportion to their numbers in the House, with the task of examining the Reports and Accounts of the nationalised industries, has helped to make this responsibility a little more clear.

Much more significant than the nationalising of individual industries—since the major necessities of nationalisation have now been realised—has been the development of machinery for planning the economic structure of the country as a whole. This is where the State, in the persons of the Government, has entered into the field of 'Higher Management.' The Industrial Reorganisation Corporation established in 1966 is intended to rationalise industry, promoting mergers where it is considered desirable to do so. The creation of the Economic Development Committees to work with the National Economic Development Council, established in 1962 to advise the Government on the conditions for economic growth, and of Regional Economic Planning Councils and Boards to advise on and co-ordinate plans for economic development in the regions, parallels a similar development in France—a circumstance supporting the view that economic necessity is a greater factor in national industrial organisation than the political colour of a particular Government.

4. THE DEVELOPMENT OF CONCILIATION AND ARBITRATION IN INDUSTRY

The managerial and supervisory activities of the State had now to be turned to the industrial field into which it itself was to enter. As the State began to play a more definite part in the industrial affairs of the country, and the principle of *laissez-faire* was finally abandoned, the Government looked with increasing concern at the problem of industrial relations generally. Unskilled workers were forming trade unions; a great Dock Strike took place in 1889; the Independent Labour Party was formed in 1893; Socialism was rearing its head. The prospect of disputes and strikes in industry was a daunting one.

In 1891 a Royal Commission was set up 'to enquire into the relations between employers and workmen and to report whether legislation could be directed to remedy any faults disclosed.'

The recommendations of the Commission were followed in the Conciliation Act, 1896, which gave certain powers to the Board of Trade; these powers, subsequently transferred to the Ministry of Labour and National Service, were:

(1) To enquire into the causes and circumstances of a dispute.

(2) To take steps to bring the parties together.

(3) To appoint a conciliator or board of conciliators on the application of employers or workers.

(4) To appoint an arbitrator on the application of both parties.

Conciliation Officers were appointed, and their services have proved valuable in bringing parties to a dispute to agree upon measures which have avoided resort to the arbitrament of strike or lock-out.

The First World War gave rise to much industrial unrest, and in 1916 a Committee on the Relations between Employers and Employed was set up; from the name of its Chairman, J. H. Whitley, this Committee became known as the Whitley Committee, and the device of joint consultative machinery which it recommended became known generally as 'Whitleyism.' The terms of reference of the Committee were to make and consider suggestions for securing a permanent improvement in the relations between employers and workmen, and to recommend means of securing the systematic review of industrial conditions affecting those relations, with a view to improving conditions in the future.

The Committee made five recommendations:

(1) *The formation of Joint Industrial Councils of Employers and Employed*

Joint Standing Industrial Councils were formed in those industries which had not already an effective machinery for collective bargaining, such as in coal-mining and engineering. They vary greatly in scope and structure, and have been applied with government approval to the Civil Service and to local authorities. Besides providing machinery for negotiation, collective bargaining and the settlement of disputes, these Councils have discussed other matters, such as technical education, training and research. Labour opinion was not very much in favour of this device, but it has proved effective in many instances, notably in the flour-milling industry.

(2) *The appointment of works committees representative of management and workers in individual undertakings*

This recommendation has also been carried out, though with varying success. It would appear that in many cases the workers have looked upon Works Committees, or Works Councils (often generally referred to as 'Joint Consultative Committees'), merely as means by which relatively minor grievances could be 'ventilated.' On the other hand, it is urged that it is just these so-called minor matters, such as lighting, ventilation and amenities generally, which loom largest in the life of a worker so far as his conditions within the factory are concerned. Personal investigation of various factories by the author has led him to the general conclusion that neither management nor men have interpreted the functions of Works Councils as including anything that may be regarded as being within the managerial sphere of the executives; on the other hand, the 'Happy Family' view of relations between management and men in these Councils is an exaggeration.

Works Councils must be distinguished from the Joint Production Councils set up during the Second World War with a more definite and technical scope.

On the wider issue of how far workers have taken a share in management in recent years, it must be remembered that from the definition of terms, there is an inherent contradiction here: somebody must be the 'boss.' Certainly, a number of profit-sharing schemes have proved successful in individual industries, notably in the gas industry. As long ago as 1884 the Industrial Co-partnership Association was founded to propagate the principle of a worker sharing in the profits of industry and, by accumulating such shares of profits, becoming a shareholder.

But profit-sharing is not synonymous with co-partnership. No genuine co-partnership between workers and owners, between 'Labour' and 'Capital,' can occur if workers do not share losses as well as profits; and this the workers have proved unwilling to do. Apart from the Co-operative movement, co-partnership in industry has made little progress in this country. In 1910 there were 121 firms with co-partnership schemes, with 57,000 participant-employees; in 1952 there were little over 300, with 200,000 participants; less than half of the total employed population participate in such schemes. Co-partnership schemes were operated in 1948, before nationalisation, by about 60 gas, water and electricity supply undertakings; by about 40 metal, engineering and shipbuilding undertakings; some glass, chemical and soap undertakings; and by a few financial firms.

(3) The statutory regulation of wages in badly organised trades

The Trade Boards Acts, 1909 and 1918, gave the Minister of Labour power to establish Trade Boards for the fixing of minimum rates of wages where he was of the opinion that no adequate machinery existed for the effective regulation of wages throughout the trade. These Acts were replaced by the Wages Councils Acts, 1945–59; Wages Councils, with wider powers than the old Trade Boards, replaced the latter: they determine a statutory minimum wage by a process of negotiation, the Minister then making an Order which is legally binding. The Wages Councils Act, 1959, consolidated the law relating to wages councils.

In agriculture, County Agricultural Wages Committees were set up by the Ministry of Agriculture and Fisheries to fix minimum wages, under an Act of 1924. In 1942 these powers were transferred to an Agricultural Wages Board constituted by the Minister of Labour and National Service.

(4) The establishment of a permanent court of arbitration; and (5) The authorisation of the Minister of Labour to hold enquiries regarding disputes.

These two recommendations were followed in the Industrial Courts Act, 1919, which established an Industrial Court as a permanent and independent tribunal appointed by the Minister of Labour and National Service from representatives of employers and workmen and indepenedent persons, and in addition one or more women. Either of the parties involved in a trade dispute may refer the matter to the Minister, who must then take such steps as appear to him to be expedient. With the consent of both parties he may, if he thinks fit, refer the matter for arbitration to the Industrial Court; though, if the parties prefer it, he may refer the matter to an arbitrator or a Board of Arbitration with equal representation of employers and workpeople. Arbitration awards under the Conciliation Act or Industrial Courts Act are not legally binding on the parties, but they are usually accepted by them.

Even during the Second World War, voluntary negotiation as opposed to State compulsion was maintained so far as possible, as in the Conditions of Labour and National Arbitration Order, 1940, and the Restoration of Pre-War Trade Practices Act, 1942. The policy of the Government has been to allow disputes to be settled by the negotiating machinery built up by the industry. Where such effective machinery has been built up, the Ministry of Labour normally does little else but appoint independent chairmen, and in other industries, only when the usual negotiation methods have been found to fail will the Ministry intervene, its conciliation officers operating locally and the Ministry dealing with nation-wide disputes.

The Industrial Courts Act laid it down that action under the Act was to be taken only where the normal procedure of negotiation possible to the parties was exhausted. The Act also provided for the

1891: Royal Commission set up to enquire into industrial relations
CONCILIATION ACT, 1896
Appointment of Conciliation Officers
1914–18: FIRST WORLD WAR
1916: WHITLEY COMMITTEE
Recommendations:

The formation of Joint Industrial Councils	The statutory regulation of wages in badly-organised trades	The establishment of a permanent Court of Arbitration	The authorisation of the Minister of Labour to hold enquiries in cases of dispute

Joint Standing Industrial Council formed ('J.I.C.s')

Trade Boards Acts, 1909 and 1918

superseded by Wages Councils Acts, 1945–59

INDUSTRIAL COURTS ACT, 1919: Established an Industrial Court; Courts of Inquiry
1939–45: SECOND WORLD WAR
1940: FALL OF FRANCE—restraint in wages demands abandoned
1940: Joint Consultative Committee
1940: Conditions of Employment and National Arbitration Order (Order No. 1305)

The formation of Works Committees

Works Committees or Works Councils formed

National Arbitration Tribunal

1951: Order No. 1305 replaced by Industrial Disputes Order
National Arbitration Tribunal replaced by Industrial Disputes Tribunal
1958: Industrial Disputes (Amendment and Revocation) Order Abolition of Industrial Disputes Tribunal as from 1 March, 1959
1959: Terms and Conditions of Employment Act

CHART 14—*The Development of the Machinery for Conciliation and Arbitration in British Industry* establishment of Courts of Inquiry composed of independent members appointed by the Minister: where any trade dispute exists or is apprehended the Minister may, whether the dispute has been reported to him or not, enquire into the circumstances, and may refer the matter for investigation to a Court of Inquiry. The recommendations of the Court are not enforceable at law; but until 1951 there was practically no known record of a recommendation being rejected—in that year the railwaymen rejected a recommendation of a Court of Inquiry.

Introduction of the compulsory arbitration principle into industrial relations came during the Second World War; after the Fall of France in 1940 it became imperative for the safety of the State that war production should be maintained and increased. In May 1940 a Joint Consultative Committee, consisting of representatives of the British Employers' Federation and representatives of the Trades Union Congress, was appointed by the National Joint Advisory Council to advise and assist the Minister on matters arising during the period of emergency. As a result of the recommendations of the committee, a Defence Regulation empowered the Minister of Labour and National Service to make an order prohibiting a strike or lock-out in connection with any trade dispute. The Conditions of Employment and National Arbitration Order came into force in July 1940. Amending orders were subsequently made without changing the principle or main provisions of the 1940 Order.

The Order established a National Arbitration Tribunal, to which the Minister was obliged to refer a dispute where there had been failure to reach a settlement, there was undue delay in the making of a settlement, or there was no suitable joint machinery in existence and conciliation attempts had failed. Any agreement, decision or award resulting from references by the Minister to existing joint machinery or to the National Arbitration Tribunal was made binding upon the parties.

Strikes and lock-outs were prohibited unless the disputes had been reported to the Minister and had not been referred by him for settlement within 21 days from the date on which they were reported. Employers were required to observe terms and conditions not less favourable than 'recognised terms and conditions,' i.e. terms and conditions of employment which had been settled by machinery of negotiation or arbitration to which the parties were organisations of employers and trade unions.

The Restoration of Pre-War Trade Practices Act, 1942, provided for the post-war restoration of trade practices departed from during the war. The trade unions cordially disliked the 1940 Order (known as Order No. 1305), especially Part Two, prohibiting strikes and lockouts unless they had been reported to the Minister and had not been referred by him for settlement within 21 days; they felt that the competence of the National Arbitration Tribunal should be limited.

After considerable agitation the 1940 Order was revoked by a Labour Government a little time before its defeat in October, 1951. The Conditions of Employment and National Arbitration Orders, 1940 to 1950, were repealed in August 1951 and replaced by the Industrial Disputes Order, 1951. The provision relating to the illegality of strikes and lock-outs was omitted, and the National Arbitration Tribunal was replaced by the Industrial Disputes Tribunal, whose decisions were, ultimately, unenforceable against the unions; so that a Minister might refuse to adopt the arbitration procedure and refer a matter in dispute to a Court of Inquiry.

In the meantime, in February 1951, a number of dockers had been charged with conspiring to incite others to take part in an illegal strike, no trade dispute between the Merseyside dockers and employers having been reported to the Minister under Order No. 1305. Nearly 7500 London dockers staged a token strike in support of the accused men, and 73 ships were idle and 32 undermanned as a result in the West India and London docks. The incident is important as illustrating the feeling provoked against the implementing of the principle of compulsory arbitration.

The machinery set up by the Industrial Disputes Order, 1951, for the compulsory settlement of disputes was brought to an end by the Industrial Disputes (Amendment and Revocation) Order, 1958: the Order of 1951 was not to apply to any dispute or issue not reported to the Minister before 10th December 1958, and the Order was revoked as from 1st March 1959. The Terms and Conditions of Employment Act, 1959, provided machinery for the determination by the Industrial Court of questions concerning recognised terms and conditions of employment, in place of that formerly provided by the Industrial Disputes Order.

Stoppages of work arising from disputes in the United Kingdom during the first three years following the Second World War caused the loss of 2 million working days each year at the establishments where the stoppages occurred. During succeeding years, the time lost was less than 2 million, but rose to $2\frac{1}{2}$ million working days in 1954–5. In 1955–6, nearly 3,800,000 working days were lost, three-quarters of them in transport and coal-mining.

The longest rail strike in British history took place in 1955, ending on 14th June after seventeen days. It cost the British Transport Commission over £15 million in forfeited revenue, and caused a great diversion of traffic from rail to road—some of this diversion, no doubt, to prove permanent. The Associated Society of Locomotive Engineers and Firemen, which had been responsible for the strike on a question of 'differentials' in wages, obtained little enough materially for their efforts, though it might be claimed that morally ' 'twas a glorious victory.'

Meantime, in May 1955, a dock strike had been called, as a result of a dispute between the National Amalgamated Stevedores and Dockers' Union and the Transport and General Workers' Union over a question of 'poaching' of members. It lasted six weeks—one of the longest, costliest and bitterest strikes since the war.

In July 1956 occurred a significant development: a strike—a most reluctant one, it would appear, as far as at least half the men in it were concerned—was called by the unions against summary dismissal of men by the British Motor Corporation on the ground of redundancy. Questions of compensation and consultation were raised by the unions; and, on the other side, there was brought up the suggestion of a secret ballot in relation to strike action.

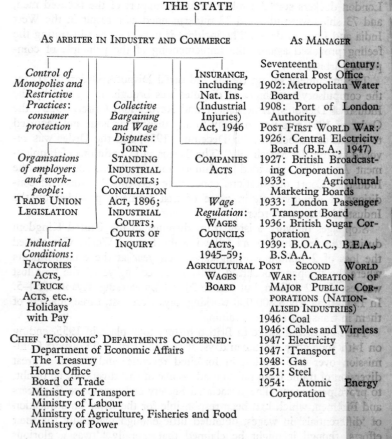

THE STATE

	AS ARBITER IN INDUSTRY AND COMMERCE		AS MANAGER

AS ARBITER IN INDUSTRY AND COMMERCE

Control of Monopolies and Restrictive Practices: consumer protection

Organisations of employers and work-people: TRADE UNION LEGISLATION

Industrial Conditions: FACTORIES ACTS, TRUCK ACTS, etc., Holidays with Pay

Collective Bargaining and Wage Disputes: JOINT STANDING INDUSTRIAL COUNCILS; CONCILIATION ACT, 1896; INDUSTRIAL COURTS; COURTS OF INQUIRY

INSURANCE, including Nat. Ins. (Industrial Injuries) Act, 1946

COMPANIES ACTS

Wage Regulation: WAGES COUNCILS ACTS, 1945–59; AGRICULTURAL WAGES BOARD

AS MANAGER

Seventeenth Century: General Post Office
1902: Metropolitan Water Board
1908: Port of London Authority
POST FIRST WORLD WAR:
1926: Central Electricity Board (B.E.A., 1947)
1927: British Broadcasting Corporation
1933: Agricultural Marketing Boards
1933: London Passenger Transport Board
1936: British Sugar Corporation
1939: B.O.A.C., B.E.A., B.S.A.A.
POST SECOND WORLD WAR: CREATION OF MAJOR PUBLIC CORPORATIONS (NATIONALISED INDUSTRIES)
1946: Coal
1946: Cables and Wireless
1947: Electricity
1947: Transport
1948: Gas
1951: Steel
1954: Atomic Energy Corporation

CHIEF 'ECONOMIC' DEPARTMENTS CONCERNED:
Department of Economic Affairs
The Treasury
Home Office
Board of Trade
Ministry of Transport
Ministry of Labour
Ministry of Agriculture, Fisheries and Food
Ministry of Power

CHART 15—*The State in its Relation to Modern Industrial Organisation*

In February 1960 a railway strike was narrowly averted; and men stayed underground at a coal mine as a protest against the threat of redundancy. 'Redundancy' was in fact becoming a problem of more significance than mere 'unemployment.' The State had involved itself in the world of management in industry, and found itself drawn into a still more complex direction of national affairs. The Managerial Revolution moved into the problems of organisation not only of industrial and commercial enterprises but also of the whole complex of planning of the economic life of the community.

Because wealth cannot be divorced from welfare, this planning had to comprise also the organisation of the social services and the means of combating the insidious effects of State intervention as it was put into effect by the Departments. A Council on Tribunals was set up by the Tribunals and Inquiries Act, 1958, to control the administrative tribunals which had been deciding cases in dispute between citizens and the Departments—the State had been obliged to manage itself in the interests of democracy as it had been worked out in Britain over the hundreds of years of its constitutional history.

It is necessary to review now the facts of our subject in relation to the broad social and economic consequences of the Industrial Revolution.

CHAPTER XI

THE SOCIAL AND ECONOMIC CONSEQUENCES OF THE INDUSTRIAL REVOLUTION

1. POPULATION CHANGES

The evolution of modern industrial organisation cannot be studied as an isolated phenomenon; it must be related to the larger social and economic background: the effects of the Industrial Revolution generally are part of the whole body politic in which the cells of industrial enterprises have their growth. Large industrial undertakings require for their very being a labour force for production and a market for their products. The study of population is, therefore, relevant to the study of the history of industrial organisation.

For over a thousand years the population of Britain was related closely to the agricultural system: a self-sufficing economy kept a population of under 6 millions more or less adequately, if coarsely, fed. In 1670 the population of England and Wales was, it has been estimated, about $5\frac{3}{4}$ millions. When the first census was taken in 1801 the population was found to be nearly 9 millions; by 1921 it was nearly 38 millions; by 1931, nearly 40 millions.

In 1700 the population of Great Britain was about $6\frac{1}{2}$ millions; the most densely populated areas were the Home Counties agricultural areas—near the London market—and the woollen areas of the Cotswolds, the Severn valley, Norfolk and the West Riding of Yorkshire. Less than one-fifth of this population lived in towns.

Between 1760 and 1820 the population of the country increased to over 12 millions. London increased its population rapidly; the populations of Liverpool, Manchester and Bradford doubled themselves in twenty years: by 1850 half the population was living in towns. Besides the London area, the increases took place in the coal-fields, north and west of a line from Bristol to Hull. The population grew beyond the capacity of home agriculture to feed it, even although farming methods improved during the nineteenth century; the imports of food were being paid for by the products of the new manufacturing industries.

In 1798 appeared the first edition of Thomas Malthus' famous essay, *Essay on the Principles of Population as it Affects the Future*

Improvement of Society; a revised version was published in 1803. Malthus was influenced by his survey of the miseries of the peasants before the French Revolution, and his work did much to earn for Economics the title of 'the dismal science.' His thesis was that population tended to outstrip food supply, and that disastrous over-population could be prevented only by two kinds of checks, positive and preventive. The positive checks are war, disease, famine and vice. The preventive checks are prudence and self-control.

Malthus has been criticised on the ground that he did not foresee the vast strides which would be made in agricultural and industrial techniques (in 1872 arable farming reached its highest acreage: 18·4 million acres and better varieties of seeds and improved methods of cultivation were in vogue), so that a greater population could be sustained with a higher standard of living. It is easy to be wise after the event; and in any case Malthus was substantially right: no doubt, being a clergyman of his age, he would have classified modern methods of contraception as 'vice.' Certainly, in our present age the East tends to fulfil his predictions; and even in modern Western civilisation acute uneasiness is expressed about the food position when strategic considerations arise.

In point of fact, the point where 'diminishing returns' begin to operate in agriculture has been pushed farther and farther away under modern techniques. Nevertheless, even if numbers in themselves have not proved so serious a cause for alarm as Malthus anticipated, the comparative densities and distribution of population have had results serious enough. The manufacturing towns that grew up so often contained the 'dark, satanic mills,' the squalor and ignorance, the insanitary dwellings, the moral and spiritual filth, that were to stir the consciences of the reformers. Beneath the pious respectability of the Victorian manufacturing middle-class society, there groaned the dark misery of the poorer classes. Industry was concentrated—to provide new problems for statesmen when the prosperity built up by nineteenth-century captains of industry began to fade.

The spread of popular education, the reforms in factories, the rise of trade unions, the development of scientific thought, the awakening of social conscience and consciousness in the mass of the population, all interacted with the crude effects of death-rate and birth-rate changes to produce changes in the distribution and organisation of industrial structure. The improvement in the public-health services throughout the nineteenth-century, the scientific achievements in inoculation, antiseptics, anaesthesia, the improved nursing services pioneered by the genius of Florence Nightingale, all these reduced the death-rate, which fell from 35 per 1000 in 1750 to 12 per 1000 in 1931.

The great *rate* of increase in population which characterised the nineteenth century has been halted. During the past few decades the total of population in Britain—and indeed, in Western Europe, America and the 'white' portions of the world generally—has come to be determined, not by changes in the death-rate, but by changes in the birth-rate. The decisive factor today is fertility, or actual reproduction.

The birth-rate began to drop in the 1870s in Britain. The extent of the decline is indicated by the net reproduction rate: a population is stationary when the net reproduction rate falls below 1·0. It is this rate, which is below 1·0 in most European countries, the United States and Canada, and the 'white' world generally, which determines the total population of these countries.

A Royal Commission on Population was appointed in 1944, and reported in June 1949. The Commission surveyed the growth of population from about 7 millions in 1700 to 49 millions. The fall in the birth-rate was not the result of a fall in the marriage-rate, but of a decrease in the number of children born per marriage. In Victorian days there was an average of $5\frac{1}{2}$ to 6 live children per marriage. This average had fallen to 2·2 children; the deficiency below that required in the long run for replacement was of the order of 6%.

Calculations based on various assumptions indicated a progressive decline in future population; the future course of births will depend mainly on the future size of the family. The age grouping of the population will alter. In 1947 there were fewer people under 20 than between 20 and 40. The average age has risen from 27 to 35 since 1891; and the proportion of people over 60 has doubled in recent years. In its earlier stages the decline developed fastest among the higher occupational categories; between 1900 and 1930 the families of manual workers were about 40% larger than those of non-manual workers. Families of six children were formerly very common.

The Royal Commission concluded from its survey that the total population would continue to grow, perhaps for another generation; after that it would decline. The working population would remain at its present size for about 30 years, though forming a smaller proportion of the total. During the following 15 years the population of young adults aged 15–39 would fall by about 1,400,000, whilst the number of people over 65 would increase during the next 30 years by about 2,300,000. There would thus be a considerable increase in the proportion of old people.

Changes of this kind have already raised, and will raise, problems for industrial organisation—there will be, as it were, a larger demand for bath-chairs and a lessened demand for toys; gardening tools would appear to be a better proposition for a small firm than play-pens or perambulators. In the wider sphere, the reluctance of firms to employ older people is already being overcome by the force of circumstances as well as by urgings on the part of the Government; such information as there is available regarding a comparison of the work of older people with that of younger would seem to indicate that the older man is slower, but more reliable, more punctual, steadier in application. The employment of women, a common factor since two world wars, has tended to confuse the problem somewhat. Research on absenteeism, sickness, productivity in relation to age and sex, will give industry more guide to future trends in desirable organisation.

The Report of the Economic Committee of the Commission* suggested that among the advantages of a growing population are the increase in the scale of production and the stimulation of technical improvements, and a greater flexibility in the economic system, so that obstinate mass unemployment is avoided; a disadvantage is the diversion of productive resources, which would otherwise go to raising the standard of living, to the supply of such capital equipment as houses, public utilities and industrial plant.

In the Report stress was laid on the distinction between quantity and quality; the average size of family of the unskilled worker is twice as large as that of the professional and administrative workers. To maintain stable numbers and improve the state of the population generally, the Report recommended economic reliefs for parents, a housing programme, better health services, and education for family life.

Some of the assumptions and conclusions of the Report now appear to lack validity; and the question of 'quality' has to be carefully examined.

Though there is no fear of a great drop in Britain's population in the near future, the increasing number of older people has given rise to anxieties relating to pension provisions, such as those of the Phillips Committee of 1954,† which suggested that the age at which the National Insurance Retirement pension can be claimed at standard rate should be raised—a remarkably pessimistic suggestion in view of the increasing resources available and the tendency towards shorter hours of work in industry.

Though the population of Britain continues to rise, the actual rate of increase has slowed down. The position reached by the sixth decade of this century would seem to indicate that Malthus's predictions are not so very wide of the mark, if we express 'food supply' as including the comforts and amenities of life in towns where traffic and road accidents on the scale of casualties in a minor war mount daily. The population of the United Kingdom is a very large one for the size of the country: 53,670,000 in an area of 93,024 square miles.

* *Papers of the Royal Commission on Population, Vol. III: Report of the Economic Committee* (H.M.S.O., 1950).

† *Report of the Committee on the Economic and Financial Problems of the Provision for Old Age* (Cmd. 9333, 1954).

Sweden, with an area of 173,624 square miles, has a population of only 7,600,000. Comparisons may be odious, in that such factors as climate and usable land area have to be taken into account; but the fact remains that with such a population to maintain the United Kingdom, with all her wealth of materials and technological resources, has a hard task, under present conditions of industrial organisation in the face of intense foreign competition, to preserve her economy—a Greek word which, it must be remembered, means good housekeeping. Yearnings have been expressed that Britain, now shorn of her Empire, should be 'like Sweden'—not only in its industrial prosperity and its aloofness from great world commitments but also in its general sociological features. Short of exporting a large proportion of its population, it is difficult to see how Britain could become 'like Sweden.'

The 'population explosion' which is troubling the world, and particularly the Asian countries and the less developed countries, has gone on in spite of intensive and near-frantic efforts in birth-control and contraceptive propaganda, the failure of which raises dangerous political possibilities. In Britain the basic economic problem of the allocation of scarce resources has had to be examined in the light of the possibility of State direction and control of the economy.

2. The Localisation of Industry

The principle of the division of labour the application of which marked a stage in the progress of mankind comparable with that marked by the control over fire or the invention of writing, has caused not merely the specialisation of occupation of persons but also the specialisation of occupation of areas. Climate, geographical features and the relative advantages of the development of shipbuilding in the Clyde valley, determined the location of the cotton industry in Lancashire rather than the Clyde. The woollen industry became localised in Yorkshire.

Once an industry has been established in a particular area, the building of a tradition of skill and the setting up of commercial machinery tend to keep it there, even though the original advantages have become less important. The presence of local grindstones is no longer important to the Sheffield steel industry; Staffordshire's pottery industry obtains better clay from Devon and Cornwall than from its own deposits. Moreover, specialisation within areas tends to occur; the northern towns of Lancashire tended to specialise in weaving, the southern in spinning.

It was inevitable that the heavy industries of Britain should be established on or near the coal-fields. The heavy transport costs of coal and iron determined the place of production of iron and steel goods at the source of the fuel and raw material. The Lancashire cotton industry drew its machinery from the conveniently situated nearby resources. It was inevitable that the port of Liverpool should become a centre for the cotton produce markets, that Manchester should develop a tradition of merchanting skill. Such localisation, with the proximity of raw materials, labour supply and subsidiary industries, permitted the survival of the small-scale undertakings which have so bedevilled the development of the Lancashire cotton industry.

A feature of the early period of the Industrial Revolution was the concentration of industry in the North and Midlands: the heavy industries in the coal-fields, the woollen industry in the West Riding of Yorkshire. These industries attracted large populations. In the period between the two world wars the development of alternatives to coal as sources of power—gas, electricity, oil—made proximity to coal-fields of less importance. The newer industries were 'light' industries engaged in the manufacture of such articles as radio sets, patent foodstuffs, gramophones—consumers' goods rather than producers' goods.

Statistics indicate the changes taking place in British industry. Between 1923 and 1938 the number employed in coal-mining fell by 29%, in shipbuilding by 23%, and in cotton manufacture by 30%. In contrast, the number engaged in electrical engineering rose by 97%; in motor-car manufacture by 104%; in silk and artificial silk manufacture by 113%; and in transport and distribution by 50%. Agriculture and the old-type heavy industries shrank; the new light industries expanded.

Between 1921 and 1934 the total population of the country increased by just over 2½ millions. Of this total, London and the south-eastern counties absorbed nearly 1,700,000. London became a great magnet for industries using electrical power and economising on transport costs by placing themselves close to their markets.

Unemployment occurred in the industrial North and Midlands, and there was some shift of population to the south and east, reversing the previous movement. A Derating Act in 1929 reduced rates on industrial premises, but the newer industries still preferred the south and east: London spread into the countryside, raising problems of a generally social as well as an economic nature. The only lightening of the darkness that began to close on the old industrial regions of the North and Midlands and South Wales was the growth of the motor-car industry in the West Midlands. Britain had lost her lead in the Industrial Revolution; Japan had captured the Indian cotton-goods market; entrepreneurs were discouraged. In Germany the crisis took a serious political turn, and events began to move towards the menace of Nazism.

But before rearmament had come to rescue, ironically, Britain's heavy industries, the great depression of the 1930s stalked its way across the land. In Merthyr Tydfil, South Wales, and in Jarrow the percentage of unemployed was 75%. No one who has travelled through the stricken town of Merthyr at the time of the depression can forget the terrible face of that town, with its shuttered, silent streets, empty save for a group or two of men talking listlessly at street corners. Throughout the 'Distressed Areas' an average of 35% of the insured workers was unemployed.

Under the Special Areas (Development and Improvement) Act of 1934 these areas were designated 'Special Areas,' and the Treasury was to manage a Special Areas Fund established to assist these areas by public-works schemes, by providing work for the unemployed on the land and by transfer of unemployed workers to other areas. The latter provision necessarily had the effect of encouraging the drift from areas now becoming derelict, and increasing the congestion in the London area. In 1936–37 factories were offered at low rents, together with relief from rates, to firms setting up in the 'Trading Estates' established in Durham, Cumberland, Central Scotland and South Wales; the Special Areas Amendment Act, 1937, made provision for loans to firms from Government funds. Training schemes for unemployed were provided by the Government.

Some hundred factories were established during the Second World War. The Industrial and Commercial Finance Corporation gave assistance to undertakings setting up in 'Development Areas,' as they now came to be called. Under the Distribution of Industry Act, 1945, a Development Areas Treasury Advisory Committee was appointed to advise the Treasury on the giving of financial assistance in the raising of capital to undertakings carried on or proposed to be carried on in a Development Area. Board of Trade approval was necessary, this approval being given to undertakings where they complied with the requirement as to the proper distribution of industry; and the Advisory Committee had to be satisfied that the undertaking was one likely ultimately to be able to pay its way. It was announced in October 1952 that part of south-east Lancashire was to be scheduled as a Development Area. The area depended on the cotton industry, and was seriously affected by the slump which began in 1951.

A Capital Issues Committee was set up in 1939; application to the Committee had to be made for a licence to issue shares or other securities. The Committee had to consider whether an undertaking wishing to raise money by the issue of securities would thereby assist the Government's investment programme, the expansion of exports, or the Government's policy of diversifying industry in Development Areas. It was abolished in 1959.

The Local Employment Act, 1960, repealed the Distribution of Industry Acts, 1945 to 1958. Scheduled Development Areas were abolished; the Board of Trade was given powers to provide employment in designated Development Districts with high and persistent existing or threatened unemployment.

It is evident that from a 'system' of free enterprise, or planning by individuals, the industrial scene generally had moved to a state of control and planning by Government agencies. Certainly, we shall see later how far we have moved from the early days of trade unionism to a time when representatives of the trade unions could sit on Regional Boards of Industry to advise the Government on industrial trends.

The legislation on Development Areas must not be regarded as a sudden leap in the Government's consciousness towards a realisation that some planning of industry was necessary to avoid the great mass-unemployment that has afflicted this country from time to time. The increasing confusion during world wars as industry became more complex, increasing dependence of the prosperity of large numbers of workers upon the state of the markets, industrial progress and invention in other parts of the world—these made some such development inevitable; for mass unemployment is dangerous politically as well as economically. Before the First World War unemployment varied between about 2 and 10% of workers; on an average, it was about 6%. The number of insured workers was $9\frac{1}{2}$ millions in 1923; $10\frac{1}{2}$ millions in 1929; and more than 12 millions in 1937. In 1929 the number of unemployed people was over 1,300,000; in 1932, over 2,700,000, about 22% of the insured workers.

In 1944 the British (National) Government published a White Paper, *Employment Policy,** in which the Government stated that they accepted as one of their primary aims and responsibilities the maintenance of a high and stable level of employment after the war. The document was a cautious one; the substantive policy proposed was in effect public works. Lord Beveridge, a few years later, in his *Full Employment in a Free Society* (Allen and Unwin, 1944), considered that the employment policy proposed was mitigating only. His remedy was a much more drastic one, a long-term programme of planned outlay by the State, involving a revolution in national finance: the estimated income and outlay of the nation as a whole would be surveyed annually with reference to man-power, not to money; and a Minister of National Finance would budget for a total sufficient to employ the whole available man-power of the country.

For a nation like ours, depending so much on exports, successful planning must be done not merely by our own Government, but by the Governments of other nations with which Great Britain has economic relations. In the long run the economic problem is a world problem. To solve this gigantic task, super-guardians of the Platonic type would be necessary. In the meantime, recourse must be had to local and national measures.

* Cmd. 6527.

The mal-distribution of industry in Britain resulted in the congestion of London and the South-east, while the North became derelict. The cure, said Lord Beveridge, was the localisation of industry, and this policy has been implemented, as explained above.

The localisation of industry in itself is not the answer to those periodic slumps which occurred, for example, in 1886, 1893 and 1904, and which so impressed some economists with a sense of rhythmic regularity in their occurrence that they gave the name of the 'trade cycle' to them, and were inclined to believe that recovery was inevitable, a part of a phase of the 'cycle.' But there was no sign of an 'inevitable' recovery from the depression which began in 1929 and reached its depth in 1931, with 2½ millions unemployed. Only by an armaments race—economically, apart from the advantage gained by technical advance, as useful as expenditure on fireworks—was Britain rescued from this unemployment crisis; and the price paid was as expensive as the depression, though it was paid in human suffering rather than in money.

The unemployment in the Lancashire cotton industry did not arise from any mysterious 'cycle,' but from world affairs, and in particular from Japanese competition. It was the price paid for over-specialisation, involving a risk which was realised in its worst form. That is the true nature of the problem of the localisation of industry.

The Local Employment Acts, 1960 and 1963, did not succeed in checking the drift to the south, though they did succeed in introducing some electrical and light industry into the Lancashire cotton towns.

In November 1963 the Government published White Papers on the development of Central Scotland and North-east England.* These are areas in which there has been much unemployment and emigration, consequent upon the dying or stagnation of industries. In Central Scotland, which has 75% of Scotland's population and 90% of its manufacturing industry, it was proposed to establish eight points as 'growth areas,' immediate attention being given to four areas each of which would have a new town. By means of public investment of about £140 million in roads, housing, transport and similar services, private industry would be encouraged to settle and grow. In North-east England, stimulating and modernising efforts would be concentrated in a 'growth zone' comprising Tyneside, Tees-side and part of County Durham, with a development programme rising from £55 million in 1962–63 to £90 million in 1964–65.

Bearing in mind that the advertising bill for this country comes to about £400 million a year, and that the gambling turnover in Britain in 1965 was £1000 million, these suggestions can hardly be characterised as 'major.'

With the advent of a Labour Government in 1964 and its corollary

* *Central Scotland* Cmd. 2188 and *North-East England* Cmd. 2206.

of planning, direction and control, came also the first steps in the fulfilment of Lord Beveridge's axiomatic suggestions in *Full Employment in a Free Society*. A Department of Economic Affairs was set up to deal with the long-term planning of the economy, the Treasury being relegated to the part of being the instrument of immediate financial measures: it had been reorganised in 1962 into two parts, one concerned with the economic and financial side of the national economy, the other with 'management' problems, its Joint Permanent Secretary thus becoming the Head of the Home Civil Service.

The subsequent story of the recognition of the need for planning the economy is given in Chapter XII (Section 4).

3. FACTORY LEGISLATION

The early concentration of workpeople into factories involved social evils on the debit side of the industrial account. The advantages were obvious enough: the reduction in costs per unit of production and the possibility of large-scale production to meet the expanding markets.

Factories were no new thing: in a sense, there had been groups of men working together from earliest times, when men set up flint factories for tool-making. The Romans had manuscript-copying factories and textile establishments. But never before had the herding together of people for mechanical work and machine-minding taken place on such a large scale; never before had the very essence of life revolved for so many people around work for an employer in a building, with leisure spent in mean houses, back-to-back in monotonous streets, without proper sanitation or water supply.

Similarly, the ill-treatment and exploitation of children were no new thing. Child labour had been common under the 'domestic system.' The toil and drudgery of the poorer classes had been endured by them for generations. It was the intensification of these evils to a degree such that the public conscience was appalled by them that gave them some chance of amelioration under the stimulus of the reformers' zeal.

The first half of the nineteenth century was lived in the *laissez-faire* atmosphere. The Government was opposed to any interference with the 'freedom of contract' between employer and employed—such 'freedom' being an obvious fallacy when the alternative to work was starvation, and especially so in the case of children, who could not by any stretch of the imagination be said to have entered into a contract with the employer. Children toiled in mines; were stifled in chimneys; it was argued that leisure would be bad for them. Another fallacy was that all profit was made in the last hours of work—a peculiar psychological doctrine hardly less remarkable than some ideas held by amateurs today. It was disproved by Robert Owen (1771–1858), who, in his New Lanark mills, built a model village round his factory, shortened the hours of work for his workers, instituted a scheme of co-partnership, and started schools for the children of his workers. His mills were as successful as his social schemes, and attracted wide attention. Not all his fellow-manufacturers approved of

---

FIRST HALF OF THE NINETEENTH CENTURY: LAISSEZ-FAIRE
THE REFORMERS:
Robert Owen (1771–1858)
Jeremy Bentham (1748–1832)
Lord Shaftesbury (1801–85)

1802	Health and Morals of Apprentices Act
1819	Children in cotton mills: employment forbidden under 9; hours of work 12 per day. Ineffective
1833	First effective Factory Act—Lord Ashley (later Lord Shaftesbury) Children 9–12; 48 hours per week 'Young Persons' 12–18: 69 hours per week Inspectors appointed
1842	Mines Act
1844	Women protected. 'Half-time' system for children
1847	Ten Hours' Day
1850	Act fixing definite hours of work '*Laissez-faire*' now abandoned
1860s	Extension to factories other than textile factories
1878	Factory and Workshops Act—classified types of establishments Provisions for cleanliness, ventilation, prevention of overcrowding, fencing of machinery, meals
1875–1901	Consolidation in factory legislation
1937	Factories Act: Health, Safety, Welfare
1948	Amendments and additions to Factories Act, 1937
1959	Factories Act: consolidating and extending Act
1961	Factories Act: consolidated previous legislation

CHART 16—*The Course of Factory Legislation*

---

such doings; and he was discredited at last through the weapon afforded by his religious scepticism.

Other great reformers were Jeremy Bentham (1748–1832) and Lord Shaftesbury (1801–85), who, among other activities, championed the 'Ragged School' movement.

The First Factory Act, the Health and Morals of Apprentices Act, was passed in 1802. This regulated the labour of pauper apprentices; and provision was made for the attendance of children at church. These pauper 'apprentices' were children placed with manufacturers by the overseers of the parishes in the towns. They were provided with food and clothing by the manufacturers, who in return exacted long hours of work from them, often obliging them to eat their meals as they worked. Their sanitary conditions were terrible; and they grew up in most cases ignorant, debased and demoralised. The Health and Morals of Apprentices Act limited their daily hours to twelve, prohibited night work, and provided for some elementary instruction; there were regulations about ventilation, cleanliness and sleeping accommodation.

But the inspection of factories for the purposes of the Act was left to magistrates who were little disturbed about such things. By this time, too, apprentice labour was being replaced by the labour of 'free' children, to whom the Act did not apply. 'Free' children were obliged to work often as long as sixteen hours a day to bring in something to keep the home going, for the wages of the adults were small enough.

The evidence given before Committees examining the situation in factories* makes harrowing reading to a modern reader of sensitivity. Robert Owen, giving evidence before the Committee on Children in Manufactories, 1816, mentioned a little girl who was employed in a mill at Stockport at the age of four. Other and later Committees obtained evidence of the forcible waking of children, so fatigued by their labours that they fell asleep with the food they were taking still in their mouths. Stories of beatings and of cruelties practised in the name of Production were common.

The result of these investigations was that an Act was passed in 1819, applying to children in cotton mills, forbidding their employment under the age of nine, and limiting their hours of work to twelve per day. No proof of age was required to be given; the magistrates were lax, and evasion was easy.

The first effective Factory Act was passed in 1833, through the efforts of Lord Shaftesbury (then Lord Ashley) and the followers of Jeremy Bentham. The Act forbade the employment in textile mills of children under nine, limited the hours of work of children between the ages of nine and twelve to 48 per week, and those of 'young persons' between the ages of twelve and eighteen to 69 per week. The Act was effective because four inspectors were appointed to enforce its provisions. It was important for them to ascertain the ages of the children, and when the registration of births became compulsory in 1837 this could be done.

In 1833, too, the Government made the first grant out of public funds for public education. In 1844 the age at which children could work was reduced to eight—a retrograde step—but between eight and thirteen years of age they had to attend school for part of the day, their hours under this 'half-time' system being limited to six and a half per day. Women were protected by the Act of 1844 introducing

* See A. E. Bland, P. A. Brown and R. H. Tawney: *English Economic History: Select Documents* (Bell).

the 'half-time' system; they were included with young persons. There were certain provisions for guarding machinery.

A Commission of 1842 disclosed conditions in mines which filled the nation with horror. Children of both sexes were taken down the mines to work, in some districts at the age of four. Women and young girls did laborious and dangerous work, carrying coal in baskets up ladders, some crawling on all fours with chains between their legs. The Mines Act of 1842 prohibited the underground employment of women and girls and of boys under ten. Sir Humphry Davy's safety-lamp was invented in 1815; haulage was improved after 1840; and a series of Mines Acts from 1850 onwards compelled better ventilation.

After the passing of the 1833 Act there was agitation for a ten-hours' day; and in 1847 an Act embodying this limitation of hours was passed. But the working day extended over fifteen hours—from 5.30 a.m. to 8.30 p.m.—and the shift system of work made evasion of the Act an easy matter. Lord Ashley was not one to let this pass. In 1850, an Act specified that the working day for women and young persons should extend from 6 a.m. to 6 p.m. (or from 7 a.m. to 7 p.m.), with one and a half hours for meals, the factories to close down at 2 p.m. on Saturdays. The weekly working hours were limited to sixty. There was a slight loss to the workers in the increase in hours, but a great advantage gained in that provisions were made for enforcing the legal standards laid down.

The middle of the century had thus been reached without any legis-lation directed to the improvement of the conditions of adult male workers. But indirectly the men benefited, for their work was depen-dent upon that of the women and young people. The attitude of laissez-faire had been abandoned—at least as far as textile factories were concerned.

The employers tried to turn the clock back; but not only did the pace of Government intervention increase; its scope was also enlarged. In 1860 a Bleach and Dye Works Act was passed: it was followed by other Acts, and the law relating to factories in which bleaching, dye-ing and printing were carried on was consolidated in an Act of 1870.

In 1864 the scope of factory regulations was extended to factories having no connection with textiles, including those engaged in manu-facturing lucifer matches, percussion caps, cartridges and earthenware. The Factory Act of 1864 also made provision for ventilation and sanitation. The 1867 Factory Acts Extension Act extended the applica-tion of the law to other industries, including iron and engineering, paper, glass, printing, book-binding and tobacco. This Act applied to the processes mentioned in the Act whatever the number of persons employed, also generally to all other establishments in which 50 or more persons were employed. Previous legislation had been limited to factories employing more than 50 workpeople and using motive power, and unscrupulous employers could evade the provisions of the Acts by claiming that they employed less than 50 persons. The Workshop Regulation Act of 1867 defined a workshop as a place other than a factory in which a handicraft was carried on by children or young persons or women under the control of an employer, and the regulations applied only to such places if fewer than 50 persons were employed.

This Workshop Act repeated the faults of early factory legislation; it was permissive only; and its enforcement was left to the local authorities, whose outlook was still that of the first half of the nineteenth century. The Factory and Workshops Act of 1871 transferred the general duty of enforcement of the law to factory inspectors appointed by the Home Office; the local authorities retained their supervision of sanitary conditions under the Sanitary Act, 1866.

The Factory and Workshops Act of 1878 classified various types of establishments; workshops were now distinguished from factories by the non-use of mechanical power. The work of children in 'domestic workshops'—rooms in private houses where work was carried on—was regulated. Women's workshops and domestic workshops were exempted from sanitary regulation, except that laid down in the Public Health Act of 1875. There were regulations for the fencing of machinery in factories. The exemptions relating to women's workshops were abolished under an Act of 1891.

The last quarter of the nineteenth century was one of consolidation in factory legislation. The Home Secretary was given powers relating to dangerous trades under the Factory and Workshops Act of 1891, a consolidating Act making provisions for sanitary arrangements; it raised the age at which children might work in factories to eleven (an Act of 1874 had raised it to ten). The Factory Act of 1895 brought under control docks, wharves, quays and laundries; it limited the hours of work of children to 30 a week and forbade the employment of children under fourteen in night work.

The Factory and Workshop Consolidation Act of 1901 made further provisions for health and safety, and raised the minimum age at which children might be employed in factories to twelve; the age was raised to fourteen in 1920. The Factories Act of 1937 followed broadly the lines of the 1901 Act, which it replaced, but contained many new provisions based upon current practice. It reduced the permissible working hours for women and young persons, basing the hours on a 48-hour week, with a 44-hour week for persons under sixteen. It abolished the old distinctions between a factory and a workshop and between a textile and a non-textile factory, only one term, 'factory,' being employed. It was altered and added to by the Factories Act, 1948; the Factories Act, 1959, consolidated and extended existing legislation. In 1946 the functions of the Home Secretary in relation to factories legislation were transferred to the Ministry of Labour and National Service. The Factories Act, 1961, consolidated previous legislation.

The history of factory legislation, like the history of the railways, exhibits the reluctant abandonment of the old *laissez-faire* principle in the fact of the compulsion of circumstances, and the subsequent co-operation and control by the Government in industrial affairs. It illustrates a fact so often forgotten in academic discussion of historical processes: that the 'Government' is not an abstraction but a number of people of flesh and blood who, in general, are the result of their upbringing and environment; who have a niche in life which they want to maintain; and whose prejudices and passions will be determined accordingly. In the nineteenth century the 'Government' consisted of a distinct ruling class, a class which contained, after the 1832 Reform Act, a number of wealthy industrialists whose interests were in many ways opposed to those of the mass of the people. Though the Party system had been already established, and there was a distinction to be drawn between Liberals and Conservatives, the differences between them were minor compared with the differences between them and the great majority of the population. Both Parties represented wealth and power; both were determined to keep that power; and both were afraid of the revolutionary ideas which were spreading from the Continent. These facts are strikingly illustrated in the early history of trade unionism.

4. TRADE UNIONISM

Though too close a parallel must not be drawn between the modern trade union movement and the gilds of medieval times, it is too great an exaggeration to say that they were totally dissimilar. Attempts to over-emphasise the differences may arise from an inclination on the part of academic historians to ignore the modern industrial scene as a regrettable excrescence having little in common with the course of the interplay of kings, policies and politicians which have formed so large a part of the study of national history. The journeymen of medieval times who had little hope of achieving the status and wealth of masters were conscious of the need for combination against the power of the employers; and, indeed, an Act passed in 1548 was a medieval counterpart of the Combination Acts of 1799 and 1800 in that it was an attempt to suppress the journeymen gilds formed to protect the interests of the journeymen as against the power of the masters.

In point of fact, we must look at the medieval scene to see the beginnings of the capitalist system—a system in which the greater part of the national resources was originally in the hands of a comparatively few people, who exploited those resources for the sake of private profit. The expanding market, the rise of the merchant class, were the features of a commercial revolution which paved the way for the Industrial Revolution. It was only when the Industrial Revolution was in full tide that tendencies already discernible could also achieve a flood recognisable as 'movements.'

It was only natural that employers, who reserved to themselves full freedom to try to force down wages and to apply the *laissez-faire* doctrine as it favoured their interests, should attempt suppression of acts calculated by the workers to force up wages. Already, in 1749, an Act had been passed prohibiting unions of workmen in the textile industry, in metal-working and in other specified industries. When the French Revolution broke out, the fear of popular combination was intensified, and the Combination Acts of 1799 and 1800 declared unions illegal: it was a criminal offence for workmen to combine to try to secure an improvement in their conditions of work, and for a man to persuade another to leave his work. Funds raised for such purposes were liable to confiscation—half of the money going to the informer. Friendly societies, in the form of local clubs only, were permitted.

An effect of the Combination Laws was to drive the trade unions 'underground': workmen's associations were formed as secret societies or disguised as friendly societies. In some districts the unions were regarded with a certain amount of tolerance; but in the industrial districts the law was enforced with severity by the masters, who were themselves nominally subject to the laws against combination, but against whom no prosecutions ever took place.

The acute dissatisfaction felt by the workmen against these repressive measures found expression in riots and conspiracies, especially when the brave new world expected at the conclusion of the Napoleonic Wars failed to materialise. The Luddite machine-breaking of 1811–12 in Nottinghamshire, Derbyshire, Leicestershire and Yorkshire, was the response to unemployment consequent upon the introduction of machinery. The acute unrest following the conclusion of peace led the Government to pass the Six Acts of 1819, restricting public meetings, placing a heavy stamp duty on workmen's publications, and prohibiting the possession of arms and the practice of military training for unlawful purposes.

But Radical leaders, placing more faith in constitutional reform than in violence, pressed for the lifting of repression. At their head were Joseph Hume and Francis Place. Their efforts resulted in the setting up of a Commission of Enquiry and the subsequent repeal of the Combination Laws in 1824. The Commission had pointed to the dangers likely to arise from the formation of secret societies and the violence which might result from suppression. In point of fact, the lifting of restriction seemed to call forth this violence, for the repeal

F

of the Combination Laws was immediately followed by an outburst of strikes which convinced the employers that the workers were going to make the maximum use of their new freedom. The Combination Repeal Act was therefore amended by an Act of 1825 which continued to make the combination of workers for dealing with questions of hours and wages legal, but which contained clauses prohibiting 'molestation' and 'obstruction' which could be given a very elastic interpretation by the judges. Intimidation, molestation and obstruction were not to be used to force a workman to leave his work, nor to induce a workman to belong to any club or association, nor to prevent him from accepting employment, nor to force a manufacturer to make any alteration in the way he conducted his business. The result was to make common effective action by workmen within the law exceedingly difficult.

The Reform Act of 1832 disappointed the workmen. Attempts were now made to form a general trades union covering all workmen; a leading spirit in this movement was Robert Owen, whose efforts resulted in the formation in 1834 of the Grand National Consolidated Trades Union. Its inspiration, under the leadership of Owen, was socialist; it aimed finally at taking over industry and reorganising it co-operatively. As usual, Owen was ahead of his time; and a depression in trade following the formation of this Union until 1840 was unfavourable to its further development. Its prestige suffered enormously when, under a practically obsolete Act of 1797 making punishable the administering of an oath to members of an association, six Dorset labourers who had joined the Union were sentenced in 1834 to transportation to Australia. Demonstrations against the severity of the sentence failed to save these 'Tolpuddle Martyrs.' The workers were given a lesson which they never forgot—and have not forgotten to this day.

The project for a united trades union for the country failed; but this was merely a line of development which circumstances made it undesirable to follow. Another line of evolution was taken. Many of the local trade clubs forming the structure of the Grand National Consolidated Trades Union remained in existence; and in the forties there was a revival of trade unionism. In 1845 a National Association of United Trades for the Protection of Labour was formed. This was intended to be, not a national trades union, but a central machinery for common consultation and protection, seeking an understanding with employers, and trying to improve conditions without resort to strike action. The depression of the 'Hungry Forties' militated against its success, and it lasted only until 1867.

The National Association was, however, an indication of how the spirit of trade unionism was changing. The culmination of the change was fulfilled in the formation, in 1851, of the Amalgamated Society of Engineers. Here, indeed, was an association with strong likenesses to the medieval gilds. It consisted of the aristocracy of workers: the skilled workers. The contribution was a shilling a week—quite a substantial sum in those days. The society was not merely a union for the protection of labour and providing for strike pay; it was also a friendly society, providing sick, superannuation and other benefits.

The Amalgamated Society of Engineers became the model for future trade union organisation—hence the name sometimes given to the movement which followed: the 'New Model' Trade Unionism (though it may be a source of confusion that the trade union movement for skilled workers is also called the 'Old Unionism' to distinguish it from the trade unionism comprising the unskilled workers: the 'New Unionism'). The carpenters and joiners reorganised themselves on similar lines to form the Amalgamated Society of Carpenters and Joiners; the boilermakers formed the Boilermakers' and Iron Shipbuilders' Society. For his weekly shilling in the sixties, the artisan carpenter got unemployment benefit up to 10s. a week, sick benefit up to 12s. a week, accident benefit up to £100, funeral benefit of £12, a pension up to 8s. a week and emigration benefit of £6. The day of the trade union officials had come; and from this time onwards the union official began to exercise an increasing influence on the affairs of Parliament.

In 1867 the Second Reform Act gave the vote to the skilled worker of the towns. In the following year the first Trades Union Congress was held in Manchester to co-ordinate the activities of the trade unions. In 1869 the Congress appointed a Parliamentary Committee to further the interests of the trade unions in Parliament; in 1900 a conference convened by the Trades Union Congress to find means of securing working-class representation in Parliament initiated the Parliamentary Labour Party. The Congress became the 'annual parliament' of the organised workers.

In the meantime events were moving to somewhat dramatic climaxes. The employers had viewed the growing power of the unions with alarm, and were casting about to find means of discrediting them so that further repression could be undertaken. The 'Sheffield Outrages,' consisting of attacks on non-members by certain small unions, seemed to support their case. In 1867 the verdict in a case, *Hornby* v. *Close*, came as a blow to the unions. The Boilermakers' and Iron Shipbuilders' Bradford branch instituted proceedings against its treasurer for wrongfully withholding £24. It was decided that a trade union, being a body formed 'in restraint of trade,' was illegal at common law, and so could not take proceedings in a court of law. The larger unions were astounded to learn that they were not protected against defaulting officials by the Friendly Society Act of 1855, under which they had been registered.

The affairs of the unions seemed to be in a sombre state. But they soon began to mend. The Trade Union (Protection of Funds) Act, 1869, gave the unions protection in relation to their funds. To a Royal Commission of Enquiry appointed to enquire into the position of trade unions it was demonstrated that the larger unions had nothing to do with the Sheffield Outrages, and that there was a case for making the unions legal. The majority report was far from enthusiastic in the cause of trade unionism, but the minority report, signed by the Earl of Lichfield, Thomas Hughes and Frederic Harrison, was more favourable, and contained constructive suggestions for the amendment of the law.

A Liberal Government accepted the proposals of the minority report; the Trade Union Act of 1871 removed the character of criminal conspiracy from membership of a trade union. But at the same time a Criminal Law Amendment Act was passed, giving magistrates power to pass a term of imprisonment upon a workman using 'threats' to another: in effect, the Act virtually made strike action impossible. A number of workmen were, in fact, punished during the next few years for picketing.

It says much for the growing power of the trade union element in the community that the refusal of the Liberals to modify the law relating to picketing cost them the trade union vote in the general election of 1874; and that it was a Conservative Government which repealed the Criminal Law Amendment Act of 1871 and replaced it by the Conspiracy and Protection of Property Act, 1875, under which an agreement between two or more persons was not criminal if the action agreed upon would not be criminal were it done by one person: the effect was to legalise picketing, and, in general, to enable the unions to carry on trade union activity without the fear of constant threats of being taken to law.

The depression of the seventies was not favourable to trade union activities; indeed, some of the smaller unions disappeared. Through the efforts of Joseph Arch, a union of agricultural labourers was founded in 1872, but the combined opposition of the propertied and feudal-thinking classes, the landlords, farmers and clergy, were for a time too strong for it: it died in 1894. Efforts were made to revive trade union activity among farm labourers, and an Eastern Counties Agricultural Labourers' Union was formed. Close control of agriculture during the First World War gave little scope for development. Trade union activity in agriculture has not been carried on with the intensity with which it has been pursued in the towns. In 1924 the Minister of Agriculture and Fisheries was required to set up Agricultural Wages Committees to fix minimum rates of wages; and wage adjustments and Holidays With Pay arrangements have been made subsequently by an Agricultural Wages Board constituted by the Minister of Labour.

In industry the growing power of the unions induced employers to form, in 1873, a National Federation of Employers to safeguard their own interests: the wheels of destiny had indeed turned.

In the 1880s yet another phase of trade unionism was begun. In 1888, under the inspiration of Annie Besant, a theosophist, girls engaged in match manufacture came out on strike, and gained their demands. The trade union movement surged in the ranks of the unskilled, under the leadership of such men as Ben Tillett, John Burns, Tom Mann and Will Thorne. The gas workers, under the leadership of Burns, obtained their demands for shorter working hours without a strike; but the dock workers, led by Burns and Mann, were refused a minimum wage of 6d. an hour, and hastened to form themselves into a union. There was much public sympathy for the dockers, as there had been for the match girls—indeed, £48,000 was raised by public subscription for a strike fund, £30,000 of it coming from Australia. The Dock Strike of 1889 was successful, and the 'New Unionism,' the combining of unskilled workers into unions, was successfully launched.

This was the age of the idealistic–Socialistic body of thinking which was to form the intellectual part of the new Labour Party movement, the actual sinews of war being provided by the subscriptions and activities of the trade unionists. The Fabian Society was founded in London in 1883, among its earliest members being Sidney Webb (later Lord Passfield) and George Bernard Shaw; H. G. Wells joined, but proved an awkward colleague. The Fabians showed themselves to be an earnest body of intellectuals whose conception of democracy would appear to be a kind of benevolent dictatorship directed by only the best theoretical Socialist thinkers; but the philosophical and mental background of which their ideas formed a part had a great deal to do with the subsequent somewhat curious alliance of the theoretical type of Socialists, often coming from the best families and with a public-school education, with the trade union official and labour leader who actually conducted the work of organising the unions of the rank-and-file workers. It is of these two diverse elements that the British Labour Party is composed; and in the 1950s the beginnings of the conflict of these two elements could be discerned.

Karl Marx's drab if formidable writings on Socialism began to bear fruit in England in the 1880s, when his teaching was expounded by enthusiasts in this country. But the British working-man, suspicious of pseudo-intellectual revolutionary creeds, preferred the solider method of constitutional progress. In 1888 Keir Hardie helped to found the Scottish Labour Party, the first Labour Party in Britain, with a Liberal programme. The Fabians supported the new movement; and in 1892 three Labour candidates were returned at the General Election. In 1893 the Independent Labour Party was formed, its ultimate aim being the collective ownership and control of the means of production, distribution and exchange. Its trade union members were drawn mainly from the new unions; and they had to work against the apathy of the older unions. At the 1899 Congress it was decided to call a conference of trade unions, co-operative societies and socialist organisations so that Labour representation in the House of Commons should be promoted. This Conference met in 1900, and the Labour Representation Committee was formed; its Secretary was J. Ramsay MacDonald, later to become Prime Minister.

As a parliamentary force, the Labour Party reached a position of political influence in 1906, when 29 out of its 50 candidates were elected. Until 1918 its membership was drawn mainly from trade unions and socialist societies, but in the new world born after the First World War it widened its scope to include people of all social grades.

It would seem that this 1906 political triumph was the result of the blow given to trade unionism by the Taff Vale Judgment of 1901. The Taff Vale Railway Company sued the Amalgamated Society of Railway Servants for damages caused through inducing workmen to strike. The case was carried to the House of Lords, and, to the consternation of the unions, who believed that they were protected by the 1871 and 1875 Acts, the House of Lords held that trade unions were liable for the acts of their officials, when those acts were done by the officials acting on behalf of the union. Damages of £23,000 were awarded against the Amalgamated Society of Railway Servants. The unions found themselves faced with the prospect of losing their funds if they organised a strike.

The Trade Disputes Act, 1906, made the unions free of this danger of civil liability; it was passed by a Liberal Government influenced by the Labour members.

A year to two later, another blow was struck at the unions, this time from within. The Labour Party depended for financial support for its political activities mainly on the levy made on members of the unions. In 1909 Mr W. V. Osborne, a member of the Amalgamated Society of Railway Servants, obtained a judgment in the House of Lords that trade unions had not the power to levy contributions from members for the purpose of securing parliamentary representation. Until this judgment was cancelled by the Trade Union Act, 1913, most of the important unions were precluded by injunctions from contributing to the funds of the Labour Party. The 1913 Act stipulated that the objects of a levy must be agreed to by a majority of members, and that the minority should be able to 'contract out,' i.e. to state specifically that they did not wish to contribute.

The First World War gave an impetus to trade unionism, especially among women, who were now employed intensively in industry, as they were to be again during and after the Second World War, this employment resulting in the creation of social problems with which it is beyond the scope of this book to deal. After the post-war boom, depression set in. Unemployment occurred and wages fell. Unrest was rife. A reduction in miners' wages led to a strike of all trades in their support. The General Strike of 1926 was broken by the new middle classes, the smaller professional and 'black-coated' workers, who manned the trains and other essential services. The strike lasted only ten days.

In consequence of the General Strike, which was obviously aimed at forcing the Government to subsidise wages, the Trade Disputes and Trade Union Act of 1927 was passed. Its terms reflected the intensity of feeling aroused by the strike in the Government. It declared illegal strikes and lock-outs which went beyond the purposes of a trade dispute, being designed to coerce the Government directly or by inflicting hardship upon the community generally; it made it illegal to apply sums in furtherance of an illegal strike or lockout; criminal proceedings could be instituted against any person who incited others to take part in an illegal strike. The law of picketing was made more rigid. The principle of 'contracting-in' was substituted for the principle of 'contracting-out': no person could be compelled to subscribe to the funds of a political party unless he specifically gave notice of his desire to do so.

The Act contained clauses which indicated the determination of the Government that there should not again occur the possibility of a national breakdown in industrial organisation. Members of the Civil Service were prohibited from becoming members of a union with political objects, and Civil Service unions were prohibited from becoming affiliated with any other industrial or political organisations. Local or other authorities were not allowed to make it a condition of employment that any person employed by the authority should or should not be a member of a trade union; an employee of a local or other public authority who broke his contract of service with the authority knowing that by so doing he would be likely to cause danger or grave inconvenience to the community was liable to prosecution.

The Act was cordially disliked by members of the Labour Party. When, for the first time, the Labour Party reached a position of power (as distinct merely from gaining office) in 1945, one of its first acts was to repeal the Trade Disputes and Trade Union Act of 1927. This was done in 1946, and the trade unions were placed in the same position as they were in before the General Strike of 1926.

Thus, the trade unions reached a position of great importance in the State. On the nationalisation of the great basic industries, coal, gas, electricity, transport, representation on consultative councils to the Boards was given them as a matter of course.

At the end of 1962 the total membership of British trade unions was about 9,872,000. There were 623 unions, but about two-thirds of all trade unionists were in the eighteen largest unions; over half were in eight large unions with a membership of over 250,000.*

Less than half of the country's 24 million employees are in unions affiliated to the Trades Union Congress. Yet the power of the unions has been stretched to the point of changing the law. In 1964 occurred the now famous House of Lords decision in the case of *Rookes* v. *Barnard*. In 1955 Rookes resigned from his union, the Draughtsmen's and Allied Technicians' Union, and refused to rejoin. The other draughtsmen threatened to strike unless Rookes was dismissed. Rookes was dismissed by B.O.A.C. in 1956. Rookes sued Barnard and the other union officers for damages. The Queen's Bench Division of the High Court awarded him damages of £7000 in 1961. The case went to the Court of Appeal in 1962 and to the House of Lords in 1964. Rookes was upheld, but the amount of damages was in question; and eventually in 1965 damages were settled out of court for £4000.

The subsequent story followed the pattern which we have seen being built up in the history of the unions. A Bill was introduced by the Labour Government to protect the unions from being sued for intimidation. The Bill, the Trades Disputes Bill, was defeated in the House of Lords, but became law in 1965.

The political activities of trade unions have not been without their critics. There have been those who have stated it as their view that the unions have gone beyond their true functions in concerning themselves directly with politics—their objects are essentially economic. Certainly those prominent members of unions who have taken up political posts have often been embarrassed by the activities of the rank-and-file, who have, in their turn, complained that those who have reached high positions in the State have tended to forget the interests of their more lowly placed comrades. The flinging wide of the net of the Labour Party to include men and women of all social grades has tended to make it much less of a trade union Party; while many trade unionists and other wage-earners belong to other parties (two-thirds of the electorate are wage-earners and their dependants, but until 1945 the Labour Party never secured more than 37% of the votes cast). The Labour Party has thus become more 'Socialist' than 'labour'; and a Labour Government may be as much embarrassed by trade union activities in industrial disputes as a Conservative one.

The National Incomes Commission established by the Government in 1962 to review wage claims and advise on their justification did not

*See *Labour Relations and Conditions of Work in Britain* (Central Office of Information Pamphlet 31, H.M.S.O., 1965).

find favour with the unions. Even less to their taste was the National Board for Prices and Incomes which succeeded it in 1965. The appointment of an ex-Tory Minister as Chairman of the Board (illustrating once more the somewhat fictitious character of Party labels) did nothing to alleviate their apprehension that the new Board was going to be 'tough.'

Trade union leaders had gone to Sweden to observe the working of national wage agreements with a legal framework, such as obtained

1799 ⎱ Combination Acts
1800 ⎰

1824 Combination Acts repealed (Joseph Hume and Francis Place)

1832 FIRST REFORM ACT

ATTEMPTS TO FORM A NATIONAL TRADES UNION		1850: THE 'NEW MODEL' TRADE UNIONISM	
1834: Grand National Consolidated Trades Union (Robert Owen)		1867: SECOND REFORM ACT; *Hornby* v. *Close* 1871: Legal Recognition of Trade Unionism	
'Tolpuddle Martyrs'	1845: National Association of United Trades for the protection of labour	1880s: THE 'NEW UNIONISM' (unskilled workers)	
Movement collapsed		1900s: Restrictions on Union Action	1872: UNION OF AGRICULTURAL LABOURERS
	1867: Petered out	Rise of Labour Party 1901: *Taff Vale Judgment* 1906: Trade Disputes Act 1909: *Osborne Judgment*	Trade Unionism in agriculture not very successful
1914–18: FIRST WORLD WAR		1926: General Strike 1927: Trade Disputes and Trade Union Act	
1939–45: SECOND WORLD WAR		1945: Labour Government in power. Repeal of Trade Disputes and Trade Union Act *Labour Governments*: 1964 and 1966 1965: Trade Disputes Act (following *Rookes* v. *Barnard*, 1964)	

CHART 17—*The Lines of Development of British Trade Unionism*

also in Holland and West Germany, and had reported that the system would not 'work' in Britain. The British people, tired of the occurrence of unofficial strikes, often over trivial matters, and of the determined resistance to change shown by the trade union leaders, were inclining to the view that it was time the British trade union movement became a responsible one, recognising that its own health depended on that of the country as a whole. The bitter experience of the past still lay heavy, it seemed, on the attitude of the trade unions.

5. THE DEVELOPMENT OF THE SOCIAL SERVICES

The 'Welfare State' of twentieth-century Britain is the culmination of the social and economic consequences of the Industrial Revolution. In no other way could British society have retained its cohesiveness in the face of industrial expansion and social stress, for that industrial expansion was based upon the profit-making motive which is a fundamental economic aim of humanity. *Laissez-faire* is human instinct; and it is only by the taming and directing of instincts that human progress is made.

The unequal division of wealth and the social and political features resulting from it might have been fairly tolerable in a previous more simply organised age—though the Peasants' Revolt of 1381 had shown that there were limits to human toleration of toil and servitude. Under the Feudal System the peasant possessed security, and could rely on a certain amount of protection from the lord of the manor. Such destitution as occurred was relieved by the Church, and the gilds exercised the functions of friendly societies as well as those of professional associations.

The spread of pasture farming and the displacement of the villeins caused unemployment and vagrancy; and the end of the Wars of the Roses let loose on the countryside the survivors of the baronial retinues. The decay of the gilds and the dissolution of the monasteries by Henry VIII intensified the problem. Severe laws were enacted against able-bodied beggars, and a compulsory poor-rate came into existence in 1572. The Poor Law of 1601 consolidated previous legislation; the parish was the unit of poor-law administration.

During the last quarter of the seventeenth century statesmen adopted the idea of 'farming out' the poor; the 'managers' of workhouses were able to undertake the relief of destitution in the surrounding parishes in return for an annual payment. This system was abolished in 1792. The Speenhamland system has already been mentioned.* Its cessation came with the appointment of the Poor Law Commission of 1834.

The first half of the nineteenth century, though it brought wealth

* See p. 77.

to the rising new middle class, was a period of widespread distress for the working classes. During the war period of 1793–1815 prices rose faster than wages. The drift of agricultural workers to the towns, the bearing down by employers on wages to meet competition, the turning of ex-soldiers to civilian life—these influences tended to force workers' wages down. Resentment of the labour-saving machinery resulted in outbursts of machine-breaking organised by the Luddites; and the Government retaliated by passing, in 1819, the Six Acts, which among other things restricted public meetings and placed a heavy stamp duty on workmen's pamphlets.

Parliamentary reform was demanded by the Chartists; their last petition was presented, and rejected, in 1848, and the coming of better times resulted in the dying out of the movement—but not before public opinion had been so influenced that eventually the reforms demanded by the Chartists came to pass.

The pressure of events broke down the *laissez-faire* attitude of the Government in the second half of the nineteenth century. The first effective Factory Act was passed in 1833; the first Act of Parliament regulating conditions in coal-mines, prohibiting the employment of women and children, was passed in 1842. Successive Truck Acts from 1831 onwards had as their object the ensuring of payment to work-men in cash and the prohibition of unwarrantable deductions from wages in respect of food, fuel, etc. The Trade Boards Acts, 1909 and 1918, fought 'sweating' in industry by providing machinery for wage negotiation in badly organised trades; they were subsequently super-seded by the Wages Councils Acts, 1945–59.

The 'nineteenth century' went on until 1914, a year which saw the outbreak of the First World War and the beginning of an era of rapid change whose nature began to be apparent only in the inter-war years and after the Second World War. It was, and is, an era in which Man's control over his physical environment seems to have limitless possibilities, and the problem of poverty seems absurdly anachronistic. But the problem appears to have been tackled not on the lines of increasing wealth so much as sharing out more equitably what there is.

The conception of the social services comprising what is called the 'Welfare State', as distinct from dealing with particular problems as they occurred, such as factory hours of works and conditions, had its origin in conscious attempts to meet the perennial and fundamental problem of poverty, poverty as it was experienced in a new world of congested towns, slums, factories and ill-health. In the 'Hungry Forties' of the nineteenth century, a pathetic and tragic army shuffles despondently through the pages of history—a boy of eleven, charged with breaking into a house and stealing oatmeal, sentenced to fifteen months' imprisonment and dying in gaol from starvation; a report of

60 out of 220 'female child paupers' in St Pancras sick from want of proper food; 10,085 child paupers recorded as having Christmas dinner of beef and potatoes in London in 1848; children charged in the Courts with sleeping at night on roofs, under arches, in pigsties.

The springing up of new towns to accommodate the increasing population of industrial workers led to the provision of houses without the decencies of life, to diseases like cholera, typhus and small-pox—conditions which received scant attention from the Government until the well-to-do were threatened.

The question of sanitation occupied a large part of the attention of Edwin Chadwick (1800–90), a lawyer who was associated with the work of the reforming philosopher, Jeremy Bentham. Chadwick's future career was decided when he was offered a post as one of the assistant Commissioners appointed in 1832 to enquire into the Poor Law. The Speenhamland system* was pauperising the country. The 'farming-out' system, by which people were hired out to farmers and others who would pay the parish a contribution towards their keep, had been abolished by Gilbert's Act of 1782. The Poor Law distinguished between those paupers who were able-bodied and those who were not; for the latter there was the workhouse erected by the parishes, for the former the Speenhamland system. By the end of the century the general 'mixed' workhouse was the common type of institution for the poor.

The Report of the Poor Law Commission, largely Chadwick's work, was published in 1834. A Poor Law Amendment Act was passed creating a Poor Law Board, of which Chadwick became the Secretary, employing a ruthless administration by which the 16,000 parishes were combined into 660 Poor Law Unions, providing workhouses into which a man wanting relief had to go unless he could find work. Chadwick's suggestion that there should be separate institutions for the separate classes of the destitute—the aged and infirm, the children of paupers, the workless—was not adopted. Parishes were grouped into Unions under the control of elected Boards of Guardians.

The horror of the workhouse, the 'institution,' has lasted in the minds of old people until the present day; entering a workhouse was the last degradation. Its memory, its legend, still influences the poor genteel who are shy of accepting the 'national assistance' or 'social security payments' offered by a benevolent State. Independence is dear to the hearts of the old-type 'middle classes.'

As far as the rural areas were concerned, the Act was successful: the confusion between what was wages and what was poor relief disappeared, and the workers were absorbed into agriculture or industry. But in the towns, and in the industrial North particularly, there was violent resistance from the under-employed workers, agitation which

* See p. 77.

was not quietened until better times came following the repeal of the Corn Laws in 1846.*

Abuses in the administration of the poor law were disclosed by the never-tactful Chadwick, and he paid the usual penalty by losing in 1846 his post as Secretary of the Board.

The poor were by no means all content to suffer the slings and arrows of outrageous fortune without making some effort to mitigate their plight. Small benefit clubs and fraternities to provide funeral insurance against the dreaded pauper burial expanded into Friendly Societies, some of which, like the Oddfellows and the Foresters, became national organisations: they were to be made use of later in the national health scheme promoted by Lloyd George in 1911. The trade unions also organised provident society activities; and insurance companies entered what they saw to be a profitable field by offering 'industrial insurance': insurance in which the small weekly premiums were paid to house-to-house collectors. The first such company was the Prudential Assurance Company, founded in 1854.

In 1892 Charles Booth published his *Life and Labour of the People in London*. It was beginning to be realised that the problem of poverty was of such a magnitude that only the State could deal with it; but the State was somewhat reluctant. A Royal Commission on the Aged Poor reported in 1895, exposing evils but suggesting no solutions. It was not until 1908 that an Old Age Pensions Act was passed; it gave 5s. a week to all over 70 whose means were below £21 per annum.

In 1908 there was a Report of the Poor Law Commission appointed in 1905; there were in fact two Reports, a Majority Report and a Minority Report. The Majority Report was inclined to retain the stigma attached to poverty; relief out of the workhouse, outdoor relief, was to be given only in cases of dire necessity. It recommended the abolition of the Boards of Guardians and the taking over of their functions by the local authorities, the counties and county boroughs. This did not happen until the reorganisation of local government under the terms of the Local Government Act, 1929.

The Minority Report, largely the work of those famous reformers, Beatrice and Sidney Webb, was much more revolutionary—so revolutionary as to frighten the Liberal Ministers. It ranged beyond the suggestions of the Majority Report relating to the reorganisation of poor law administration, advocating the setting up of Labour Exchanges and a Ministry of Labour. The basic idea of the Poor Law was to be scrapped: in effect, the State should provide a minimum standard of subsistence.

It took the First World War to change even the name of the workhouse; and a Second World War to abolish the old Poor Law.

In the meantime, a sudden increase in the death-rate in the industrial

* See pp. 76–77.

centres, further attacks of cholera and the adding of occupational diseases like lead poisoning and anthrax to the list of diseases resulting from foul living conditions pointed to the necessity of action for public health. In 1832 James Kay published *The Moral and Physical Condition of the Working Classes*. Edwin Chadwick, as indefatigable in the pursuit of public health as in getting some order out of the Poor Law, published in 1842 his *Report on the Sanitary Condition of the Labouring Population*. Dr Southwood Smith wrote in 1844 on the results of overcrowding, his findings being endorsed by a Report on the *Housing Conditions of the Working Classes*. The first effective Housing Act was passed in 1890—though, again, it was not until after the First World War that practical steps of significance in public housing were made.

The first Public Health Act was passed in 1848—the year Chadwick was awarded the C.B. for his labours. A Central Board of Health was constituted, with Chadwick as one of the members and in effect running the Board. It lasted for six years, supervising the sanitary law for the towns and populous districts. By that time the authorities had decided that they could bear Chadwick's forceful ways and determination no longer. *The Times* said: 'We prefer to take our chance with cholera and the rest, than be bullied into health.' Chadwick was retired at 54, his conception of the sanitary idea lying dormant with the authorities until its realisation became inevitable.

The political pressure of the newly enfranchised working class spurred the authorities to new efforts in the causes of public health and the treatment of the poor. By the end of the nineteenth century the number of hospitals was increasing, adding to the facilities of the Poor Law Dispensaries. The plight of the aged poor was engaging the attention of the Government. The old Poor Law received its first death-blow when the Old Age Pensions Act of 1908 was passed; it had been delayed by the Boer War. The cost was £8½ million.

The Liberals of the early twentieth century projected reforms which were held up by the Lords. Lloyd George's Budget of 1909 started a battle between Lords and Commons which culminated in the Parliament Act, 1911: the power of the Lords over finance was abolished and their power to delay Bills reduced to two years—to be further reduced to one year by the Parliament Act, 1949.

Inspired by the German scheme initiated by Bismarck, Lloyd George in 1911 introduced a national insurance scheme: the National Insurance Act, providing for insurance against sickness, using as his agencies the 'Approved Societies': the friendly societies which had already built up administrative services. This machinery was to last until 1946.

As for his pension scheme, old people today are still heard to speak gratefully of 'the Lloyd George pension.'

The Chamberlain Government of 1925 introduced a contributory pension scheme. Though the Government did not go so far as to provide a single scheme for health and unemployment and pensions, the pension scheme was linked with health insurance. In 1937 people who were outside the scope of the national scheme, the 'black-coated' workers, were admitted as 'voluntary contributors.' The insurance idea and the flat-rate contribution were to persist in the story of Britain's social services reforms.

A Royal Commission on Unemployment reported in 1932, and distinguished between insurance and relief. Under the Unemployment Act, 1934, those who had lost their entitlement to insurance benefit were placed under the care of an Unemployment Assistance Board. No longer did the able-bodied have to go to an institution to receive relief. The Public Assistance Committees which had been established in 1930 were linked in the public mind with the poor law; and the 'transitional payments' system, with inspectors calling round to enquire into means, had done nothing to remove that impression.

The chairman of the Unemployment Assistance Board was Sir William Beveridge, who had created effective Labour Exchanges and who was trying to mitigate the hardships of the years of depression of the 1930s. It changed its title to 'Assistance Board' in 1940, and its benefits were dispensed to the accompaniment of a household means test. It lasted until 1948.

But this was the period of the Second World War; the abolition of the means test came in 1941. In 1941 an Interdepartmental Committee on Social Insurance and Allied Services was set up to survey the existing national schemes of social insurance. Its chairman was Sir William Beveridge. In 1942 appeared *Social Insurance and Allied Services** : the Beveridge Report, for he alone was responsible for its findings.

The mood of the country can be judged by the fact that the Beveridge Report was a 'best-seller.' Beveridge caught the imagination of the people. The Government was cautious and in fact disapproving of this revolutionary plan. Though recommending the establishment of a single Ministry of Social Security—realised at last in 1966—Beveridge regarded his Report as not a complete plan for social security in itself: it was concerned with only one of the 'Five Giants' that barred the way to reconstruction and social progress. It dealt with Want; the other Giants to be tackled were Disease, through a comprehensive health service; Ignorance, through reforms of the educational system; Squalor, by a housing programme; and Idleness, by an organisation of the labour market and securing a stable economy.

The Government plans appeared as White Papers in 1944: *A National Health Service*; *Employment Policy*; *Social Insurance*. In 1944, too, an Education Act set up a Ministry of Education.

* Cmd. 6404, November, 1942.

National health insurance, the public health work of local authorities, their housing activities, and the hospital administration of the Poor Law had been brought together by the creation of the Ministry of Health in 1919. The Poor Law administration had gone to the local authorities in 1929. The hospital service was a confusion. It was not until the Public Health Act of 1936, which replaced the 1875 Act, that public hospitals were given power to provide out-patient departments. In 1944 a comprehensive hospital scheme was envisaged.

In 1946 the modern 'Welfare State' was ushered in by legislation. The National Insurance and National Health Service came into being on 5th July 1948. The old Poor Law was at last dead, replaced by 'social assistance'; by 1966 the Government was in the strange position of appealing to those who were ignorant of the new benefits and those who were still chary of receiving what they obstinately regarded as 'public assistance' to come forward and claim their rights. Family allowances were available for all but the first child. Yet, it seems unaccountably, poverty still exists, especially among those whose fecundity outruns their ability to deal with it.

Insurance guards against the worst effects of illness, industrial injury, unemployment, retirement with its reduced income. Hospitals have been grouped under Regional Hospital Boards; the services of general practitioners and specialists have become freely available; research in medical science steadily decreases the number of diseases which have been scourges in the past. The local authorities dispense a host of personal services, especially in such preventive services as are connected with midwives, maternity and child welfare, health visitors, the disabled.

The cost of the National Insurance, Pensions and Assistance schemes rose from £825 million in 1952 to over £1800 million in 1962. The National Health Service cost £450 million in 1952; £950 million in 1962: the latter figure was 3·8% of the Gross National Product. The Guillebaud Committee of Enquiry into the National Health Service had been expected in its Report of 1956 to recommend a cutting down of expenditure (£430,500,000 in 1953–54); but it recommended instead increased expenditure.

In 1966 the insurance, pensions and assistance administrative machinery came together into the Ministry of Social Security.

Giants Want and Disease were and are being vigorously attacked. Giant Idleness has not been much in evidence since the coming of full employment since the Second World War and the coming of the Affluent Society. But the 1966 depression in the motor-car industry in Britain reminded the country that he could revive unless notice was taken of the advice of his foe, Lord Beveridge: *Full Employment in a Free Society* is still relevant to the age.

Giant Squalor has been attacked first by the Ministry of Health and by its successors in housing policy, the Ministry of Local Government and Planning in 1951 and now the Ministry of Housing and Local Government. Various Housing Acts have provided dwellings for what were called until the Housing Act 1949 removed the expression, the 'working classes.' The Housing (Finance and Miscellaneous Provisions) Act, 1946, provided for a general standard subsidy for housing by local authorities in England and Wales. The clearing of slums and of overcrowding was allocated to the local authorities. Rent rebate schemes have reduced rents to what a family may be considered to afford. The principles of housing management, first realised and advocated by Octavia Hill in the middle of the nineteenth century, have been studied and increasingly applied.

In town planning, Ebenezer Howard's *Garden Cities of Tomorrow* (1898) with its ideas of cities limited in size and each surrounded by a green belt may seem remote from the congested industrial areas of today. A Ministry of Town and Country Planning was created in 1943 to implement the major proposals of the Barlow Committee on the Geographical Location of the Industrial Population (1940), the Scott Committee on Land Utilisation in Rural Areas (1942) and the Uthwatt Committee on Compensation and Betterment (1942). The Town and Country Planning Act, 1962, consolidated previous legislation. The New Towns Acts, 1946 to 1949, were concerned with the creation of new towns initially through the agency of Development Corporations; the Town Development Act, 1952, provided for the settling of 'overspill' populations.

The details of such social planning have become too numerous, involved and technical to be more than indicated in outline in such a work as this, concerned mainly with the relationship of the social services to industrial organisation. That relationship itself has become so complex, with its threads stretching to factory legislation, the activities and aspirations of the trade unions, the organisation of industry with its monopolies and combinations and restrictive practices, its communications, the organisation of the managerial and supervisory activities of the State, that it would require a very knowledgeable and all-embracing mind to comprehend all its implications.

There does appear to have been too intimate a relationship between the 'Welfare State' and the 'Affluent Society.' There are implications of danger in the latter expression; and if it is to be of real value, the Welfare State itself must tend to be self-liquidating: its activities must be so successful that, for example, there would be no part of it dealing with 'problem families' because 'problem families' would no longer exist. The Welfare State or Social Services State is not an end in itself; it is a means whereby each individual may be enabled best to pursue what he regards as the Good Life. It is because of the terrible power possessed by the Giant Ignorance that the words attributed to Gladstone can be aptly applied in a democracy which has witnessed the triumph of the 'working classes':

> *You will have temptation sent you—you, the labouring people of this country, and when you have become supreme to such a degree that there is no other power to balance and counteract the power you possess you will have approaching you a deep and searching moral control.*
>
> *You will have to preserve the balance of your mind and character when you have fought the struggle with the capitalist and aristocrat and great mercantile classes. When you have become in a sense the political masters you have still before you one achievement to fulfil, one glory to attain and to appropriate to yourselves—to continue to be just.*

6. The Education of the People

Education can hardly be described as a 'social service': it is a necessity of life. Instruction is a prerequisite; it may be described as a service which the State owes to the people. What they do with instruction once they have acquired the facts of a given subject is the individual's affair as far as his own personal education is concerned.

By the eighteenth century there were endowed grammar schools, some with a history extending back to the sixteenth century; many of them became 'public schools,' catering for those who would become the natural leaders in industry, commerce, the Church and the professions. Elementary instruction was given to 'Dame' and Charity schools, established under the auspices of such societies as the Society for the Promotion of Christian Knowledge. In 1780 Robert Raikes established Sunday Schools, which not only imparted religious knowledge but also gave instruction in reading, writing and arithmetic; for the poor there were 'ragged schools,' founded by John Pounds, a schoolmaster, providing for destitute children; though it is also held that Robert Raikes was the pioneer of this movement.

For girls there were private schools, Charity schools and Sunday schools.

Apprenticeship training and trade gilds provided some sort of technical education. In the late eighteenth century a small number of schools of industry were established, combining elementary instruction with technical training. Robert Owen founded in 1816 an infant school for his employees, and his example was followed by a few enlightened industrialists.

Oxford and Cambridge provided opportunity for the further study of the classics pursued at the public schools.

Charity schools and the schools of industry were declining by the end of the eighteenth century. The Industrial Revolution had produced a crop of 'wild and mischievous' child workers, catered for by the Sunday school movement.

Public Health	Poverty	Housing and Town Planning	Child Care
1842: *Report on the Sanitary Condition of the Labouring Population* (Chadwick) 1848: First Public Health Act; Central Board of Health 1875: Public Health Act: permitted the setting up of municipal hospitals; provision for by-laws relating to housing standards 1911: National Insurance Act (Lloyd George): Part I: National Health Insurance. Use of 'Approved Societies' in adminstration 1919: Creation of Ministry of Health 1936: Public Health Act, superseding 1875 Act and consolidating previous legislation. Public hospitals given power to provide out-patient accommodation 1946: National Health Service Act; National Insurance (Industrial Injuries) Act 1948: National Health Scheme came into operation	1834: Poor Law Amendment Act: Boards of Guardians, supervising Poor Law Unions Origin of Friendly Societies Industrial assurance from 1854 1895: Report of Royal Commission on Aged Poor 1908: Old Age Pensions Act 1908: Majority and Minority Reports of Poor Law Commission 1911: National Insurance Act. Part II: a limited scheme of unemployment insurance. 1925: Contributory Pension Scheme 1929: Local Government Act: abolition of Boards of Guardians; C. councils and C. boroughs Poor Law authorities 1930: Public Assistance Committees; means test. 1934: Unemployment Act: Unemployment Assistance Board 1940: Assistance Board; household means test 1941: Abolition of household means test 1942: Beveridge Report 1944: Ministry of National Insurance created 1945: Family Allowances Act 1946: National Insurance Act 1948: National Insurance Scheme came into operation 1948: National Assistance Act 1966: Ministry of Social Security: insurance, pensions, national assistance	First effective Housing Act, 1890 1919: Housing and Town Planning Act: subsidised houses 1924: Housing Act: a million 'Council houses' built between the wars 1930: Slum clearance scheme 1935: Housing Act: set out an official standard for overcrowding 1946: General standard subsidy; special subsidy for agricultural workers' houses 1951: Ministry of Local Government and Planning took over housing functions from Ministry of Health (subsequently Ministry of Housing and Local Government) 1916–65: Various Rent Acts 1946: New Towns Act 1952: Town Development Act 1962: Town Planning Act	1906: Provision of Meals Act: permitted local authorities to provide school meals 1907: Compulsory medical inspection of schoolchildren 1934: Milk Act (cheap milk) 1944: Education Act: duty of L.E.A. to provide milk, meals, etc., for day pupils Children and Young Person Acts, 1933–1963: 1948: Children Act: Home Office became Govt. Dept. responsible for care of deprived children Each county borough and county council to appoint a Children's Committee and a Children's Officer. Boarding out and institutional care for deprived children 1963: Children Act: extended the power and duty of local authorities to promote the welfare of children and young persons

CHART 18—*The Development of the Social Services*

In the nineteenth century were established two groups of schools run by religious bodies: elementary schools for boys and girls were established by the nonconformist British and Foreign Schools Society and by the National Society, sponsored by the Church of England. Warfare broke out between the two groups on the question of religious instruction—warfare which bedevilled the course of English education and for a hundred years hampered and confused the cause of the education of the people in any sort of Platonic sense: 'seeing things in proportion' and the 'education of the whole man' were far from the ideas of people who believed that education should be propaganda rather than instruction.

By 1820 the necessity for some sort of education of the people if they were to attain to anything like the efficiency of dumb machinery was evident. Parliament appointed a Select Committee on the Education of the Lower Orders. A Bill introduced by Brougham in 1820 was opposed by both the religious groups.

In 1832 came the first Reform Act; and Parliament received petitions for the reform of education. The 'Children's Charter,' the Factory Act of 1833, laid down that the hours of work of children of nine to thirteen should be limited to eight a day; they were to attend schools provided by their employers. The under-nines were not to be employed at all.

In 1833 Parliament granted £20,000 to the societies for buildings, and after a debate on the paucity of the sum, added another £10,000. The societies opened training colleges for teachers with this money.

The Church was hostile to the idea of training colleges set up by the State, where undenominational religious instruction would be given; and neither group could bear the idea of contributing through taxation money which would be used to aid the educational efforts of the other group.

Dr Kay, of sanitary and housing fame (he was to change his name later to Kay-Shuttleworth) was also interested in the education of the young and education in the Mechanics' Institute which had been founded. His work with the Poor Law Commission and his search for enlightenment led him to study schools and teaching methods in England, in Scotland, and on the Continent. He became convinced that the monitorial system used in the Church and nonconformist schools was useless. The pupil training system which he introduced in 1846 lasted to within living memory. He himself started a training college for teachers at Battersea, adopting Swiss models. The college was not a success and was eventually handed over to the National Society; by 1845 the Church school authorities had established 22 training colleges.

It was generally agreed at the time that religious instruction was an essential part of education. By the 1840s the National Schools were more numerous than the nonconformist schools; the Church based its religious teaching on the Catechism. The Oxford Movement strongly supported Church teaching as a condition of entrance to the schools. Until 1870 the acrimonious battles between the rival religious groups frustrated attempts to found a system of national elementary education.

In 1846 the Committee of the Privy Council concerned with public education became the Education Department.

Grants to schools by the Government were made on a payments-by-results basis: attendance and examination results. It was many years after the cessation of the system in 1897 before the cloud on the relations between the teachers and the Government Inspectors raised by this unhappy system was dispersed.

In the meantime, Durham University was founded in 1832; and the University of London, at that time as an examining body only, in 1836. New public schools were being established.

In 1867 came the Second Reform Act. Reform of the educational system could no longer be delayed. In 1870 came the first Education Act for England and Wales, the 'Forster Act.' Locally elected School Boards were to provide elementary schools in areas where there were insufficient voluntary schools. There was thus a dual system of 'Board' and 'Voluntary' Schools.

By the Board of Education Act, 1899, the Board of Education was established; it never met as a Board. By this time there were 20,000 schools, a quarter of them under School Boards set up by the 1870 Act and three-quarters under religious or voluntary bodies, maintained by rates and Government grants in the case of the Board Schools and by subscriptions and grants in the case of the voluntary schools. There were no public secondary and technical schools; but the Science and Art Department and the county and county borough councils gave grants in aid of this kind of instruction. Adult education existed in the form of university Extension work. There were 62 training colleges; and special schools for blind and deaf and handicapped children under relevant legislation. There was no system of medical inspection and treatment for children of the normal public system.

The course of public education at this time was influenced by Sir Robert Morant (1863–1920), an official in the Education Department who had acted as tutor to the Crown Prince of Siam and who familiarised himself with educational developments in France and Switzerland, and with the Bryce Report on Secondary Education, published in 1895. The Report recommended that there should be a central authority for public education and that Local Education Authorities should be instituted.

The first recommendation was implemented when the Board of Education was created. The second was more difficult of attainment.

Morant was concerned with promoting a sound secondary education system in the country, welding it out of the confusion of the 'higher grade' elementary schools catering for the more advanced pupils, the endowed schools under the care of the Charity Commissioners, and the 'science' schools and classes which were operating under grant from the Science and Art Departments in all sorts of places like grammar schools and evening continuation schools. He realised that the School Boards had to be abolished, and that the voluntary schools, much more numerous than the Board Schools and urgently in need of funds, had to be aided out of the rates. Naturally enough, the Boards were fiercely opposed to their own abolition; and the non-conformists were bitterly opposed to the aiding of the voluntary schools, the greater part of which were National Schools.

Morant forced the issue by an ingenious manoeuvre; at his instigation, a local government auditor, a Mr T. Barclay Cockerton, ruled that the London School Board had acted illegally in providing 'higher' education out of the rates. This 'Cockerton Judgment' was upheld in the Court of Appeal.

Something had to be done; and it was done by the Education Act, 1902. It constituted the county and county borough councils Local Education Authorities, dealing with higher education; and the councils of boroughs with a population of over 10,000 and of urban districts with a population of over 20,000 became Local Education Authorities for elementary education. Thus the Board Schools became 'Council' Schools, also known as 'provided' schools because the buildings were provided by the Local Education Authorities; the voluntary schools were 'non-provided' schools.

The First World War had as its inevitable result the stimulation of ideas on the reconstruction of the economic and social structure; a Ministry of Reconstruction was created in 1916. In 1918 an Education Act, the Fisher Act (H. A. L. Fisher was President of the Board of Education) abolished fees in secondary schools, extended the powers and duties of the Local Education Authorities in relation to physical education, provided for medical inspection and treatment for secondary school pupils, stated that the period of compulsory education at school should be from five to fourteen, and gave powers to L.E.A.s to provide nursery schools—rather as a consequence of mothers going out to work than on educational principle.

Day continuation schools were envisaged; but continuation schools with compulsory attendance have never been seriously attempted (except for a brief period in the 1930s when Junior Instruction Centres for unemployed boys and girls were operated by local authorities). Not only were there difficulties in the way of providing buildings and teachers but the idea of compulsory education—itself a contradiction in terms—has proved a glamorous one neither to teachers nor to the prospective victims.

A Secondary Schools Examination Council was established, and university examining bodies; the story was begun of the School Certificate, G.C.E., and, recently, the Certificate of Secondary Education for those unable to reach the General School Certificate level.

The 200 State Scholarships which were introduced formed the first rungs in the ladder 'from school to university' which had been the dream of social reformers. An Adult Education Committee was also established.

A period of slump in economic activity after the boom years put a temporary halt to the fulfilment of educational schemes; Rugby was the only place in which the day continuation school idea came into being. Attempts to raise the school-leaving age to fifteen failed.

In 1926 came the Report of the Hadow Committee appointed by the Labour Government: the famous *Education of the Adolescent*. It took a somewhat idealistic view of adolescence: 'There is a tide which begins to rise in the veins of youth at the age of eleven or twelve. If that tide can be taken at the flood, and a new voyage begun in the strength and flow of its current, we think that it will move on to fortune.' Its influence resulted in the 'eleven-plus' break in educational development.

There came a new terminology: 'primary' and 'secondary' schools; the 'central' or 'senior' or 'higher grade' elementary schools became secondary schools. The 1902 secondary schools became 'grammar' schools. Hadow said nothing about the technical schools, regarded at this time in the light of schools for 'rude mechanicals.' Many private firms were releasing their employees for part-time day instruction. Technical education had in fact a lowly origin: it was born out of the 'whisky money' intended to recompense publicans for the loss of their licences.

In the new grammar schools education tended to copy that given in the public schools: the classics, the organisation into houses, the prefect system, compulsory games. It was not education for a new world in which knowledge of that world and the insistence on clear thinking on the issues of that world were paramount considerations. One disadvantage of the learning of Latin was that there was little future in, say, the translation of the classics: it had all been done. Certainly there was appreciated the value of the idea of 'I teach John' instead of 'I teach John Latin'; but for the most part John got the instruction which would enable him to pass the School Certificate Examination, and was often the plaything of theorists and administrators. There was little guidance on life in general and no Careers Masters at that time. Still, John was subjected to the mental disciplines he found in the study of his subjects; and the grammar schools of his day, the municipal secondary schools, gave to the new 'lower middle' or 'working' classes the opportunities for a great expansion of mental horizons.

There was as yet no recognition that technology could also comprise education in a broad sense; science, and the history and implications of science, tended to be neglected. Academic tradition had not broken away from the medieval ideas.

But the efforts of those who were trying to find their way in a new world amid the ideas on education of the old world—the reading, writing, arithmetic instruction at the one extreme and the writing of Latin and Greek verse at the other—are not to be discounted or despised. In 1931 came the Hadow Report on the Primary Schools and in 1933 the Hadow Report on the Nursery Schools. The Education Act of 1936 raised the school-leaving age to fifteen; but with provisions for exemption for 'beneficial employment.' The War nullified its proposals.

The Spens Report of 1938 was concerned with the organisation of secondary education in three forms of schools: grammar, technical and modern. It considered the possibilities of the 'multilateral' school —now called 'comprehensive.' The idea of the 'comprehensive' school did not find favour with the Committee.

In the 1940s came the Norwood Report (1943) on the relations between the different types of secondary school; the Fleming Report (1944) on the question of the relations between the public schools and the general educational system; the McNair Report (1944) on the training of teachers and youth leaders; the Percy Report (1945) on the co-ordination of the work of the bodies concerned with technological education: the warning of the competition of other countries in using applied science was beginning to be heeded.

A comprehensive attempt to reform the educational system was made in the Education Act, 1944. The old division into elementary and 'higher' education was replaced by a new classification of public education into three progressive stages: primary education, secondary education and further education. It shall be, said the Act, the duty of every local education authority to secure that there shall be available for their area sufficient schools for providing primary and secondary education, 'and the schools available shall not be deemed to be sufficient unless they are sufficient in number, character and equipment to afford for all pupils opportunities for education, offering such variety of instruction and training as may be desirable in view of their different ages, abilities, and aptitudes, and of the different periods for which they may be expected to remain at school, including practical instruction and training appropriate to their respective needs' (Section 8).

Section 36 said: 'It shall be the duty of the parent of every child of compulsory school age to cause him to receive efficient full-time education suitable to his age, ability, and aptitude, either by regular attendance at school or otherwise'—the latter provision to cause later some trouble to an education authority disapproving of a parent giving personal instruction to her children. The section, in fact, could give rise to reflections whether the local authorities which, in the 1960s, imposed their systems of comprehensive education on the schools in their area were not contravening the law.

The Act provided for the raising of the school-leaving age to fifteen, and for the compulsory inspection and supervision of private schools. It raised the question of the day continuation school again, announcing the intention, 'in due course' to establish 'county colleges' for young people who had left school before reaching the age of eighteen.

From now on came a spate of reports on various facets of the educational scene. Among them the demands of technology were of significance in a world in which other countries, including the U.S.S.R., had shown an increasing awareness of the opportunities available for gaining a greater command of the material environment. A revolution similar to that in which the men of the Stone Ages turned to metal was in progress.

The universities, if not Stone Age in outlook, retained much of the spirit of medieval exclusiveness. The Chairman of the Percy Committee which reported in 1945 had proclaimed, by his denial that it existed, the existence of the universities' suspicion of, and antagonism towards, the technological institutions which threatened their claim to represent the heights of knowledge. The universities by now included a number of recently established institutions, many of them former 'university colleges' whose students took the external degrees of London University. They looked upon their charters as certificates of promotion to the status of institutions of Higher Learning. They enjoyed a favoured position as drawing their funds from the University Grants Committee financed by Parliament, and claimed an 'academic freedom' in some instances very broadly interpreted—a pleasant status which later the Teachers' Training Colleges, as distinct from the Education Departments of universities, sought vainly to achieve. The question which the universities resented was that relating to the suggested award of a degree to successful technological students. A university degree, the universities felt, was something more than a certificate that the holder had passed certain academic examinations.

In 1951, in the statement *Higher Technological Education*, the Government accepted the recommendations of the National Advisory Council on Education for Industry and Commerce. It proposed the establishment of a College of Technology to grant awards to students taking courses in higher technology.

In 1956 the Government announced a five-year programme in technical education, and announced a classification of technical colleges into Local Colleges, providing courses up to 'Ordinary National Certificate' level; Area Colleges, providing varying amounts of ad-

G

vanced work; Regional Colleges, doing a substantial amount of advanced work; and Colleges of Advanced Technology, providing a broad range of work exclusively at advanced level. Subsequently, several of the Colleges of Advanced Technology achieved the status of universities. In 1965 the National Council for Academic Awards, which took over the work of the College of Technology, announced its intention to award first and higher degrees.

News of what was going on in the universities, apart from advanced work in science, seemed in the Press to be concerned mostly with demands by students for complete freedom in everything. Proposals that students should repay loans from the authorities for their maintenance and tuition by instalments from their salaries when they secured jobs, met with vehement denunciation from the students.

By this time the implications of a technological age for the social and economic structure generally of society were becoming apparent. The myth of the illiteracy of scientists and technologists was finally dispelled; the meaning of the term 'culture' was being re-examined. The more progressive of the universities discouraged early and extreme specialisation on the part of their students, demanded that the arts students should know something about science and that science students should know something about the arts.

The Crowther Report, '15–18' (1959) made proposals for the further education of people between these ages, and recommended that the school-leaving age should be raised to sixteen. It advised the postponement of the establishment of 'county colleges' to the 1970s, but supported part-time day attendance of young people at centres of further education.

The Albemarle Report of 1960 was concerned with the Youth Service; the Anderson Report (1960) dealt with the question of awards to university students; the Robbins Report (1963) with higher education.

In 1961 there were in England and Wales 3837 secondary modern schools, 1268 grammar schools, 130 comprehensive schools, 251 technical secondary schools, and 620 others.

Amidst the general enthusiasm for giving better and better educational facilities to more and more pupils and students, the Newsom Report (1963), with the somewhat pathetic title, 'Half Our Future,' and dealing with secondary modern education, remained neglected. Yet the Newsom Report was perhaps the most significant of all; for it recognised the fact that not everybody—half the schoolchildren, in fact—is endowed with ability to reach the academic heights. This consideration was entirely ignored by those who, in the 1960s, fiercely advocated the cause of comprehensive schools not on educational grounds (though this was not admitted) but from doctrinaire political motives. There was a compassion in the Newsom Report which gave nobility to what could have been a very dull document—a compassion for those who, having no aptitude for the 'grammar' heights, are happier if they are not pushed up them, and who are as entitled to love and care on the part of society as the 'brighter' ones.

And there (because an attempt at appraisal of educational trends is rendered difficult by the educationalist's own prejudice, the effects of tradition, upbringing and environment, of even his own intellectual calibre, and probably of obscure biological forces) we must break off this account of the still continuing story of education and its relation to modern industrial organisation.

CHAPTER XII

THE STATE OF THE NATION

1. The National Debt

The National Debt is the debt owing by the Government; the internal National Debt is debt owing to people within the country who have lent money to the Government, which is therefore required to pay principal and interest. It is this internal debt which is generally spoken of as the British National Debt; the external debt is that owing abroad.

The British National Debt stood in 1964 at about £28,000 million, or over £500 per head of the population. The payment of interest on this debt is raised by taxation and does not take wealth out of the country, though it redistributes the national income. The greater part of it has been incurred in the financing of wars during the past 250 years; there is, therefore, little in the way of real assets represented by the debt. Moreover, the debt increases in war much faster than it can be repaid, so that only by the application of technical knowledge and skill to productive work over a long period of peace is there hope of extinguishing it. On the other hand, the creation of such assets as roads and schools by the Government reduces the actual burden.

Though the National Debt may be said to have had its beginnings during the reign of Charles II, when the London goldsmiths advanced money to the Exchequer on the security of the public revenue, it was on the incorporation of the Bank of England in 1694 that the National Debt became an institution; it will be remembered that the charter of the Bank was granted in consideration of a loan by certain financiers of £1,200,000, on the security of certain duties on liquors and tonnage of ships. Parliament reserved the right to redeem the debt at any time after 1705, but the indebtedness was increased by succeeding governments. By the end of the war with France in 1697 the debt amounted to over £20 million, and after a reduction to £16 million at the end of William III's reign, rose to £54 million in Queen Anne's reign as the result of the expenses of the War of the Spanish Succession. After the Seven Years' War it reached £146 million in 1763; in 1816 it was £900 million, costing over £30 million a year in interest and management expenses. The First and Second World Wars caused the great rises to its present fantastic size.

Though, as has been said, in an internal debt the money is owed to the citizens of the country by the Government, and does not take wealth out of the country, yet its growth is a real burden on industry: the money spent on war materials could have been invested with profit in industrial undertakings, and the payment of interest involves taxation which will affect industry and enterprise. Consolation is found in the fact that, but for this expenditure, British industry might perhaps not be in existence at all.

2. The Growth, Decline and Revival of Free Trade

During the eighteenth century the amount raised and spent by the Government rose from about £4 million annually to about £18 million. The wars of 1793–1815 caused this sum to rise to nearly £60 million. Until 1842 the money was raised mainly from Customs and Excise

Eighteenth Century	Income and Expenditure of British Government £4 million ⟶ £18 million
1776	Publication of Adam Smith's *Wealth of Nations*
1793–1815	Wars. Income and Expenditure £60 million
1815	Budget £100 million. Corn Laws passed
1816	Budget £66 million
1816–42	Money raised mainly from Customs and Excise duties. In 1816 abolition of Income Tax imposed in 1798
1840s	The 'Hungry Forties'
	Reduction and simplification of Customs duties by Peel
1841	Recasting of system of national finance by Peel
	Introduction of Income Tax of 7d. in the pound
1846	Abolition of Corn Laws
1849	End of Navigation Acts
1853–60	Gladstone's reforms—reduction and removal of duties
1850–70	Prosperity
1894	Death duties introduced
1909	Super-tax on incomes over £5,000 per annum
1914–18	First World War
	'McKenna' duties. Abolished 1924, restored 1925
1921	Safeguarding of Industries Act
1932	Protection
	Ottawa agreements
1934	Budget £700 million
1936–38	Deficit in Britain's trading position
1939–45	Second World War
	Bilateral trading agreements; trade restrictions
1947	Marshall Aid
1948	General Agreement on Tariffs and Trade
1950	European Payments Union, superseded in 1958 by European Monetary Agreement
1957	Rome Treaty establishing the European Economic Community ('Common Market')
1959	European Free Trade Association Convention
1961	Britain's application to join E.C.M. rejected
1967	Britain again applied to join E.C.M.

Chart 19—*The Growth, Decline and Revival of Free Trade*

duties. It is interesting to know that bonded warehouses for tea and coffee (the duty being paid on the goods when they were taken out of the warehouses) were established by Sir Robert Walpole in 1724.

After 1787 the national revenue was paid into the Consolidated Fund, and it became possible to set out an annual national balance sheet to show income and expenditure. At first a number of Commissioners were employed to audit public accounts; but in 1866 an official called the Comptroller and Auditor-General was appointed for this purpose.

Reformers like William Cobbett had been agitating for an overhaul of the Parliamentary system so as to give effect to the wishes of the increasing numbers of workers; but a government frightened by the excesses of the French Revolution was in no mood to listen to such proposals; and, in fact, a cavalry charge scattered a crowded meeting at St Peter's Fields, Manchester, in 1819—hence the name of the 'Peterloo Massacre.' With the coming to power of the industrialists, the factory owners, pressure for reform—in favour of the industrialists, not the workers—was exerted. The Reform Bill, 1832, which gave power to the middle classes, was passed after the wealthy people had threatened to withdraw their money from the Bank of England.

The shifting of power from the landowners to the industrialists enabled the latter to put into practice the free-trade ideas advocated by Adam Smith. In the 1840s Peel reduced and simplified the Customs duties; and the Corn Laws were abolished in 1846. Pitt had introduced an income tax in 1798, graduated according to income. It had been imposed to help pay for the French wars, and was abolished in 1816. In the last year of the war, 1815, the budget exceeded £100 million. In 1816 it fell to £66 million, £31 million of this being interest on the debt Peel had raised. Huskisson, who became President of the Board of Trade in 1823, abolished bounties on exports and reduced a number of duties on imports. Peel became Prime Minister for the second time in 1841, and in this Ministry he recast the system of national finance, reducing and abolishing duties; to make up for the revenue from them he introduced for three years an income tax of 7d. in the pound on incomes over £150 per annum. At the end of the three years the experiment had become so successful that Peel decided to reduce or abolish yet more duties and continue the income tax. In 1853 Gladstone, Chancellor of the Exchequer in Lord Aberdeen's Ministry, removed and reduced further duties; and after the Crimean War he continued his policy in his 1860 budget.

The policy of free trade was, of course, of great benefit to the industrialists, who wanted to exploit all means to obtain the great advantage from Britain's leadership in the Industrial Revolution. The policy was of great benefit to the country as a whole; and from 1850 the country entered upon a twenty-year period of prosperity.

Income tax was imposed in the hope and expectation that it would prove a temporary measure; but the increasing scope of government activity, and the increasing expense in national defence and social reform, caused the hope to recede; all hope was, indeed, abandoned officially by Asquith in 1907. In that year Asquith extended the scale of death duties introduced in 1894. Lloyd George imposed a super-tax on incomes over £5,000 per annum in 1909.

In 1902 a protectionist policy was adopted by Germany. The free-trade tradition of Britain was opposed to the attitude of 'fair-trade' or retaliation suggested in some quarters, but the arguments of Joseph Chamberlain were beginning to weaken this tradition. During the First World War the 'McKenna' duties on clocks, watches and motor-cars were imposed to economise shipping space. These duties were abolished by the Labour Government in 1924, but restored by the Conservative Government in 1925. The Safeguarding of Industries Act of 1921 was passed to protect 'key' industries and those suffering from foreign 'dumping.' The abandonment of Free Trade was marked by the protection of 1932: a general duty of 10% *ad valorem* was passed, subsequently raised to 20%.

In 1932, too, was established on a broad scale the principle of Imperial Preference; under the Ottawa agreements Customs duties on goods imported from the Empire countries were charged at a lower rate than those from other countries, and the Dominions granted preferential duties on United Kingdom manufactured goods and Colonial produce.

In the years after the war, strangling restrictions had been imposed on trade by the countries of the world; 'bilateral' trading agreements were made between countries which, in effect, went back to a system of barter. The 1937 Report of the Bank for International Settlements showed that while at the end of 1936 world industrial production was 20% above the 1929 level, the volume of world trade was 10% below it. It was evident at the end of the war that the process going on was one of national and international suicide. In 1947 international tariff negotiations took place in Geneva; and 33 countries signed an agreement for the general reduction of tariffs. In 1948, at Havana, a Charter of the International Trade Organisation was drawn up and signed by 54 countries. In 1952 a Commonwealth Economic Conference was held, and British representatives proposed a revision of the General Agreement on Tariffs and Trade signed in 1948 by twenty-three countries so as to allow new and increased Commonwealth Prefer-ences; but the Commonwealth countries did not take kindly to the idea of a new Empire Free Trade policy, with tariffs against outside countries. The 'Kennedy Round' of international negotiations to agree on tariff reductions was initiated by President Kennedy in 1962.

The slow strangulation of trade resulting from bilateral agreements was combated by a European Payments Union (superseded in 1958 by the European Monetary Agreement) set up in 1950 under the Organisation for European Economic Co-operation (superseded in 1960 by the Organisation for Economic Co-operation and Development) to enable countries which were members of the organisation to set off surpluses and deficits with one another.

In 1944 the Governments of Belgium, the Netherlands and Luxembourg concluded a customs union agreement which came into force in 1947. In 1950 these 'Benelux' countries together with France, West Germany and Italy, formed a Coal and Steel Community, in which the member countries pooled their coal and steel resources. In 1956 it was proposed that these countries should form an European Economic Community abolishing their internal customs duties and imposing a common tariff on the countries outside. Negotiations resulted in an agreement, signed in Rome in 1957, to set up a European Common Market, which in the course of the twelve to fifteen years suggested for the full abolition of internal tariffs, will comprise about 160 million people.

In 1957 Britain suggested the formation of a wider organisation, the Free Trade Area, comprising the European Common Market countries and the other members of the O.E.E.C. Britain's suggestion of an industrial Free Trade Area was intended to enable her to continue to protect her agriculture and to maintain her Commonwealth relationships. The scheme was not established; but in November 1959 Ministers from the United Kingdom, Sweden, Denmark, Norway, Switzerland, Austria and Portugal (the 'Outer Seven'), met in Stockholm and approved a Convention to establish a European Free Trade Association. The EFTA plan envisaged the abolition, by 1st January 1970, of all protective tariffs and quotas on industrial goods which originate in the EFTA area. This area comprises a rich and diversified market of 88 million people. By 1963, 50% of the tariff barriers had been removed; and the 'Seven' agreed that a completely free industrial market should be created by the end of 1966.

In 1961 the United Kingdom applied for membership of the European Common Market, but this application was rejected after strenuous French opposition. A second application was made by the Wilson Government in 1967.

3. THE NATIONAL FINANCIAL POSITION

Inflation, the extension of social services, the increase in debt interest, the expanding and devastating expenditure on armaments, raised the Budget figures to nearly £700 million by 1934. The Second World War gave a few more twists to the spiral of inflation; the total defence expenditure reached over £1400 million; the total Ordinary Revenue and Expenditure came to over £4000 million.

Already, before the Second World War, Britain was barely paying her way in her trading. The average total cost of Britain's imports for the years 1936–38 was £884 million. The visible exports (exports of goods) were £496 million in value. Of the 'invisible' exports, shipping services accounted for £105 million, and banking and miscellaneous services for £44 million; the income from overseas investments was £203 million. There was thus a deficit of £36 million, which was met by borrowing from other countries or from the sale of investments owned abroad.

The Second World War had a disastrous effect upon this somewhat precarious economy. Workers were transferred to armament factories, at the expense of the export trade; British ships were sunk faster than they could be replaced, and over £1000 million worth of investments were sold before 'Lend-Lease' started; by 1945 the income from investments was halved. Britain's overseas debt was £750 million in 1938; in 1945 it was £3355 million.

Great efforts on the part of the British people reduced a net trading debt of £630 million in 1947 to £150 million in 1948. 1948 showed a surplus with the Sterling Area—the countries conducting their trade in sterling and comprising mainly Commonwealth countries. The European Recovery Programme—'Marshall Aid'—helped certain European countries with loans and gifts of dollars, and Britain turned a deficit with these countries into a surplus; with the countries of the world generally, apart from America, the deficit was comparatively small. But with the Western Hemisphere generally there was a large deficit—six out of every ten shillings' worth of imports from the Western Hemisphere was not being paid for by earnings: it came from European Recovery Programme aid.

In the years immediately after the war the 'terms of trade' moved against Britain: less imports could be obtained for exports than in 1938, because while the world generally was still short of the manufactures which Britain could supply, she was one of the many customers urgently in need of the food and raw materials which Europe could not supply so abundantly as before, so that food prices rose higher than the prices of manufactured goods.

Rationing, limitation of supplies, food control, financial control—all kinds of control were combined with government direction of industry to combat the economic consequences of the Second World War. The longer-term results of such control and taxation have been such as to surprise even Chancellors of the Exchequer. Purchase Tax was levied on consumers' goods delivered on or after 21st October 1940, and was applied to a large variety of commodities, the rate varying from $16\frac{2}{3}\%$ on essential and household goods to 100% on luxury articles. Originally applied as a means of curtailing expenditure and so combating inflation, the tax proved to be a source of income to Chancellors of the Exchequer such as the holders of this office had not dreamed of. The tax is regressive, falling, when it is imposed on essential articles, with equal weight on rich and poor; it imposes a burden on the retailer; it leads to anomalies, some of them absurd; it has compelled manufacturers to direct their efforts to producing 'utility'-type products not suitable for the export markets and has prevented their trying out new products on the home market. But in 1962 the revenue from purchase tax amounted to over £570 million; and with the vast expenditure on social services which the State has undertaken, any suggestions for the abolition of purchase tax are met with the enquiry as to an alternative source of income.

In 1946 the United States Congress agreed to make available to Britain a credit of £1100 million; Canada lent £280 million. These credits were insufficient; and in 1947 the scheme of Marshall Aid, the European Recovery Programme, was initiated: the United States would help Europe if the European nations could work out a joint recovery programme. Marshall Aid was suspended in 1951, American aid to Europe then being merged into a general defence contribution.

Meanwhile, pressure of events had forced that closer co-operation between the government financial machinery and industry which the Macmillan Report had advocated. In 1945 the Chancellor of the Exchequer announced the creation of two new corporations which were established to promote this cooperation: the Finance Corporation for Industry, Ltd., to provide finance to industrial enterprises for their rehabilitation and development in the national interest; and the Industrial and Commercial Finance Corporation, Ltd., to supply medium- and long-term financial facilities of from £5000 to £200,000.

In 1945, too, the problem of those areas of the country in which changes in the organisation of industry, previously discussed, had caused unemployment and distress came under review. A Development Areas Treasury Advisory Committee was appointed by the Treasury to advise on the giving by it of financial assistance to industrial undertakings for capital development in a 'Development Area.'

Immediately after the war British industry could sell its goods easily in response to the urgent demands of overseas buyers. But when this era of a 'sellers' market' came to an end British industrialists found that their goods were priced too high in relation to United States goods or goods sold by countries tying their currencies to the United States dollar. It was necessary to reduce the value of the pound sterling in relation to the dollar; and in September 1949 the British pound sterling was devalued from 4·03 U.S. dollars to the £1 to 2·80 dollars to the £1.

The immediate effect in Britain was an increase in the price of bread, the wheat and flour obtained by Britain from Canada being now dearer. The goods from countries of the Sterling Area, those countries tying their currencies to the British pound sterling, and comprising mainly the Commonwealth countries except Canada, did not increase in price, nor did the goods from those countries devaluing their currencies to correspond with the devaluation in sterling.

The necessity of examining the persistent rise in prices since the end of the Second World War, and of finding some means to stop the process of inflation which has troubled the British economy, gave rise to the appointment in August 1957 of a Council on Prices, Productivity and Incomes, the Cohen Council. The terms of reference of the Council were:

> Having regard to the desirability of full employment and increasing standards of life based on expanding production and reasonable stability of prices, to keep under review changes in prices, productivity and the level of incomes (including wages, salaries and profits) and to report thereon from time to time.

The First Report of the Council was published in February 1958, the Second in August 1958 and the Third in July 1959.

4. THE PLANNING OF THE ECONOMY

The great increase in the number of private motor-cars on the roads of Britain which gave rise to the fears expressed in the Buchanan Report of 1963 was an aspect of the Affluent Society so long dreamed of. But the affluence was based on a precarious economy. Britain was no longer a manufacturing country with imports consisting almost entirely of food and raw materials. A third of British imports now consisted of manufactured or semi-manufactured goods; and during the ten years 1954–64 the imports of consumer goods grew relatively faster than the imports of investment goods like plant and machinery, so that by 1964 they amounted to a third of imported manufactured goods.

The trading figures had been causing alarm; there was perennial anxiety about the balance of payments, the rises in wages, the state of production. In 1962 the Government appointed a National Economic Development Council, comprising Ministers, industrialists, trade union representatives and two independent members, to advise the Government on the conditions necessary for economic growth. It was established that a 4% growth was necessary to double Britain's output in eighteen years and that for this, investment would have to rise by an average of 5·3% a year, exports by 5%, while consumption would rise by only 3½% per year. The expected yearly increase had in fact been achieved in 1959 and 1960; but thereafter had declined to nothing at all in 1962.

In the view of various authorities, including the Bank for International Settlements, the heart of the problem lay in the fact that money incomes had been rising very much faster than the increase in output per person—an average of 5 or 6% over the period 1948–61.

In 1962 the Government appointed a National Incomes Commission to advise the Government whether claims for increases of wages were justified in view of the position ascertained by the National Economic Development Council.

The trade union leaders had accepted the creation of the National Economic Development Council and were willing to let their representatives sit on it. A proposed 'freeze' on wages was a different matter; it savoured too much of a national wages policy which might be working well in foreign countries like Sweden and Holland, but was not at all 'suited' to British conditions. They did not take at all kindly to 'Nicky.' They spoke loudly of the need to 'freeze' dividends and other emoluments and rewards of capitalistic enterprise—as far as the much-abused 'expense accounts' of executives were concerned, with some justification.

In 1964 a Labour Government was elected with a small majority. It quickly demonstrated the fact that Governments do not create policies but are subject to the circumstances of the times, particularly to economic forces. The new Labour Government put the blame for the country's difficulties on its Tory predecessors, and announced its intention of putting things right. 'Nicky' was superseded—by a National Board for Prices and Incomes. That its Chairman was an ex-Tory Minister might have struck an ardent Socialist as curious.

In October 1964 the Government set up a Department of Economic Affairs, intended to be primarily responsible for the long-term aspects of economic policy; short-term measures to regulate the economy or the balance of payments were to be the affair of the Treasury. The Department of Economic Affairs became responsible for achieving a policy for productivity, prices and incomes.

As part of the machinery of the N.E.D.C., Economic Development Committees ('Little Neddies') were established to consider the problems and obstacles to growth of individual industries. Economic Planning Councils and Boards were established to consider the problems of regions, the country being divided into Economic Planning Regions. Arrangements were made for an 'early warning system' by which voluntary notice of intention to increase prices and to change pay and conditions of work would be given to the Government.

In September 1965 the Government published *The National Plan*, a plan for achieving a 25% increase in national output between 1964 and 1970; a plan, it stated, which had been worked out in very close consultation with industry.

The machinery set up by the Labour Government for regional planning was accompanied by a programme designed to 'cover the human effects of industrial change': it included redundancy compensation, wage-related unemployment benefits and better industrial training.*

The Government was returned with an increased majority after the General Election of March 1966; evidently the country, including the trade unions, had come to the conclusion, however reluctantly, that a Government which proposed to take steps to direct and control the economy in the interests of prosperity was worth supporting in spite of the unpleasant consequences of direction and control.

A 'pay freeze' policy was applied more stringently in July 1966; it applied increases in tax to a wide range of consumer goods and tightened up hire purchase regulations. Legislative support for the policy was subsequently imposed.

A 'wages freeze' was a bitter pill for the trade unions to swallow, and the Government's policy in fact proved too much for the General Secretary of the Transport and General Workers' Union, a union with a massive membership: it is the largest organised group of workers in the United Kingdom. He had accepted the post of Minister of Technology under the Labour Government, but returned to his trade union leadership and began an active campaign against the Government policy.

The Government made efforts to implement the National Plan to increase productivity and regulate prices and incomes. In 1966 a Selective Employment Tax was introduced to divert labour from the service industries to the manufacturing industries and at the same time to curb expenditure. These not very successful moves to link prosperity with effort were regarded with some dismay by the trade unions and the country generally.

What had happened was that the lessons Lord Beveridge had taught twenty years before in his *Full Employment in a Free Society*—the direction and control of industry, the long-term planning of the economy—were beginning to be learnt. The sending back to power of the Labour Party with an increased majority would seem to indicate not so much a popular enthusiasm for Socialism as a doctrinaire creed but a recognition that only by planning, direction and control of the economy by a Government endowed with powers to fulfil these functions could the economy in the new industrial conditions be made to work. The Socialism part of the proceedings could be left to H.M. Opposition and the resistance of non-Socialists to deal with.

Thus we have to break off our account of the evolution of modern

---

* See *The National Plan* (Cmd. 2764, September 1965 (H.M.S.O., 30s.). A short 'popular version' of the Plan entitled *Working for Prosperity* has also been published (H.M.S.O., 1s.), itself an example of the way in which modern Governments attempt to arrive at satisfactory 'communication' with the general body of citizens. See also D. E. A. *Progress Reports* (Central Office of Information), published (free) from January, 1965; it succeeded the Treasury *Bulletin for Industry*.

industrial organisation at a point where the affairs of the people of this country have entered upon a new phase. It is probable that if the policy of 'social priorities' advocated by Lord Beveridge is followed, great changes will occur in the lives and work of the people, changes that will have far-reaching and deep implications. The imposition of 'social priorities,' as determined by a Government, may not be to the taste of many of the citizens; it may be that much waste and mismanagement of human resources, including personal resources and personal integrity, may vanish.

The alternative to going into the European Common Market with which the British people are faced in 1967 is a reconstruction of the economic and social system, and a determined planning of the economy. Such a planning would involve the abolition of restrictive practices on both sides of industry, and changes in the lives of ordinary British men and women going beyond the mere rise in the cost of living frankly admitted as accompanying entry into the Common Market. Change often involves personal discomfort; but it is better for changes to be foreseen and provided for than for economic priorities to be imposed by a blind 'system' which cares nothing for human suffering —suffering such as was imposed in the recession in the motor industry in 1966 and even worse, in the horror of the 1930s.

CONCLUSION

It is part of the fascination of the study of history that the story one reads is continued into one's own life and that one is part of the events that will shape the lines of the future. As has been stressed in this work, it is difficult to obtain a proper perspective of the course of events near to one's own day; and this is especially true of the specialist; to the cobbler there's nothing like leather, and to the industrialist the fact of industry seems to be the most important fact in the picture of his own times.

Yet one may ask whether the evolution of modern industrial organisation is in many aspects the evolution of new ways by which men and women may make themselves unhappy. This is an age in which economics is one of the principal preoccupations of mankind. But economics is an extremely limited and partial social science; and it may even be disputed whether it is worthy of the description of science to the extent that physics and the other exact sciences are science. Only in so far as 'science' is conceived to be scientific method, a means of discovering relationships between facts, can economics be regarded as a science.

Certainly a 'science of living' is of far greater magnitude and complexity than the mere study of the ways in which communities make use of their material and mental resources, in so far as these ways can be expressed in money prices, which is all that economics is, as a 'science.'

Many more people have suffered in many more different ways in the course of the evolution of modern industrial organisation than might have been believed possible by a student of industrial affairs watching the developments of the nineteenth century and expecting that an era of material prosperity for everybody would follow the promise of Man's greater control over his material environment as invention followed invention, as transport and communications spread, as a greater understanding of the possibilities of currency and banking problems came to men. There followed the era of dark, satanic mills, of population overflowing our little island, of conflicts between 'capital' and 'labour' the story of which is not yet done.

In our own day we see in our own country the struggling of groups for economic power, the demands of industrial workers for a greater share of the product of industry, the grinding out of the lower middle and professional classes striving to preserve a standard of economic

189

independence in the face of an ever-increasing burden laid on them by a State (whatever its political colour) in which economic and political functions are inextricably intermingled.

'Social classes' today refer, as they have done for some time, not primarily to incomes, but to cultural levels; the term 'standard of living' has come to mean much more than mere consumption of food and entertainment services, but has reference also to the dignity of maintaining one's own house; to providing a suitable environment for one's children; to the employment of one's leisure, whether in the pursuit of organised sport or of the graces of life in music, art and literature.

Modern industrial organisation has made possible for many more people the opportunity of enjoying a higher 'standard of living' in this sense; and it is precisely this which is, or should be, the *raison d'être* of any industrial organisation at all. Man does not live by bread alone; a factory is a tool for better living, as indeed, is the State itself, for government is not an absolute Good, an end in itself, but a means to an end.

Such observations as these would be irrelevant in this work, or at least superfluous, if there were not a danger that industrialists, and many other people, come near very often to forgetting the theme to which they relate. Social conditions, the physical and mental quality of the people, the part which the State is allowed to play in the organis-ation of community life, all are very real influences in the evolution of modern industrial organisation. Conversely, the development of in-dustry itself, the progress of industrial relations, the operation or otherwise of the private profit motive—all have a considerable influence upon the social structure of a community. Such problems as the inter-action of atomic energy for industrial purposes, and of the prospect of tremendously increased sources of power, upon the tendency of both employers and employed to indulge in restrictive practices to suit their own personal ends, will have to be faced; and the solving of this problem alone will tax to the uttermost the capacity of men and women to adapt themselves to changed circumstances.

It is related of Henry Ford that a famous remark of his was to the effect that: 'History is bunk.' If it should prove that men generally have learned nothing from the procession of events which have been described in this work, that waste of human resources and effort through efficiency in organisation, conflicts, self-seeking and limited vision shall continue, then indeed it may be feared that Ford's criticism will be justified. If the study of 'history' is the expenditure of time, effort, enthusiasm and resources on the investigation of the details of the past of the slightest or no material significance to the brief span of life of men and women of the present time seeking happiness and fulfilment in their daily lives, it is useless.

Mary Parker Follett, one of the pioneers in the theory of industrial administration and 'scientific management,' said that conflict arises not from the differences between individuals but from the failure of individuals to make their differences contribute to the common cause. In Britain there are differences enough, differences not merely between 'classes' and between 'capital' and 'labour,' but between the very temperament and character of the various types of people making up the 'British' people. One can think at once of, for example, the hard-headed practicality of the Northern people, the softer geniality of the West Country folk, the caution but essential kindliness of Norfolk men and women. The 'British' are a united nation only in so far as the people have learned to integrate their differences.

The changes that are taking place around us call for an effort on the part of every man and woman to study the trend of industrial affairs in order that he may play a part, however humble, in helping to integrate the differences between individuals and groups that must inevitably arise or become accentuated as more complex industrial forms are evolved—forms that, as we have seen in our study of combines and monopolies, reach out far beyond the nation's shores. The contribution which the ordinary man can make to his industrial civilisation can be made clear to him only by his study and appraisal of the events which have gone to make up what has been called in this work the evolution of modern industrial organisation. In his estimate of the significance of certain events he may make mistakes. But those very mistakes, if recognised and subsequently pondered over, help to free the thinking person from the danger of acquiring an academic sterility of mind, preoccupied mainly with the fear that it may in some small matter be proved wrong.

BIBLIOGRAPHY

Books on British economic history are legion. Most of them contain bibliographies which will enable the reader to find references to particular periods and the student to pursue historical aspects of economic life in which he is most interested. The advanced student might care to note the selection of official Papers given below as illustrative of the historical 'highlights' in official publications.

The following books are recommended for general reading and basic study. For general reading:

Allen, G. C. *The Structure of Industry in Britain: A Study in Economic Change* (Longmans, 1961) surveys the changes that have occurred in the structure of British industry from 1900 to 1960.

Ashworth, William. *An Economic History of England, 1870–1939* (Methuen, 1960).

Bland, A. E., Brown, P. A. and Tawney, R. H. *English Economic History: Select Documents* (Bell).

Clapham, Sir J. H. *An Economic History of Modern Britain* (3 vols.) (Cambridge University Press, 1964).

Deane, Phyllis, and Cole, W. A. *British Economic Growth 1689–1959* (Cambridge University Press, 1962).

Knowles, L. C. A. *The Industrial and Commercial Revolutions in Great Britain during the Nineteenth Century* (Routledge, 1937).

Lipson, E. *The Economic History of England* (3 vols.) (A. & C. Black, 1964).

Mantoux, Paul. *The Industrial Revolution in the 18th Century* (trans. Marjorie Vernon) (Jonathan Cape, 1952).

Warner, Townsend. *Landmarks in English Industrial History* (Blackie & Son, 1949).

Worswick, G. D. N. and Ady, P. H. (Editors): *The British Economy, 1945–50* (1952) and *The British Economy in the 1950s* (1962) (Oxford University Press).

On the history of science and technology, Sir Wm. Dampier's work, *A History of Science* (C.U.P., 1946) is a clear and well-written account. The Oxford *History of Technology* by Singer, Holmyard, Hall and Williams (1954–58) is a monumental work.

On the development of the social services, Maurice Bruce's *The Coming of the Welfare State* (Batsford, 1965) gives a broad review from the days of the Victorian Poor Law. M. Penelope Hall's *The Social Services of Modern England* (Routledge & Kegan Paul, 6th Edition, 1963) is a survey of contemporary services. On education, H. Curtis's *History of Education in Great Britain* (University Tutorial Press) reached its 6th Edition in 1965.

Official documents of current interest have been mentioned in the text. The following is a selection of Papers of historical interest:

A SELECTION OF OFFICIAL PAPERS OF RECENT HISTORICAL INTEREST

TEXTILES

Report of the Committee on the Textile Trades after the War, 1918 (Board of Trade).

Committee on Industry and Trade: *Survey of Textile Industries,* 1928.

Economic Advisory Council: *Report of the Committee on the Cotton Industry,* 1930.

Report of the Cotton Textile Mission to the United States of America, March–April, 1944 (Platt Report).

Reports of Working Parties on Cotton (1946), Hosiery (1946), Lace (1947), Wool (1947), Jute (1948), Carpets (1948).

IRON AND STEEL; METALS; SHIPBUILDING

Report of Committee on the Iron and Steel Trades after the War, 1918 (Board of Trade).

Committee on Industry and Trade: *Survey of the Metal Industries,* 1928.

Iron and Steel Industry: Reports by the British Iron and Steel Federation and the Joint Iron Council to the Minister of Supply. 1946.

Report of Committee on the Shipping and Shipbuilding Industries after the War, 1918 (Board of Trade).

COAL

Reports of Royal Commissions on the Coal Industry, 1910 and 1925.

Coal Mines Reorganisation Commission: *Memorandum on Colliery Amalgamation,* 1931.

Report of Technical Advisory Committee on Coal-mining, 1945.

TRANSPORT

Report of Royal Commission on Transport, 1928.
Report of the Royal Commission on Shipping Rings, 1909.
Report of the Imperial Committee on the Deferred Rebate System,
    1923.
The Co-ordination and Development of Transport: Final Report of
    the Royal Commission on Transport (1931).
Report of the Conference on Road and Rail Transport (The Salter
    Report), 1932.

FINANCE AND BANKING

Report of Committee on Finance and Industry (the Macmillan
    Report), 1931.
Report of the Committee on the Working of the Monetary System
    (the Radcliffe Committee Report), 1959.

MONOPOLIES AND RESTRICTIVE PRACTICES

Collective Discrmination: a Report on Exclusive Dealing, Collective
    Boycotts, Aggregated Rebates, and Other Discriminatory Trade
    Practices (Cmd. 9504), June 1955.

INDEX